To: E. Mac Edington

with my best wishes,

[signature]

LEST I FORGET

MY LIFE AS A BOY · SOLDIER · FBI AGENT

BY

Larry Ford Thomas

PUBLISHED BY

Thomas Publishing Company
Columbia, Tennessee

Library Of Congress Cataloging-in-Publication Data
Thomas, Larry F.
      Lest I Forget
      ISBN 0-9711215-0-8
      Library Of Congress Control Number 2001 130573

Edited by Lynnette Ingram, Peggy Thomas, and Martin Ramsay.
Printed and bound by Vaughan Printing, Nashville, Tennessee.

Dedicated to the memory of
my late wife, Nina, and to
our children, Elizabeth,
Susan, and Larry. A gift
from God and a joy and
blessing in our lives.

Acknowledgment

To my son, Lawrence Gray
Thomas, without whose
encouragement, suggestions,
and hours at the computer
this would not have been possible.

The God-given ability to remember is very fragile. It can be lost in the moment of an accident, through illness, or even deteriorate with the mere passage of time.

So, "lest I forget"...

CONTENTS

PREFACE

My parents never seemed especially interested in their ancestry. My father, who was born on a farm, spent his entire life working on a farm. His goal was to feed and care for his family. There was little time for anything else. Questions about where my grandfather came from got no further than, "Well, he was born in an adjacent hollow." Questioning where my father's grandfather came from netted even less information.

My mother was orphaned at eleven years of age so she knew little about the history of her family.

I felt the need to research my family history as far back as I could and to leave the results as a legacy for my children and grandchildren.

Children born recently cannot, in most instances, begin to comprehend how rural life was in the 1920's and for a period thereafter. A nephew, after reading a manuscript of this book said, "Mama, no one ever lived like that."

Without any of the present conveniences we take for granted, life on a remote farm was not bad. We were never hungry. Maybe a little cold in the worst of winter because our homes were not insulated and we lacked proper outer clothing, but we all survived. From birth, I was taught to honor my father and mother. To defend this nation was considered a privilege. I was taught honesty and integrity and to always respect those in authority. I must confess this latter principle has been tested in recent times, particularly with the behavior of the Clinton administration. Still, I strongly defend these principles, have endeavored to instill them in my children, and feel confident I have succeeded.

I now live in a different world. One with all the comforts modern society offers. God has blessed me with sufficient funds to pay for it all and leave my children a remembrance.

When I depart this earth my greatest hope is that I can leave a heritage equal to that of my mother and father.

My initial objective was to do nothing more than record my family history as I knew it and to include what I recall of my childhood. It was at my son's urging that I decided to make this book what it is. Much of the credit goes to him because without his inspiration and endless hours at his computer I would never have completed it.

INTRODUCTION

This endeavor was not undertaken for the purpose of revealing my literary talents (or the lack thereof), but only to record some events important to me in my life, and in the lives of my family members, and hopefully of some interest to those who follow after me.

Hickman, Tennessee, located in the southern part of Smith County, was, in the 1920's, a thriving little town. The Tennessee Central Railroad literally ran through the center of town. Hickman had a factory that made soap, a small hotel, bank, post office, general store, and a blacksmith shop. There was even a drug store complete with a soda fountain and marble-top tables. Of these, only a post office remains and it is now in a new building, removed from its earlier location.

Downtown Hickman, Tennessee, c.1950

The one-room schoolhouse, in 1925, stood on the western edge of town. Here, one teacher taught all grades, from the first through the eighth. It was the teacher's responsibility to arrange for wood to fuel the pot-bellied stove used to heat the building, bring the wood for the stove,

1

start the fire, and keep it going. It was also the teacher's responsibility to keep the building clean.

Willie Geneva Dillard (who was to become my mother) was a native of Marshall County, Tennessee. She was the new schoolteacher and was the object of attention of all the eligible young men in the community.

East of town about a mile, was "Thomas Hollow." George Nicholas "Nick" Thomas and wife, Allie Bates Thomas, owned a large farm of more than 300 acres, which they operated with four sons, two daughters, and two or three tenant farmers and their families.

Nick and Allie with Loyd, John Melvin, George, and Henson, c.1905

Their oldest son, John Melvin Thomas (who was to become my father), had the distinction of owning one of the first automobiles in the community – a Ford Overland, much to the chagrin of his father, who felt it was ridiculously extravagant. Nick Thomas maintained that the horse and buggy was more than adequate transportation, much more reliable and cheaper to operate. He steadfastly refused even to get into the new machine. He chose to walk the mile to town and to church, rather than ride in the "new contraption," as he called it. One Sunday when it was pouring rain, Nick was about halfway to town when his son came along in the automobile and offered his father a ride, which he grudgingly accepted. Apparently this one ride changed Nick's mind. He was never known to have condemned "the contraption" again. My dad was a bit reluctant to talk much about this period, but did admit he was a bit rebellious where his dad was concerned. Having an automobile, he was "the boy about town." My mother was reluctant to admit that my Dad's automobile was what initially attracted her to him.

Willie Geneva Dillard and John Melvin Thomas were married on Thanksgiving Day, November 23, 1923. They began housekeeping in one of the tenant houses on his father's farm.

All the roads in this part of Smith County were gravel. The one from Hickman to "Thomas Hollow" was one-lane, with that lane becoming more narrow as it got closer to the Thomas enclave. The last quarter mile ran through the Thomas farm and ended, almost, at the big barn. On past the barn and up the hill to the left was the "big house" where Nick and Allie lived. Past the barn and literally behind it, as you approached along the roadway, was a small three-room tenant house where Willie and Melvin lived. Other tenant houses were scattered about the farm.

The little house behind the barn sat on an incline. One side touched the ground. The other side was supported by large rocks, loosely stacked, one atop the other. There was adequate room under the lower side of the house to shelter the dog and afford a young boy a place to play on rainy days. There were two levels to this house. Downstairs consisted of three rooms. The one facing the front and referred to as the "front room," served as the living room and master bedroom as we might refer to it now. Behind the front room was the dining room, with the kitchen behind that. A second bedroom was located upstairs, above the front room. A large fireplace, fed with wood, served as the source of heat for both bedrooms. A wood-burning stove heated the kitchen and was used to cook the meals.

Air conditioning, unknown to us, consisted of opening the windows with hope that the wind would blow. During the summer the upstairs bedroom would often get so hot it was uncomfortable to touch the sheets until well into the night. The roof was covered with tin. There was no insulation in the walls or ceiling, except for the wallpaper. The more layers of paper on the walls, the warmer the room.

Water for drinking came from a spring located near the rear of the house. Where the water came out of the hill a rock-walled "spring house" had been built. It had a tin roof over heavy timbers, which served to maintain a somewhat even temperature. A thick door faced our house. It was big enough to walk through stooped down a bit. A pool had been fashioned by cutting into the solid rock where the water came out of the hillside. The cool

The remaining rock walls of the spring house.

water coming forth in generous quantities served as drinking water, and also as a refrigerator of a sort for milk, butter and other perishables. Less perishable items

4

were stored on three or four shelves inside. A large crock, holding ten to fifteen gallons of sauerkraut, sat on the cool rock floor.

A large metal storage tank at the back corner of the residence caught water running off the roof. This water was used to wash clothes and dishes. It was "soft" water that made suds easily. A pipe through the wall brought water into the kitchen in the summer. It had to be disconnected in the winter because it would freeze and burst.

Clothes were washed by hand, using what is called a "wash board." This task was especially difficult for my mother, since she weighed only 95 pounds. When I became large enough I would come in from the field and wring the water out of the heavy pieces on wash day, which was each Monday. A heavy "flat iron," heated on the cook stove or in front of the fireplace in the winter, was used to iron the clothes. The iron was hot enough to use when it would make a drop of water sizzle. Every time the iron was used, whether on the stove or before the fireplace, the bottom had to be cleaned with a moist cloth. Otherwise, the garment would be soiled with ash or bits of grease from the stove. Imagine, if you can, ironing on a hot summer day.

Food came from either the garden or the farm, and was preserved by canning for use in the winter. Corn and wheat would be taken to the mill and made into cornmeal and flour. Little was purchased from the store, and the standard grocery list consisted mainly of sugar, coffee, and laundry soap. Groceries were almost always paid for by selling eggs to the general store. If the eggs didn't bring enough, something had to be omitted from the list.

Hogs were fattened and slaughtered for hams, bacon, and sausage. Pork was cured in salt. We rarely had beef, since there was no way to preserve it. Occasionally, a young steer would be butchered and shared with other members of the community.

I was born in this little house on January 6, 1925, at about 3:30 p.m., according to my mother, who had a very difficult delivery. I weighed a little over 9 pounds, much too large a child for such a small woman. Dr. Thayer S. Wilson, a young physician from Carthage, Tennessee, attended my mother. He had come to the house prepared to stay until I arrived. I was one of the first babies he ever delivered.

The house in "Thomas Hollow" in which I was born

Mama and Dad had not yet settled on a name for their new arrival. Since Dr. Wilson needed to submit a certificate of birth, he simply named me William Melvin Thomas. It was not until I was about 25 years old that I learned of this when I applied for a birth certificate. The Bureau of Vital Statistics had never heard of Larry Ford

Thomas. Fortunately, Dr. Wilson recalled it all and set the record straight.

Summer brought the annual county fair, a large and important event to the community. It afforded everyone in the area, mostly farmers, an opportunity to show off their prized animals, very best ears of corn, other products, and even their babies. The women involved themselves baking cakes and pies, making preserves, quilts, and just about everything needed for their daily lives. I never learned whether politics or true opinion determined that I was the best-looking baby at the fair, but I won first prize, nonetheless.

"Best-looking Baby"
Smith County Fair, 1926

I was three years old when my sister, Adelyn Kerr Thomas, was born in this same house on August 13, 1928.

My first recollections are of the years when I was about 5 or 6 years old. By then Mama and Dad had purchased a farm a few miles west of Carthage alongside Highway 70. The back portion of this farm was bounded by the Cumberland River. This farm, therefore, was always referred to as "the farm on the river."

As I recall, some of the most pleasant times were the Sundays when we all got into the Overland Ford, a four-door car with eisenglass curtains, and went to visit my paternal grandparents, Nick and Allie Bates Thomas, known to me as "Pappy" and "Mammy."

Nick & Allie ("Pappy" & "Mammy")
c. 1930

ANCESTORS

For years, I have been interested in attempting to establish the Thomas lineage. To date I have been unable to complete it, but I hope to do so before I die. I have, however, determined the following:

My late father and other members of the family have said that the late General George Henry Thomas, the Civil War general known as the "Rock of Chickamauga," was a cousin. Dad first thought he was told the General was a first cousin, but on further consideration felt that he might have been a second cousin. The late Reverend Johnnie Thomas, son of Lewis Franklin Thomas, referred to the General as a first cousin.

In any case, my father, John Melvin Thomas, was born August 2, 1899. He died August 21, 1993. His father was George Nicholas "Nick" Thomas, who was born February 10, 1877, and died February 17, 1945. Nick Thomas's father was George G. Thomas. George G. Thomas was born September 28, 1848, and died June 10, 1906.

The father of George G. Thomas was James "Jimmy" (no middle name) Thomas. James Thomas was born February 2, 1811, somewhere in Virginia. He reportedly came to Tennessee as a small boy. James Thomas died July 16, 1895, and is buried in the cemetery across from the Hickman Baptist Church, Hickman, Tennessee.

Historians have written many books about General George Henry Thomas; but little is known of his ancestry, due to the fact that the Union Army burned most of the county court houses and public records in their march South in the Civil War. It is said that General Thomas ordered that no damage was to be done to

Southampton County, Virginia, the General's birthplace.

In August 1995, I traveled to Courtland, Virginia, the county seat of Southampton County. Here I learned that General Thomas was born at "Thomaston," which is located just off Highway 674 north of Newsom, Virginia. His place of birth still stands and is now the home of Lisa Skeeters.

The General was born July 31, 1816, the son of John C. Thomas and Elizabeth Rochelle. It is believed that General Thomas's father was born in 1784. He was killed in a farm accident on April 20, 1829, at 45 years of age. His mother was a descendent of the French Huguenots. In addition to George Henry Thomas, John and Elizabeth had the following children:

    John William Thomas (_____, 1809 – May 2, 1889)
    Judith Elvira Thomas (August 19, 1812 - _____, 1902)
    Benjamin R. Thomas (_____ - March 12, 1876)
    George Henry Thomas (July 31, 1816 – March 28, 1870)
    Lucy Thomas (____ - _____)
    Elizabeth Thomas (____ - _____)
    Anne Thomas (____ - _____)
    Juliet Thomas (____ - _____)
    Francis C. Thomas (August 20, 1827 - _____, 1903)

Southampton County Will Book #4, page 671, reflects the will of William Thomas, offered for probate on February 12, 1795. In this will William Thomas divided his land, known as "the Sarah Carter place," among his children in differing amounts. He refers to his children:

        Son – Henry Thomas
        Son – John Thomas
        Daughter – Lucy
        Son – George Gurley Thomas
        Son – William

The will also directed that William's sister, Elizabeth, be supported by his son Henry.

I was told by Mrs. Adeline Kitchens, Southampton County Court House, that "Thomaston" was originally a part of the Sarah Carter property.

I find it interesting to note that on July 29, 1805 (Deed Book 11, Page 128) George Gurley Thomas and wife Hannah B. Thomas sold 223 acres of land. There is no record subsequent to that date placing them in Southampton County. Could they have migrated to Tennessee? Further, it is interesting to note that my Great Grandfather was George G. Thomas, though it has never been conclusively established whether this was the same man or not.

It is known that the General Thomas had no children. Historians record that following the Civil War Battle at Murfreesboro, Tennessee, where General Thomas was the Commanding General of the Union Forces, he took three days to visit his brother Benjamin.

It has been established that one Benjamin Thomas and wife Leanna, both born in Virginia, lived in DeKalb County, Tennessee at that time. This was easily within a day's horseback ride from Murfreesboro. It seems logical that if Benjamin Thomas lived in this area less than ten miles from my birth place, that other members of his family may have also migrated to this area.

"The Thomas and Bridges Story, 1540 to 1840," written by Edison H. Thomas, and published in 1972 by T&E Publishers in Louisville, Kentucky, contends that the first Thomas to enter America was John Thomas, born in Wales about 1585. He arrived in America at Jamestown, Virginia on May 14, 1610. It is contended that practically all the Thomases in this country descended from this John Thomas. Note also that my father was John Melvin Thomas.

In the recent past I visited the Antietam Battlefield in Virginia. In the visitors' center there was a large portrait of General George Henry Thomas hanging behind the Welcome counter. I looked at it and said, "Hello, Cousin." One of the Rangers overheard me and asked if I was in fact related to General Thomas. After explaining the relationship I was asked to sign a special guest register and was told that if any time I, or any member of my family, visit there we are to be considered "special guests".

Little is known about my mother's family, the Dillards. My mother, Willie Geneva Dillard Thomas, was born March 20, 1898, and died December 27, 1993. Her father, Joseph Henry Dillard, was born January 8, 1852, and died January 11, 1910. Joseph Henry Dillard's father is not

Seated: John Hay, Herschel Dillard

Standing: Willie Geneva Dillard, and John Hay's sister (name unknown)

Dec 31, 1913

known. His mother was Peggy Halliburton Dillard. Nothing more is known about her.

My mother's maternal grandfather (and for whom she was named) was Will Dillard, who was born, lived, and died on the family farm located near Club Springs, Tennessee which is located near the Chestnut Mound community, Smith County, Tennessee. Mama contended that the Will Dillard Family was not related to the Joseph Henry Dillard family.

My Mother was born in Marshall County, Tennessee, near what she knew as the Flat Rock community. This community no longer exists. Her mother, Elizabeth Ann Dillard, died when my mother was nine years of age. Her father died when she was eleven years old. She was left with an older half-sister, Daisy Dillard, and half-sister Cleo Dillard along with two brothers, Hershel Dillard and Elmore Dillard. Hershel Dillard, at age 15, was the oldest brother. For three or four years Hershel tilled the family farm, which was not very fertile land, and kept the family together. Economic conditions were very poor.

My mother recalled that in the Fall of the year, my Aunt Daisy picked field peas for income. She would pick peas all day and the family would shell them at night. When she had accumulated $10.00, Daisy purchased a sewing machine. Aunt Daisy could neither read nor write, so it fell my mother's lot to assemble the new "White" brand treadle sewing machine, and then learn to operate it. At nine years of age, my mother made her first dress. At 95 years of age, just before her death, she could still describe the fabric and exactly how the dress was made.

Word soon spread that Mama could sew and people would show up at her home with fabric asking her to make a dress. One "cousin" in particular showed up often. They would make a dress and the cousin would wear it home, all in the same day.

Economic conditions became increasingly difficult. Mama learned of a family in Carthage, Tennessee, Billie and Betty Ford (now deceased), who were searching for a live-in "domestic." She secured that position and lived with them throughout her education and up to the time she began teaching school. It is from them that I get my middle name, Ford.

FARM ON THE RIVER

In the fall of 1928, Mama and Dad bought a farm along the Cumberland River just west of Carthage, Tennessee. It was a good, productive piece of land. The dwelling was of wooden construction, but much more substantial and comfortable than was the house in "the hollow."

Mama and Dad always worked from dawn to dusk. In addition to general farming, Dad developed a strong interest in raising white leghorn laying hens. He approached this enterprise rather scientifically, trap nesting to record the number of eggs each would lay, endeavoring through this method to develop the most productive of laying hens.

Leghorn roosters can develop into very dominant animals, almost to the point of that attained by game roosters. Not only do they obviously rule over the hens and smaller roosters, but often everything and everyone that enters their domain. We had one such rooster that seemed to develop a special dislike for my mother. He tried not to be too obvious, but simply took his time in stalking quietly from the rear before making his final charge. Mama found it necessary when going into his pen to take a strong stick. Even so, he attacked her more than once about the legs, bringing blood. This afforded a special challenge to a six-year-old boy. At that time, one could purchase firecrackers of just about any size. Some were almost like a small bomb. Choosing what I thought was the appropriate time, I entered the pen with a very large firecracker. I didn't know until after the fact that my mother was watching from the kitchen window.

Just as soon as I entered the pen, this particular rooster came running toward me in a fighting stance with his wings spread out. He stopped before he got to me, but near enough that I felt I could toss the firecracker at him.

I lit it and threw it in his direction, but it fell short, about three feet in front of him. Defiantly, the rooster hopped forward, stopping astride the firecracker. When the firecracker exploded, the rooster was blown or jumped three or four feet in the air, enveloped in a huge cloud of feathers. He turned and slowly walked away, no longer looking for a fight. Mama declared often, with obvious delight, that when the firecracker exploded, the rooster was blown at least six feet in the air. I doubt whether it was that high, but then I couldn't see very well because of the cloud of feathers. This completely demoralized the rooster to the point he was no longer an asset in the chicken yard. He was relegated to chicken and dumplings a short time later. What surprised me most was that Dad never scolded me for this, not even once.

⁓ ⁓ ⁓ ⁓

It was about this time, during the summer, that tragedy almost struck. It was is in the mid-afternoon when threatening, angry-looking clouds moved in. They were very dark and the wind was blowing fiercely. It was obvious that a severe storm was brewing. Mama remembered that the baby turkeys were out. Turkey chicks are especially susceptible to drowning in heavy rain, so Mama went out to get them in. She instructed my sister and me to stay inside. I stood by the window watching her. Just as Mama got under the outstretched branches of a huge oak tree not far from the house, the storm hit. The moment she stopped under one of the long, lower branches, lightning hit the tree. I watched as the ball of lightning ran down the tree trunk, out the limb, and hit Mama. She fell instantly as though she had been killed.

Dad, coming in from the field, saw what happened and ran to her. I also ran outside. Her face was literally black with no sign of life. Dad sat on the ground in the driving rain holding Mama's head in his lap. A neighbor had also seen what happened and came running. He was carrying an umbrella and wanted to hold it over Mama. But Dad told him to let it rain on her face. Within a short time she began to revive. It is easy to understand that from that day until the day of her death, when a storm approached she preferred to, and often did, sit on the bed hoping to insulate herself from the lightning.

The economy following World War I had improved steadily, but then disaster approached in 1932 during the "Great Depression." Times became especially hard for Mama and Dad, who worked even harder trying to simply pay the interest on the money Dad had borrowed to purchase the farm. He grew further and further behind.

Tobacco was considered the cash crop and provided the money to pay interest and other debts. When Dad sold

Dad (Melvin) in tobacco, with the tobacco barn behind

his tobacco crop in 1931, it brought him only twelve dollars, not enough to pay the cost of selling it. Mama and Dad did everything they could think of, even churning butter by hand and taking it into Carthage, along with selling eggs in an effort to generate some cash. Often they could not even sell what they took in. No one had any money. In spite of all their efforts, they could not meet even the interest payment on the mortgage.

If Dad had only known what was to come, he could have held out a few months until President Roosevelt issued an order to the banks that would have saved his farm. Not knowing this, he simply had no choice but to default and turn it over to the bank. Little did he suspect that one of the bank officials would end up with the farm, which within a few years would be a very valuable piece of property.

17

BACK TO THE HOLLOW

Just before Christmas in 1932, with no hope of saving the farm on the river, there was no place to go but back to Thomas Hollow. Dad started moving the farm machinery, a few head of stock, chickens, and furniture by wagon and a team of mules. It was a long one-day trip each way. I don't remember how many trips he had to make, but he made several.

Once we were all back in the hollow, we could not move back into the house where I was born. It was then occupied by my Uncle George Thomas, who had just married Frances. So we had to move into the "Big House" and share it with Mammy and Pappy and Dad's youngest sister, Alta Thomas. Even though it was a large house, it didn't seem big enough for all of us. We had a rather separate part to live and sleep in, but meals were shared with Mammy and Pappy, since there was only one kitchen and dining area.

Because I was still young, all this did not affect me a great deal, but I was well aware that it was of major importance to Dad, and especially to Mama. I recall little about this period, except for Christmas in 1932. This holiday is indelibly imprinted on my mind. With the excitement that only a child can have, I awoke early on Christmas morning and went to Mama and Dad's room after being unable to find my overalls. It must have been very early, because they weren't up yet. My overalls were hanging on the end of the mantle. I didn't recall leaving them there but thought nothing of it, since the fireplace used to warm our part of the house was in this room, so we spent most of our time in there. There was nothing in view to indicate this was a special holiday season.

I was not aware that Dad was awake until he suggested I look in my overall pocket. When I put my hand inside the pocket, I still remember the thrill of touching a new pocket knife. This was the only gift I received from anybody that year, yet I was ecstatic. I can only feel that this was probably all my mother and Dad could afford. What touched me even more was the fact that Mama lay in bed, crying softly.

When uncle George and Aunt Frances moved out of the "little house," we moved in, back to where I was born. This was home for about the next eleven years. It was not always pleasant, but it was dry when it rained. It was hot in the summer and cold in the winter.

Some twenty years later I sat in a restaurant in New York City with a group of FBI colleagues listening to their stories of early childhood. When my turn around the table came, I chose to tell them about "the house in the hollow" – how the wide boards in the floor around the fireplace had worn to the point you could see through the floor to the ground below. I told them how a rug would have been nice, but that we couldn't afford one then. We had to settle for a 9 x 12 piece of linoleum pulled up over these boards. Even then, at times when the wind blew hard, it would lift the linoleum off the floor to the point we had to put furniture on it to hold it down. To this day my friends believe this was a total fabrication. The truth of the matter is that we sat right there, as close to the fire as we could get, with long underwear and coats on but still could barely stay warm.

The middle room in this house was the dining room. We used it mostly when we had guests (which wasn't often) or on Sundays if the weather wasn't too cold. Otherwise we ate in the kitchen.

The kitchen, located at the rear of the house, was Spartan, to say the least. Cooking was done on an "Enterprise Range," a wood-fired stove. Later on we got a stove that had a reservoir alongside it. This was great.

We could have warm water without having to heat it on top of the stove. Also in the kitchen was a portable cabinet, probably called a hutch today. Except for that, there was only the breakfast table and chairs. There were a couple of open shelves along one wall that served as a storage place and a place to hang coats and hats. Even so, the kitchen was such a hospitable place, especially in the winter. It was always warm and the aroma of cooking food was so inviting. There was a small sink along the back wall to carry away water that came in from the large tank outside. As mentioned before, this pipe would freeze in the winter, so we had to disconnect it every year. Water from the sink simply ran out on the ground outside. There were no closets in the house. Illumination came from a kerosene lamp or lantern. Electricity was something people had who lived far, far away.

The toilet was a small framed "two holer," sitting right on top of the ground back from the rear of the house. Toilet paper, as we now know it, was nonexistent. The substitute was the Sears & Roebuck catalogue, but only the black-and-white pages.

There was always sufficient food. Maybe not always what we would like to have, but enough. Mama and Dad canned and preserved almost everything we ate in the winter: corn, beans, sauerkraut, and sometimes canned sausage, which I dearly loved. Dad would grow potatoes and store them in the hay in the barn to prevent them from freezing. We also had turnips, turnip greens, and mustard greens all winter until they froze out when the weather got cold.

Dad butchered several hogs and cured them in salt at first. Later on, he used a sugar-cured method. This required expert attention or the meat would spoil. We sacked and smoked our own sausage. Hog killing day and several days thereafter were great days. Our first meal would be liver, and for breakfast we would have brains and eggs, with hot biscuits, butter, and jelly. Then followed grinding and making the sausage. It was always necessary to experiment with the spices until they were just right, which we could only tell by cooking and tasting some. I can still feel the warm kitchen and smell the fragrance of cooking sausage and the joy of endless tasting. As you might imagine, one can eventually tire of eating pork all the time. So Dad would, from time to time, take a ham to the general store in Hickman, where he would swap it, usually evenly, for a case of canned salmon. This meant salmon croquettes, which I love to this day.

Since we raised chickens, there was always a lot of fried chicken and chicken and dumplings. "Country butter", milk, and cream were in abundance. It was not at all unusual for us to give whole milk and cream to the hogs.

Bathing was often confined to sponging with a wash cloth. Saturday night was serious bath night in preparation for going to church the next day. We bathed in a large, round galvanized tub, also used for washing clothes. It was difficult to impossible to get into it.

Children, no matter where they are or whatever the circumstance, will find something with which to amuse themselves. I don't recall that I ever had a toy except for one I made myself. My earliest remembrances are of playing under the house in the hollow. I would make a crude car out of a piece of wood. Wheels were made by sawing across a spool after Mama had used all the thread. I would make roads in the dirt under the lower side of the house and play there for hours. As I grew older I became fairly adept at making a pistol out of wood, some of which became very realistic. When I could get together with others my age in the hollow, we would have a good game of "cops and robbers," often extending out into the wooded areas.

I think my favorite pastime was playing with a steel rim, the bigger the better. Generally, about the largest one I could find was a foot to eighteen inches in diameter and approximately one inch across. I would then fashion a "pusher" out of a heavy piece of wire that would not bend easily. One end would be fashioned in the form of a crude handle. The other would be bent in the shape of a "U" the width of the wheel. By pushing the "U" against the wheel it could be propelled almost anywhere I wanted to go while walking or running.

Not long before Mama died she was recalling, as she often had before, my "oogie" game, as she called it. Bethel Kent, who was my age and lived in another of the tenant houses in the hollow, would come to my house. We would each get a metal pie pan and pretend that it was an automobile steering wheel. We would run "all over the place" for hours blowing the horn by saying, "Oogie." Automobile horns in those days were not as melodious as they are now. They all sounded rather like "oogah."

Cousin Ralph Thomas showed up at my house one day with his latest creation. He had made a baseball mitt out of an old felt hat. It truly was a work of art and worked just as well as the real thing. Believe it or not, it lasted for a long time.

I often thought of having a bicycle but never got one.

Soon after we moved back into the hollow, the engine in Dad's Overland Ford froze and burst, rendering it totally useless. There was no such thing as Prestone antifreeze. Alcohol could be used, but Dad didn't have any and forgot to drain the water from all parts of the engine. This meant walking the mile to Hickman to church and to catch the school bus when school was in session. There was no mail delivery, so we had to walk the mile to the post offic in Hickman to get it.

God blessed me by giving me parents who, above all else, believed in Him. "Thou shalt not" meant just that. "Honor your father and mother," "Thou shalt not steal," and "Do unto others as you would have them do unto you" were everyday principles that we followed. Mama and Dad were not inside the church every time the doors were open, as some thought one ought to be, but they were there on "The Lord's Day," rain or shine. The only thing that prevented us from being in church would be illness. A runny nose wouldn't do it — we had to be really SICK. When we had no automobile, we walked. On the rare occasion when it had rained and the creeks threatened, we would go by wagon, drawn by two red mules, Kit and Kate.

As a child it seemed to me that the "preacher's" (minister's) sole objective was to scare people into Heaven or to scare Hell out of us, and as in all teaching situations, it seems more got through to us than we thought. When I was twelve years old, I think, we were in the midst of a "protracted meeting," known today as a revival. Those meetings, held in the evenings, usually lasted at least a week each year and were set at a time least likely to interfere with farming operations, but while the weather was still favorable. One night, in the midst of such a meeting, and after the minister had preached a particularly compelling sermon, we were standing for "the invitation." It was the practice for those already a Christian to move about in the congregation during the invitation and speak to those not yet "born again," encouraging them to accept Christ.

As I stood there, I looked diagonally across the church and saw my Aunt Callie Smith leave her pew. I knew she was headed for me, and she was. I don't remember just what she said to me, but I vividly recall what happened. Whether I looked up or not, I do not recall, but I could then and can still now see clearly a wide band of light stretching from me all the way into the heavens.

God had chosen me and at that moment forgave my sins and guaranteed me a place in Heaven one day. He continues to forgive me as I go, and more than once He has shielded and protected me, according to His purpose.

Baptism was done in the Hickman Creek, which ran just at the rear of the church. Sometimes the creek would be just about dry, so we often had to wait for a rain and by then had several persons waiting to be baptized. It was an impressive event. The entire congregation (and sometimes even other spectators) gathered on the creek bank. They always sang "On the Banks of the River Jordan." One could never forget this experience.

I believe it was the winter of 1937 when we had the biggest snow I ever saw in this area. It was bitter cold. The snow in the yard in front of our house was knee-deep. We were getting very short of firewood and simply had to go cut some, snow or not. I did not have footwear suitable for such weather. Dad had some rubber boots that would fit over his regular work shoes, but he could not get enough wood by himself. Mama wrapped my feet, over my workshoes, with paper, and then wrapped me from the knees down in burlap. It was a bit bulky and awkward, but quite warm.

Dad selected a thorn tree alongside the creek not far from the house. It was close enough we could carry it to the house. The tree was frozen solid. The first blow broke a huge chip out of the axe. Fortunately, we had another one.

The years from 1932 to 1942 were difficult times, and sometimes not altogether happy. Everything was directed toward trying to save enough money to buy another place of our own. Little was said to me, but I was aware that Dad did not feel he was being treated fairly by his mother. Mammy was a very domineering person and let it be known that she felt it was my father's responsibility to stay on the farm and work as long as she and Pappy lived.

It was an open point of contention that during the early 1930's Pappy was in debt and was afraid he would lose the farm, which was in his name only. So he deeded it to Mammy with the understanding that when the crisis was over she would deed it back to him, since he had purchased it in the first place. But she never did. She held it in her name until her death. I can remember Pappy being so unhappy about this that he would walk around crying. Dad and Mama's determination to leave this farm as soon as possible came to a head when Mammy rounded up most of Dad's hogs and sold them as her own. She refused to give him any of the money.

We all worked, as did other tenant farmers, from dawn to dusk on an almost cruel hillside farm. From the time I could lift a hoe, I was expected to work in the field. Then came the turning plow and other large tools. The long corn rows around this hillside far from the house, without a person in sight all day, leave lots of time for daydreaming. I remember vividly that "The Yellow Rose of Texas" had just become popular. How easy it was to imagine, though I had no idea how, meeting a beautiful girl from Texas. How often I have remembered this fantasy, having married a beautiful, wonderful, loving wife from Shreveport, Louisiana, which is so near to Texas.

Transportation from the house and barn to the field was on the back of a mule or walking. If you have never ridden a mule bareback in the hot summertime, you cannot appreciate the effect it has on one's backside. While riding along one day, almost half-asleep, going to the house for lunch, the mule suddenly jumped, sending me straight up. While I was in effect suspended in mid-air, the mule jumped to one side so that I landed hard on the ground still in a seated position. The mule then stood aside waiting for me to get back on. I suspected I knew what caused this sudden departure from an otherwise trustworthy animal. Mules and horses are very leery of a rattlesnake and can apparently smell the presence of one, even when it can't be seen. There was a stand of canes, the rattlesnake's favorite lair, alongside the trail at this point. I couldn't find a snake at that time, but I felt sure he was nearby.

I knew that a big woodchuck (groundhog) had a den just over the fence from the cane break. So on the way back to the field I took Dad's shotgun along. It was an 1897 model Winchester pump gun. This gun has an exposed hammer. In order to get a better look over the wall and check on the woodchuck, I had to step atop a large tree stump between the trail and the fence just to one edge of the cane break. Fear seized me when I heard the "rattling" of a snake. Once you have heard a rattler up close you never forget the sound. I knew he was close, very close. Moving nothing but my eyes, I found him coiled between the stump I was standing on and the rock fence, barely inches from by legs. I knew I could never move away before he could strike. Fortunately, I was holding the shotgun in my right hand with the muzzle pointed generally in the direction of the snake. With as little movement as possible, I cocked the hammer and ever so slowly moved the barrel toward the snake, knowing it would take a lucky shot to save me. I fired the gun, holding it only in my right hand like a pistol, and fortunately severed the snake in two places, the first just behind the head.

There were many rattlesnakes around, with a story about each one. Rather than fill this narrative with snake stories, I will limit it to just two rather unusual ones. I must tell you, as I begin this first one, it is about the time I saw a rattlesnake jump over a man's head. My New York City FBI colleagues who did not believe my story about the house in the hollow found this one even more unbelievable. My Dad was there when the event occurred and verified it each time I told this story in his presence.

Living and working on Pappy's farm was a full-blooded Cherokee Indian. I never knew his first name, but his last name was Stocklin, and we affectionately called him "Uncle Sock." One spring, Uncle Sock decided he wanted to plant Irish potatoes in some "new ground." "New ground" meant the space above the tillable land generally where the wooded area began, but which was too steep to be tilled normally. It was, in some places, very rich soil. The place Uncle Sock chose was very steep, but he insisted that this was the place.

Pappy, my father, Uncle Sock, and I were busily clearing away the small bushes when suddenly I heard my Dad say, "Look out, Uncle Sock!" I turned to see Uncle Sock, a bit above me and to one side, quickly crouch and lean toward the hillside, just as a rattlesnake, on about the level of his head, started to strike at him. The momentum of the snake propelled the snake into the air and down the hill just missing Sock's face, but going over his head. The snake's tail touched his shoulders as it went down.

My second snake story took place in the big barn near our house. This barn had a couple of large corn cribs, a haven for rats and mice. Cats were of little help since the vermin could move about among the ears of unshucked corn, out of their reach. The rats were so numerous and such a problem I would go to the barn when it rained and take along my .22 rifle. The rats would literally line up for water at the drip edge of the roof. I would lie on the ground, down toward the end of the line of rats and could kill several with one shot. Over time I killed hundreds.

Somehow Pappy got the idea that a snake would help to eliminate the problem. The snake could move about in the corn and eat the little rats and mice, eventually depleting the rat population. Pappy knew of my fear and strong dislike for snakes. He explained how beneficial some were and how harmless they were to humans. His last words on the subject were, "Don't kill my snake." One of my daily chores was to take the corn shucks, piled in the corner of the crib, to the mules and cows. They ate them just like hay. One particular evening, there was an unusually large pile of shucks. In order to reduce the number of trips necessary to dispense them, I began trying to gather as many as I could hold onto in both arms. I had so many I could not see where I was going.

It was not at all uncommon to find an ear of corn in among the shucks. I got hold of an ear on this occasion. At least I thought it was until it began to move. Dropping the shucks, I realized I was holding a big, long snake just a few inches from its tail. I was literally scared stiff, I think. I was so frightened I could not let go of the snake, now twisting wildly, trying to get loose, no doubt, but seemingly trying to devour me, just as if I were another big rat. I must have screamed, because Pappy later told me he saw what was happening and called to me to turn the snake loose. I just could not let go. Nearby was a post used to support a portion of the loft. Instinctively, I began whipping the snake against this pole and didn't (or couldn't) stop until there were a mere two or three inches of snake left. This ended Pappy's attempt to rid the crib of rats by using snakes.

ے ے ے ے

The first job I ever did for which I was paid was thinning corn. I was just old enough to wield a hoe. Corn was usually planted a little too thick and then thinned to the right amount, by cutting out the excess. This was when I learned how to "thin" or "chop corn". There is only one correct way to do it, and that is to cut it off well below the ground. Otherwise, it will sprout and come out again thicker than ever. Needless to say, I didn't chop mine deeply enough. Dad made me chop the entire 14-acre field a second time, free of charge. This made the original compensation, in the amount of 50 cents per day, now only 25 cents per day.

Along with the work on the farm, we had to take a few days, usually three or four, every summer to "work the road" and "run the telephone line." In those times, neither the county nor the state made any attempt to maintain secondary roads, except for an occasional pass by a road grader. The grader usually concentrated on cleaning out the ditch, which more often than not made the road worse, since it put dirt and mud on the surface. Those living along a given stretch of road were obliged to haul gravel and fill the pot holes if they were to be filled. The various neighbors would attempt to select a day agreeable to all and everyone would take their wagons, drawn by mules, to the creek and get gravel for the roadway. More often than not, some who should have been there were not. It didn't take extensive observation to notice the same ones were repeatedly absent.

In the mid-1930's each community usually had its own telephone system, a cooperative financed by individual subscriptions. One or two paid operators handled all the calls. Unless we were calling someone on our line (a party line), we had to crank the telephone to get the operator. She would ring the party we wanted and if they answered, the operator would make the connection so we could talk. Even though we were living under the same constitution we have now, there wasn't much said, or much concern, about the right to privacy. Anyone on our party line, the recipient's party line, or the operator could listen in. Often, so many neighbors would pick up the phone when they heard it ring that the volume would be reduced. We would simply ask those listening to hang up so we could hear. Most of the time they did, but not always. Everyone knew what everyone else in the community was saying over the telephone.

The telephone lines were maintained by people living along the path of the line. More often than not, this was handled on an emergency basis, but occasionally we would walk the lines, cutting trees that threatened the wires. Trouble usually came after a storm when a tree would be blown across the line. Generally, a person would check the line from his house to the next house, and if the trouble wasn't found, he would call ahead and ask others to do the same. Sometimes we had to run the line all the way by ourselves.

∽   ∽   ∽   ∽

I clearly remember that 1937 was a banner year. My brother, Lewis Caroll Thomas was born on July 27, 1937. Dad purchased a used 1936 Ford, which meant we no longer had to walk to town and to church. This little car had a small V-8 engine and was adequately powered. It ran well except when it wanted a new fuel pump. I drove it to Nashville one day and had to replace three fuel pumps before I got it home. The car had no heater or defroster, so we did not go far in the winter time. The car was always easy to start, but stopping it was the problem. This was years before hydraulic brakes, and often it was necessary to put both feet on the brake pedal and push as hard as possible. We still had this car during World War II. Tires were so nearly impossible to get that we simply had to "make do" with what we had. All tires had inner tubes in them; some tubes would literally have patches on patches. Early on, patching was done with "cold patches" which often did not seal very well when the tire was inflated and the tube stretched. Later on, "hot patches" were available, making a more permanent seal.

~ ~ ~ ~

As I got older, I was given one row of tobacco, and the income was mine to use as I wanted. Around 1937 I chose to use my tobacco money to buy a radio, which we had never had before. Dad felt this was an unnecessary luxury and that my money could be more wisely spent. I purchased a tall console Philco radio that was advertised as being able to pick up stations a long distance away. I could very clearly get WSM radio in Nashville, and WLW in Cincinnati. This was on AM, since FM was yet to come. I paid the sum total of $15.00 for it. Since we had no electricity, I had to get a radio powered by a battery. Luckily, the radio needed a six-volt battery, the same as the one in the car. So I bought a second battery and when the radio battery needed charging I exchanged it with the one in the car.

This "unnecessary luxury" very quickly became the center of activity in the house. It introduced us to Amos and Andy, Lowell Thomas, and the Grand Ole Opry. Dad became so addicted to the Grand Ole Opry that it was imperative we listen to it every time it was on the air, usually until it went off the air, which I believe may have been around 11:00 PM every Saturday night.

A new country music star named Roy Acuff was just emerging on the Opry. Dad was so taken with Acuff that he took me to Nashville one time to meet him. I'm afraid I was not quite as impressed as Dad had hoped. He insisted I learn how to "fiddle" anyway. One of my high school teachers could play the violin and offered lessons. After a couple of years I could only play a few church hymns reasonably well, which was a clear disappointment to Dad. I blamed my slow progress on my Sears & Roebuck violin for which I paid $25.00. I really could play much better on my instructor's violin.

~ ~ ~ ~

When I was young, you went to the doctor only when you thought you might die if you did not go. The winter of 1937 was very cold, with an unusual amount of snow. Mama and Dad both developed a severe cold, followed by a lingering, terrible cough. They finally reached the point at which Dad went to see Dr. Wilson. Dr. Wilson offered to prescribe a cough syrup, but told Dad he could make a syrup of his own that would be just as effective and cost much less. He told Dad to get a bottle of whiskey and mix it with rock candy until it was syrupy and to sip on it when needed. Dad, being adamantly opposed to the use of whiskey, refused to even go in a liquor store. Dr. Wilson sent him to see the local Sheriff, who would give him the whiskey. As I recall, the whiskey was in a gallon jug, and in all probability was confiscated moonshine. Dad mixed it as directed.

I had forgotten about this until approximately 40 years later. The family was gathered around the table for Thanksgiving dinner. I asked Dad if he recalled the occasion, and he did. Intent on teasing him, I asked if he recalled how effective the cough syrup was. "Yes," he said, "when I got it all mixed just right, it was late at night, and I was so hoarse I could hardly talk. I took a couple of tablespoons of it and went to bed. Next morning my throat had improved to the point I could call the hogs in all the way from the back of the hollow." Pursuing it further, I asked that since it was so effective, "how much did you have to take before your cough was all gone?" Without the slightest hesitation and without looking up from his meal, he said, "The whole gallon." I'm not sure who was teasing whom at this point.

During the winter of 1938, Lewis, who was still very small, 18 months old I think, became very ill. Dr. Wilson came to see him and told us he had pneumonia. As he was leaving, Dr. Wilson said he did not think Lewis would live through the night. Dad had concocted a liniment composed of camphorated oil, turpentine, kerosene, and carbolic acid. The right amount of carbolic acid, the healing part, he said, was just a bit short of what it would take to blister the skin. He would test it on his arm, under the belief that the "hotter" it was, the more effective it would be. If it was too strong, he would add a wee bit more oil. Dr. Wilson said there was nothing he could do for Lewis, and that Dad could put liniment on him if he wanted to, but that it would not help. Mama and Dad sat up all night, wrapping Lewis in warm blankets soaked with the liniment. The odor was so strong that all of us got a good dose. When Dr. Wilson arrived the next morning, Lewis was not only alive, but very alert. He is still living. Dad continued to make and use his liniment until he died. More than once he considered marketing it. It was good, he claimed, for sore muscles, back aches, tooth aches, in fact just about anything that ailed a person.

My children, in due course, were introduced to Granddaddy's liniment, but not by choice. Once when we were going to Granddaddy's house, Susan began crying, not wanting to go. Finally my wife, Nina, learned that it was because Susan, our youngest daughter, had a freshly skinned knee, and knew that if Granddaddy learned of this, he would insist on soaking it with liniment. She calmed down and agreed to go when she was told to wear a pair of long pants so he wouldn't see her knee.

Mrs. Henry (Daisy) Ashe, was my mother's half sister. Their son Joseph "Joe" Ashe, was born and reared in the Salusbury Community of Wilson County, Tennessee. Joe and I grew up together.

During World War II, Joe served in the United States Marine Corps in the South Pacific. He was in every major invasion of the war in that Theatre of Operation, but never in the first wave of troops. He told me that he often had to climb over a mound of dead American soldiers just to get ashore. Joe was wounded twice.

After the war, he worked in Nashville, Tennessee and commuted by car each day. One morning in July 1957, as they passed through Donelson, Tennessee he had a sudden and compelling need to go to a rest room. The driver stopped opposite a gasoline service station. As Joe attempted to run across the Highway, he was hit by a car and suffered severe head injuries. Witnesses said that when his head hit the pavement it bounced like a basketball. Joe was pronounced dead and taken to a morgue in Nashville.

His father, my Uncle Henry, went to see him and was told the body was to be embalmed momentarily and no one could see the body until they had finished. Uncle Henry, persisted and was taken to the morgue. As he stood looking at the body, covered with a sheet, he saw slight movement of the sheet in the area of the chest. Uncle Henry, told the attendant what he had seen and said, "My son is not dead." The attendant strongly disagreed, announcing that Joe was to be embalmed momentarily.

Uncle Henry, refused to leave the room and demanded an ambulance to take Joe to the local Veterans Administration Hospital. Joe was, in fact, alive, but in a deep coma. He remained in a coma in excess of four months.

While I was visiting my parents, my mother asked that I take her to see Joe. Knowing his condition, I did not want to see him. My mother prevailed and along with my sister Adelyn, we drove to the hospital. When we arrived at the hospital a nurse tried to condition us by telling us Joe was still in a coma, would not know us, would not respond to us, and was restrained in a straitjacket.

As I stood looking at him, getting control of my emotions, I spoke his name, "Joe." Joe immediately opened his eyes, looked at me and said, "How are you Ford?" (my middle name) He turned to my sister and inquired about her two daughters, calling them by name. The nurse immediately turned around and ran down the hall in search of a doctor. When he arrived, the doctor took one look at Joe and said, in effect, "I cannot believe it." They promptly removed the straitjacket. Joe was totally calm. Joe was eventually moved to the Veterans Hospital at Murfreesboro, Tennessee, where he continued to improve.

Several years passed. I was assigned by the FBI to work at the Columbia, Tennessee Residence Agency. Murfreesboro was a part of my territory. I had not seen Joe for a long time. While I walked along the hospital corridor, I heard some one speak my name. When I turned around, Joe was walking towards me. We went to the local cafeteria and had lunch topped off with ice cream, Joe's favorite food. We carried on a normal conversation.

Joe was never able to leave the hospital and seek employment, but for 30 years lived what appeared to be a happy, comfortable existence. A potential tragedy had been averted by his persistent, loving father.

SMALL EVENTS - CHERISHED MEMORIES

The mundane life on a remote farm, in the early part of this century, was often filled with events that seemed so commonplace as to be insignificant at the time, but have become cherished memories.

It was not uncommon to make a pet out of the wildlife. My Dad once had a grey squirrel that he carried around in his overall pocket. My grandparents had a pet raccoon that, when he was good, had run of the house. One Saturday, the day we went to town for groceries, Mammy had baked three pies for dinner. Searching about for a place to store the pies that would be safe from the raccoon, she and Pappy decided the only place in the house the raccoon could not reach was the top of a very tall cupboard. The sides, Pappy said, were so slick he could not possibly climb it.

When they returned from town a few hours later and entered the kitchen door, the first thing they heard was the y-u-m-m, y-u-m-m of the raccoon. Sure enough, he had gotten on top of the cabinet and was finishing off the last of the pies. Mammy picked up the rifle that stood next to the door, handed it to Pappy, and said, "Do your thing." He did, right there in the kitchen.

❧ ❧ ❧ ❧

When I was a very young boy, I found a large dead mole in our yard, and showed it to my mother. She stroked the very smooth skin and said that she would like to make a powder puff out of it.

I skinned the mole, stretched the hide, and nailed it to a board to retain its shape. Then I scraped the inside of the skin to remove all tissue and then covered it with salt. Periodically, I would scrape off the salt and replace it with fresh salt. When it had dried out, I washed it thoroughly and softened it with a light application of oil on the inside part. My mother then trimmed it so that it was round, placed a wad of cotton on it, and sewed the edges together. It was soft as only moleskin can be, and was exceptionally durable. She used it for years.

～ ～ ～ ～

Riding the back of a mule on a hot day, going to one of the distant hillside fields to chop corn all afternoon is hardly something I looked forward to. Yet this was often a very special time for me. Dad had an interest in music, and probably could have easily learned to play an instrument if he had been so inclined. In his 30's, when I was about ten years old, he played the harmonica a great deal. I have very clear memories of him ahead of me on a mule with him going through his collection of popular songs. One in particular, and my favorite, was "My Wild Irish Rose." My brother, Lewis, must have inherited this talent, and plays the harmonica to this day.

～ ～ ～ ～

One day while we lived in "The Hollow", Dad and I had gone back to the "head" of the hollow to clean up some saplings and brush. Dad stumbled and fell backwards, landing in a seated position atop a large brush pile that had been there for some time. He had hardly hit it when he literally bounced off of it, obviously excited. Knowing something was amiss, I asked what was wrong. Dad's answer was immediate, "There is a rattlesnake in there." Neither of us had heard the rattle, nor could we begin to see the bottom of the pile, yet Dad persisted and started taking the brush away with a large fork. Sure enough, there in the middle of the pile was a large rattlesnake.

～ ～ ～ ～

Dad was as nearly ambidextrous as anyone could be. I have seen him pick up a small round rock and throw it with equal accuracy using either arm. In fact, I have seen him kill rabbits with a stone. Dad related often that when he was high school age and a bit after, he played baseball when he could get away from farm duties long enough. Dad was the pitcher. He would pitch with either arm, often pitching one ball with his right arm, and then throw the next time with his left arm. This apparently was somewhat disconcerting to the batter. He won most of the games he pitched.

꒰ ꒰ ꒰ ꒰

One afternoon Mammy, realizing that a thunderstorm was coming, sent Dad up in the "grass lot" to find the baby turkeys and bring them in. While looking for them, Dad kept hearing a loud hissing sound, which seemed to follow him about. Turning around, he was literally face-to-face with a very large black snake. A black snake, when it wants to, can stand erect with just a small portion of its tail section on the ground. They are especially defensive if they have little snakes about. Dad assumed this was the case, since black snakes are generally not aggressive. Dad was carrying a claw hammer with him and, with that being the only defensive weapon at hand, threw it at the snake. Luckily (Dad said it was skill), the claw of the hammer caught the snake just behind its head, killing it.

꒰ ꒰ ꒰ ꒰

As I have said before, there were lots of rattlesnakes about. Dad told many times about having observed a particular battle between a black snake and a rattlesnake. The black snake was the aggressor. It would wrestle with the rattlesnake, coil about it, and hold on as long as it could. The rattlesnake would bite the black snake as often as it could. Seeming to tire, the black snake would hurriedly leave the scene and go to a particular weed nearby, appear to take a few bites of it, then go back to the struggle. This was repeated several times over about an hour that Dad continued his vigil. Finally, the black snake prevailed and killed the rattlesnake. Unfortunately, Dad did not remember to identify that weed!

~ ~ ~ ~

Everyone knew Dr. Wilson's black model A Ford car. Any time I saw it, I would try to stop him in hope he would show me his shooting skills. He always carried a .22 caliber Remington pump-action rifle with him. Unless he was on an urgent mission, he would always stop. He could toss a small stone in the air and break it every time. He contended he could shoot a hole in a quarter and would ask if I wanted the hole in the center or near the edge. He explained how easy it was to do. After years of practice, the tosser, he said, knew exactly how far the target was going up, so he would be ready when it stopped at the top of its path, and shoot before it started back down. I have killed a few birds in flight with a .22 rifle, but not often. I was never able to hit a stone tossed in the air.

~ ~ ~ ~

While living on the farm on the river, Dad had a Jersey bull that was especially mean. This bull decided what and whom was welcomed in his field. He seemed to especially dislike Mama, and would have gored her one day, had she not reached the fence just in time to roll under it ahead of his horns. Not long after this event, Dad came up to the house, wet with perspiration and very upset. The bull had chased him for the first time, and Dad had barely made it to the fence. Dad was bent on teaching this bull a lesson, and he did, too. Dad removed all the lead shot from a 12-gauge shotgun

39

shell. He tightly rolled a piece of bacon rind and stuffed it inside the shell. With gun in hand, he went back to the bull's domain. The bull was waiting as if he knew Dad would be back, head down, pawing the earth, daring him to come over the fence. Selecting his position carefully, Dad fired one shot. The bacon rind hit the bull near the front of the left shoulder, coursing a path along the bull's left side, all the way to its hind leg, removing skin and hair in a path about 1 inch wide. The bull lowered his head, bellowed loudly, and walked away, never to chase anyone, or anything again.

❧   ❧   ❧   ❧

It was about this same time Dad realized some of his prized laying hens were missing. Knowing they were tightly fenced-in, he discounted the possibility of a varmint getting to them. I did not know of his real suspicions until I was awakened one night by movement in the house some time during the wee hours of the morning. I saw Dad reach above the front door and get the shotgun out of the rack. Mama stopped me from going outside with him, but let me stand just inside the door. I could hear something disturbing the chickens. Dad had stepped out onto the front porch and stood next to a large pillar with the shotgun down along his right leg. It was a moonlit night and visibility was good. I saw a person with a large burlap bag over his shoulder climb up on the wire fence about 50 yards away. When this man was atop the fence, Dad fired at him, and kept firing until the man had gotten out of range and the cloud of chicken feathers had settled. Dad had killed a couple of his hens, but the chicken thief continued on his way. Dad explained he knew the man was far enough away that the shots would not kill him, but that he suspected he knew who it was and he was determined to stop it.

The next day, Dad stayed around the house. When he saw a black Ford go down the lane leading to a shack not far from our house, Dad got his shotgun and walked over to the fence alongside the road. A short time later, Dr. Wilson came driving back up the lane. Dad stopped him and wanted to know if somebody "down there" was sick. Dr. Wilson's reply was classic. "Not very, just got a bad case of lead poisoning." Dr. Wilson had picked approximately 200 bird shot pellets out of the man's back.

Dad, much to my surprise, walked on down to this house, shotgun in hand, and knocked on the door. He said he had seen Dr. Wilson going out and wanted to know if anyone was sick, and if there was anything he could do. He never lost another chicken to thievery.

❧   ❧   ❧   ❧

Years later, not long before Dad sold his farm and moved to town, I went to visit my parents. Before Dad had come in the house, Mama showed me the mulberry tree that stood just outside their bedroom window, and asked that I not mention its condition to Dad. The tree had no leaves on it, even though it was summer. It looked like it had been in the middle of an artillery bombardment. As it turned out, this was the katydids' favorite tree. They chattered so much at night that Dad could not sleep, so he simply stuck the shotgun out the window and fired in the direction of the tree. He rid it of katydids, but in the process had shot his tree to death.

❧   ❧   ❧   ❧

When the chips were down and all else failed, we could usually count on Mama to come through. She had her usual flock of young chickens, the making of fried chicken later on, but was losing an alarming number to a chicken hawk. I tried to kill it, but I was never around when the hawk was. I came in from the field for lunch one day and Mama proudly announced that she had rid herself of the hawk. She showed me how she had taken the .22 rifle, which she had never fired in her life, out behind the house and shot the hawk off a fencepost. She pointed to a post, not near the house, but at the far end of a field behind the house. I pointed out this was at least 200 yards away and well beyond the range of a .22 rifle. She showed me how she had pointed the barrel up in the air above the bird and pulled the trigger. Disbelieving, I told her she could not possibly have hit the bird that far away. She said, "Well, when I pulled the trigger, he fell off the post and did not get up." I walked out there, and there he was, with a .22 caliber hole squarely through its middle. After Dad died, Mama gave me his shotgun, but insisted on keeping the rifle as long as she lived. I found it in her bedroom closet with a cartridge in the chamber after she died. I pity the person she might have shot at.

~ ~ ~ ~

There was a very large locust tree in front of our house in the hollow. The last time I was there, it was still standing. If it ever falls, it will be so heavy no one could carry it away. It has thousands of rounds of .22 caliber lead in it. Our favorite pastime on Sunday afternoon was to shoot at matches. The object was not to shoot the head off the match — that was too easy. The object was to light the match. Dad had filed the front sight of the rifle, which I now have, to be very narrow, so that when we sighted, the front sight was rather like a small dot, making for very precise sighting and shooting.

EDUCATION

Education through elementary and high school was rather uneventful. I started elementary school in Carthage while we still lived on the farm on the river. I was in either the second or third grade when we moved to Hickman. I don't recall how I got to school in Carthage, but know I did not walk. It was much too far. After we moved back to Hickman I had to walk the mile each way.

There were several children of school age in the hollow, among them my cousins, Roy Jackson Thomas and his brother Ralph Edward Thomas. I thought they were both very aggressive and mean. They seemed to delight in throwing small stones at me, and especially seemed to enjoy making a spear out of a tall weed and throwing it. You might think little damage would be done by a weed, but when the weed was dead, the end would be sharp and painful when it hit. So if they were along, I would spend most of my time going to and from school dodging weeds and stones. Finally, Dad had enough of this and went to his brother, Lloyd, who lived in another of the tenant houses and stopped it. Both cousins delighted in calling me a "tattletale." Both cousins were stocky in build, while I was tall and thin. There was no way I could have whipped them, especially both of them, in a fight.

Elementary education, except for the first couple of years in Carthage, was all at Hickman. All eight grades were taught by a total of three teachers, one in each of the three classrooms. So obviously, there were two or three grade levels in one room.

Each day began in the auditorium with a period of devotion followed by prayer. The course was basic: reading, writing, and arithmetic. Mental arithmetic was encouraged. I enjoyed it and was also pretty good at it. By the time I reached the eighth grade, we were adding at least three columns of figures, at the same time. Only one other student, the late Wilson High, could do it faster than I.

Work on the farm didn't stop just because we were back in school. Almost every day there would be some heavy work to do in addition to the usual chores. Often it was necessary to unload a load of tobacco, hay, or corn before I ever thought of trying to study. Homework assignments, and there were lots of them, were relegated to last place, after all the chores and supper. By now it was just about always dark, even in the long summer days. This meant studying by a kerosene lamp which gave off about as much light as a 5-watt bulb, and that's when the lamp's chimney was clean and the wick was well-trimmed. Later on I purchased an Aladdin lamp with my own money. The difference in the light output was unbelievable.

I owe what education I have to my mother. She was a good teacher. She knew all subjects equally well, but was especially proficient in English grammar and math. I had to rely upon her help because we had no reference material at all in our home. We did not get a daily paper or any magazines, except that later on we subscribed to the Progressive Farmer magazine.

After eating and being tired from a day at school, as well as the work before and after school, it was easy to want to go to sleep rather than study. My mother was always there until I had it all finished, no matter how late it was. She was patient, understanding, and an excellent teacher. I don't recall that I ever asked for her assistance when she was not immediately able to help me. I always thought it was sad she could not have pursued a teaching career. She wanted more than anything else in her life, I think, to resume teaching. She pleaded with Dad to let her teach again. Dad, rather arbitrarily I think, insisted she be at home to prepare his meals when he came in from the field. She even offered to fix his lunch before she left for school, but he would never agree to it. At one point she could have gotten a lifetime teaching permit simply by going to Carthage in person and applying for it. Dad would not even let her do that. I felt he was grossly inconsiderate in his position and told him so after I was grown and married. I can still remember how unhappy Mama was over this, and it lasted for quite a while. She often cried. Mama wasn't well at this time, either. She often had a bout of pleurisy. This may have been brought on by the environment, since in the winter the house was cold and drafty. In the summer, with the house located at the bottom of a hollow with hills all around, the sun would shine directly on the house for only part of the day. To me it always seemed damp.

Except for the Bible, there were no books in the house. When I needed a dictionary, I would call Mama. I recall one occasion when I was called to task by my teacher, Elmer Winfree, who disputed the definition of a word Mama had defined for me. He let me know in clear, unmistakable terms that his word was final and in effect, that I could disregard what my mother had told me.

You can imagine how well this was received at home that night. The next day Mama walked to school with me and confronted Mr. Winfree in front of the whole room. Needless to say, she was correct. He never challenged me again, but then it was obvious that he didn't like it. The end result was that I had to work even harder to maintain the grades I wanted.

Discipline was the absolute domain of the teacher. If he or she were not big enough, then the principal handled it. A paddle large enough to be a deterrent hung on the wall by the door. It was well known in our house that if we "got a whipping" at school that we would get another one when we got home. I always knew that the second one would be worse. When the teacher asked for quiet, it meant no talking, no shuffling of papers or feet. It meant to be quiet.

Dad impressed me with a story of an incident in his elementary school. There was a one-room school just over the hill on the back side of "the hollow". It was closer to his home than the school in Hickman, so he walked across the hill, through the woods to the school at Newbell's Branch. As the Board of Education was planning for the new school year, it came time to assign a teacher to Newbell's Branch. They asked for a volunteer, but no one spoke up. It seems that there was a bunch of "roughians," as Dad referred to them, that had dropped out of school, but who would always gather at the school on opening day, disrupting activities, even beating the teachers and running them away. The Superintendent of Schools said that unless someone volunteered to take this school, it would have to be closed.

One man, of slight stature, stood up and said he would go under one condition: that he could run the school his own way. He was given a free hand. On opening day, all the students were outside, including the group of roughians. The teacher rang the big bell that always stood on a heavy wooden stand just outside the front door and the students began filing into the one room. He instructed the smaller children to take the front seats so they could see better. The roughians were lined up in the back of the room, maybe trying to understand why this small teacher was there. When asked to take a seat, they continued to stand.

The teacher announced that classes would begin immediately, looking straight at those still standing. He walked across the room and drew a large circle on the blackboard. Inside that circle, he drew a very small one. The teacher returned to the opposite wall, drew a pistol, and fired one shot, hitting the small circle dead center.

Then he turned and ordered those still standing to sit. They sat and there were no more problems of any sort for the balance of the year. Haven't we made a lot of downhill progress since then?

Social life outside the home was practically nonexistent, except for going to church-related activities, usually on Sunday. Our only contacts with the outside world, except for the time I was in school, were limited to the radio, church, and the weekly visit to the general store.

I went to high school, grades eight through twelve, at the Gordonsville High School, Gordonsville, Tennessee. I still had to walk the mile to Hickman to catch the bus, except when my aunt Alta taught school and lived with her parents in the "big house." I really enjoyed high school. The curriculum was broader and more interesting. My basic mathematical skills served me well so that I truly enjoyed algebra, geometry, and related courses. With my mother's help, then as earlier, English grammar was easy. History was my least favorite subject. I would like to do that one over again.

Courses were offered in typing, but there was a $9.00 annual fee attached. Dad didn't see much future in typing and wouldn't pay the fee. Again the row of tobacco came into play and I paid for it myself. I didn't tell him right away that I was taking the course. He found out anyway and lectured me again on wasting money. I can only conclude he had no idea I would ever do anything but farming, and that a farmer had no need to know how to type.

Adolescence seemed especially difficult. Economic conditions contributed to it a bit, but then almost everyone in the area had little money. I had my first pair of commercially-made undershorts about the time I finished high school. Prior to that, Mama made mine. Most were made from bleached cotton feed sacks. Generally it was impossible to remove all the lettering. I must say that although the fabric was obviously not the quality of broadcloth, it surely was durable. This mattered little most of the time. But when I had to dress in the gymnasium for football or basketball, I was embarrassed. Our dressing area was in the furnace room, and I would usually work my way around the other side of the boiler and get my clothes changed quickly.

Mama even made my shirts, but not out of feed sacks. She was a good seamstress and made a very nice shirt. It fit me, too, which was more than a "store bought" shirt would do in those days, since I was very thin and had long arms.

Dad kept the shoes repaired. He had a cast iron shoe tree that got lots of use. A pair of shoes was worn until they were worn out, tops as well as soles. The soles were repaired with rubber half-soles that were supposed to be held on with cement. Adhesives then were not like what we have today. The soles would soon come unglued around the edges, and then had to be tacked down. This usually left an uneven, ruffled effect, not exactly contributing to sartorial splendor.

One summer about the time I started high school I developed a very sore big toe. You know it must have been bad, because Dad took me to see Dr. Wilson. As I have said before, a person never went to the doctor unless he was about to die. Dr. Wilson took one look and diagnosed the problem as an ingrowing toe nail. Dad wanted to know how such a thing could have happened, since he had never had such a problem. I can clearly recall Dr. Wilson's indignation. "Melvin," he said, "the boy's shoes are two or three sizes too small." Dr. Wilson reached for one of my shoes with scalpel in hand. I can still hear Dad saying, "No, NO!!!" He was too late. Dr. Wilson had already cut the toe out of the shoe for the foot with surgery. The doctor immediately cut the toe out of the other shoe also. Dad was still protesting, pointing out that they were still good shoes, not nearly worn out. Dr. Wilson was steadfast and said, "Yes, and they are both too small for him." Needless to say, I kept quiet, but was elated, even with a sore toe. I knew I would now get a new pair of shoes that fit.

❧ ❧ ❧ ❧

Much more devastating during this period of adolescence was the stern parental control. If there is one thing I feel I can criticize my father for, it would be the fact that I was given no input in making decisions which affected me. Actually, I was forbidden to even offer an opinion. My brother, sister, and I were told what to do, when, and how to do it. Objection was not tolerated. This does not build self confidence.

I wanted, in the "worst sort of way," to participate in sports in high school. It was such a hassle even being allowed to practice. This meant that I would be a little late getting home and lost to the various things that had to be done. I was never allowed to participate in a game held anywhere other than Gordonsville, unless it was played during school hours.

It wasn't until my Dad, during his later years, was talking about his high school days and the fact that he was considered an excellent baseball pitcher. Pappy took exactly the same position my Dad held toward me. Dad expressed his dislike for Pappy's lack of understanding, forgetting what he had done to me, until I reminded him.

To this day, I am indebted to my aunt Alta Thomas for teaching me how to drive a car. Fortunately, she was teaching at Gordonsville while living at home with Mammy and Pappy. This meant that I could ride to school with her. I remember when she bought a new

49

1937 Chevrolet sedan. She paid $750.00 for it. I would rush over to her house early each morning in the hope she would let me turn the car around. I learned to drive backwards before I could go forward. Soon Aunt Alta would let me drive to school. Dad found out about it and was very displeased. I got a lecture on irresponsibility and his liability to Alta if I had a wreck. I was more than 50 years old before I knew that Dad had gone to Alta and told her not to let me drive her car again, that he would not be responsible if I damaged it. Aunt

Alta Thomas, c. 1940

Alta, in telling me this, said she was offended and told Dad that it was none of his business, that the car was hers and she would decide who drove it. Even after I began driving our own car, Dad often felt the need to direct every turn and all too often would take hold of the steering wheel to steer the vehicle around a hole in the road the way he wanted to go.

❧ ❧ ❧ ❧

Dating, one-to-one, wasn't allowed until I was a senior in high school. Even then, I had to advise, on the front end, who I was dating, where I was going, and was told when to be home. It seemed I always had to be home at least an hour before any social event was over. Movies were only a bit more respectable than "the road house" (a tavern). I had no desire to go to a tavern, but invariably was warned about their evils.

According to Dad, most girls I wanted to date were no good. I never did know how Dad knew so much about all the girls around, some of which he had never heard of. Oh, there were a couple of girls that were O.K. One, a girl from Carthage whom Dad had heard play the xylophone at a church function, was at the top of his list. Any girl that played a xylophone at church had to be all right. This is to point out that by now I was afraid to make a decision for fear it would be unacceptable, and often was. I was a social dud, and I knew it.

Thanks to my mother, my grades in school remained very good and seemed to come easy. I was salutatorian of my high school graduating class, and according to Mama, would have been valedictorian had I not given so much help to my secret love, Ann Moss.

THE LAST FARM

In 1941, Mama and Dad bought a farm located between Hickman and Sykes, Tennessee, about a mile from Hickman. In December, 1941, my senior year in high school, we moved to this farm. The residence was a very old structure with a couple of additions having been added to it throughout the years.

On January 4, 1942, 21 days after moving to the house, it burned to the ground. Dad was sitting by the fire when he saw a mouse run out from behind the mantle, across the fire, and back behind the mantle. He thought the fire started that way. I was at school when the house burned. I knew nothing about it until I got off the school bus and saw nothing but a chimney standing amid smoking ruins. We lost everything, almost everything that is. Dad remembered the Winchester shotgun. He ran back to the house with flames coming out the door, reached in above the door and got the gun. One side of the stock was scorched. It was so hot it blistered Dad's hand.

Mama remembered my new graduation suit for which I had paid $18.00. It was in the rear of the house. Somehow she got through the flames and retrieved the suit, with flames now coming out of every door and window. A neighbor told me he saw Mama take a large tub full of water up a ladder to Dad on the roof. Mama did not recall doing it. At no other time could she even have lifted such weight off the ground.

Where could we go? It was winter time, soon to be dark. We had no food and only the clothes we had on. There was little money. Jimmy Thomas, a distant cousin and husband of Dad's sister, Liney, lived down the road just a little way. He invited us into his home. It was a very large, old house built almost exactly like Mammy and Pappy's house.

I shall forever be indebted to Uncle Jimmy. Some people found him difficult to get along with. He was a typical Thomas, very positive and assertive. I can't describe the chemistry, but he and I became very good friends. We lived there almost a year, just as if we were members of his immediate family. We ate his country ham, which he insisted should be on the table at every meal in one form or another, along with other food put on the table. Of course Mama helped in any way she could.

Dad had inadvertently overlooked paying the home owner's insurance and our coverage had lapsed about a month before the fire. We had little to no money with which to rebuild. It was decided that the only way it could be done was to cut trees from the farm and have them sawed. Dad and I began cutting large oak trees, some as much as three feet in diameter. This was before the advent of gasoline-powered chain saws, so we cut them with an axe and a two-man crosscut saw. We were to transport them to the sawmill, approximately 15 miles away, by mule-drawn wagon. The biggest problem we faced was how to load them on the wagon. We cut two straight tree limbs, put one end on the wagon and one end on the ground, and then rolled the logs onto the wagon. The larger cuts were simply too heavy for us to load. It was time for a bit of ingenuity. I took a heavy jute rope from the barn, wrapped it around the log, tied one end to a tree, and fastened our most trusted mule to the other. As she pulled, we slowly rolled the logs onto the wagon with little effort on our part. We did encounter a big problem once. The mule pulled a little too fast and rolled a big log over the opposite side, turning the wagon over with it.

Once the logs were loaded, we would leave about daylight, hoping to reach the sawmill before dark. We slept on the wagon or under it, and returned home the next day. We made several such trips. Then, once the logs were sawed, we had to go and get the finished lumber.

After considerable searching, Dad located a retired carpenter, "Uncle Tom Gill," who agreed to build the house for the unheard-of price of $250.00 (this was in 1942), provided that we helped. He lived in our smoke house Monday through Friday. My mother prepared lunch for us each day and we ate at the farm, not wanting to take the time to return to Uncle Jimmy's house.

While waiting for the sawmill to do its work and using only a pick and shovel, I dug a trench for the footing. Large rocks from the hillside made for a very sturdy foundation about four feet high in the front of the house.

It was there that I learned masonry and how to build a house. I also learned how heavy a piece of oak lumber eight inches wide, an inch thick, and fourteen feet (or longer) could weigh. Taking a square of shingles up a ladder was no fun either, but I was there every day until it was finished. Meanwhile, Dad tilled the fields.

We moved into our new house in September, 1943, very fast in view of all we had to do. Now we had a home, but not one piece of furniture. As they typically did, the community held a "shower" or "house warming" and brought gifts. We received all the basic furniture we needed to get started, along with linens, kitchen accessories, and a variety of things, some of which my mother still had when she died.

The last house

This house is still standing. When Mama and Dad sold the farm, the house was as good as the day it was built. I don't believe a tornado could have moved it. The oak framing and ceiling were still green when we put it in place. We used large nails, which rusted from the green wood. Once the wood dried, we could not pull a nail out of it. In fact, the wood was so hard we could drive a nail into it only with great difficulty. We generally needed to drill a hole first.

Following the attack on Pearl Harbor, December, 1941, and implementation of the military draft, Dad got an agricultural deferment for me. I really wanted to go into the service, since all my friends were already gone. I'm sure Dad's move was the better one. Had I gone into service earlier, I would have been subjected to the Battle of the Bulge, as were so many who went in around that time. Being deferred meant that I did not attend school at all during the latter half of my senior year. My mother kept right on tutoring me and I ended up salutatorian of my graduating class.

Every day except Sunday was spent working on the farm. This was for two reasons, I think. First, there was always plenty of work on a farm, especially if Dad was operating it. Second, we felt there was a need to keep especially busy to justify my deferment. Rarely did I go anywhere except to church and on an occasional Saturday night date.

Most every day was a repeat of the day before, but occasionally one would stand out. One day Dad sent me to town with the farm wagon to pick up some feed. We had been working the mules in the field, so they had only plow lines on their harness. I simply wrapped them around the hames (part of the harness) and put the leather harness on them, which was more suited to driving the wagon.

As I have mentioned before, I was very tall and thin — six feet-three inches tall and weighed one hundred forty-four pounds when measured for my graduation cap and gown. This made me a favorite target for the bullies who had nothing to do but sit around downtown. Some of them were always there.

After getting the feed, I went down to the nearby store for some candy, leaving the wagon and team of mules simply standing in the middle of the town square. As usual, several of the local boys were sitting alongside the store in the shade when I went in. When I came out and called the mules to move forward, their heads were immediately bent to the outside in a grotesque manner. I realized immediately that someone had tied one end of each plow line to the mule's bit and the other end to the front wheel of the wagon. I thought it was about to break their necks. I was livid and directed my indignation to the group by the store, knowing that one of them had done it. I challenged the guilty one to step forward. Thayer McKinney, well-built and the town bully, stepped forward and acknowledged that he had done it and wanted to know what I intended to do about it. He kept coming toward the wagon, threatening me as he came.

Sometime before that day, I had put a hickory stick, about an inch in diameter and three or four feet long, in the wagon bed for just such a time. Just as Thayer, known as "Little Dick McKinney," since his father was known locally as "Dick," started to climb aboard the wagon, I hit him on his head with the hickory stick, as hard as I could. I knocked him cold. This was one of the few times I had exerted some initiative, and it felt good. All the other boys alongside the store headed toward me. Seated there with them was Matt Thompson, an elderly Negro man everyone affectionately called "Uncle Matt." Uncle Matt had worked for Pappy Thomas for years, and still worked when needed. I had always heard it said that Uncle Matt had spent some time in jail for stealing, but I never did know if it was true.

56

Seeing I was greatly outnumbered, Uncle Matt climbed aboard the wagon, pulled a .38-caliber revolver from under his shirt, and announced that he would shoot the first one that laid a hand on me. The fight was over before it started. There will be more about Uncle Matt later.

Nick Thomas (my grandfather)
about 21 years old

Melvin Thomas (my father)
about 20 years old

Willie Geneva Dillard
(my mother) about
20 years old

Nick (my grandfather) and Allie Bates Thomas (my grandmother)
holding their first grandchild (me)

Family photo (l-r): Dad, sister Adelyn, brother Lewis,
Mama, and me, c. 1947

Sister Adelyn   Mama and Dad   Brother Lewis

Mama and Dad

"Mama"
at 90

Farm Life

Mama at the well

Foot bridge over the creek

Mama preparing Christmas
dinner

Everyone had a job to do
(even after they grew up!)

Dad planting

Dad's hands

Coming in from the field
with "Kit" the mule

TO HELL'S CORNER AND BACK

MILITARY SERVICE - WORLD WAR II
U. S. Army Serial # 34 914 147
Company A
52nd Armored Infantry Battalion

D-Day, June 6th, 1944, brought on an increased demand for new recruits. I was ordered to report to the Draft Board in Carthage, Tennessee, along with several other recruits, none of whom I knew. I was 19 years old. We were put aboard a bus that took us to Camp Shelby, Mississippi where, on June 24, 1944, I was inducted into the United States Army. Being without any special skills, I was destined for the infantry.

Uncle Sam's new recruit

This was the first time I had ever been away from home overnight, except for an occasional visit with relatives. This was my first trip out of the State of Tennessee. I soon learned what it was like to be truly lonesome, alone and homesick. To add insult to injury, indoctrination included "policing" the grounds around the barracks. "Policing the grounds" was mainly confined to picking up cigarette butts. Almost every one smoked except me. I found it repulsive to pick up what someone else had put in his mouth and then thrown away, so I simply bypassed the butts for an occasional candy wrapper or other paper. It didn't take the Sergeant long to see what I was doing. He ordered me to pick up the cigarette butts. I tried as politely as I could to tell him that I did not smoke and therefore did not pick up after those who did. I hastened to add I would pick up anything else, but no "butts". Somehow I got away with it.

After only a few days I was sent to Camp Blanding, Florida. Here I underwent basic military training. Being off the farm, "basic" was a picnic. I really enjoyed it. My attitude improved immediately and I got along well with the officers and non-commissioned officers. During one of our early marches with full field pack and carrying the heavy M-1 rifle, I jokingly challenged Captain Jack Martin, saying I could run up and down the line like he did if I were not carrying a full pack. "Let's see you try it," he said. I stayed with him every step all day still carrying the M-1, while he carried the smaller carbine. Not once thereafter did I receive any extra assignments.

As we approached time for "maneuvers", which were to be in the Florida swamps, Captain Martin called me to his office and asked if I could drive a truck. I had never even driven a pickup, but I assured him I could drive almost anything. I was surprised when he assigned me to drive a half-track. This meant no more walking and, besides, it looked like fun.

Not having any idea how to drive a half-track, I managed to get into the motor pool ahead of time and look the vehicle over. It seemed very large, and had a big artillery gun hooked to it. Thankfully, the transmission housing had a diagram of the gears right on top. I went through the gears a few times, knowing the true test would come the following morning when I turned the key and started it. If anyone ever knew how little I knew about driving a half-track, it never came to my attention.

The next day we headed for the swamps, our half-track loaded with men and pulling a 105 Howitzer. One after-

noon while racing madly through the pine trees I noticed
the vehicle in front of me sink into the earth much too
far. I elected to make a new trail around that spot. The
unit behind didn't follow me, and instead went straight
ahead. He didn't make it through. Quicksand began to
gobble up the truck. Troops scattered everywhere, trying to get out of the way. I hooked a winch onto the
sinking vehicle, pulled my vehicle against a large pine
tree, and prevented the stricken one from sinking.

Training to use the various firearms was pure fun. I had
scarcely fired the .45 caliber pistol when I was told I had
qualified. Ammunition must have been in short supply.
Every recruit was issued a new Garand M-1, 30-06 caliber
auto-loading rifle, except for the few who wanted the old
Springfield bolt action. Each of us had the responsibility
of "zeroing" our own rifle. When we had it done to our
satisfaction, we progressed to what was called "the
record round". I took somewhat longer than most getting mine adjusted, knowing I wanted to be certain I
could shoot it accurately. When finished, I was ready to
fire for the "Sharpshooter medal" at 300 yards. As I
recall the bull's eye was a ten-inch circle. At 300 yards it
looks very small. After firing my five shots, I requested
the spotter "in the pits" to mark the hits. He waved his
marker all over the place, but showed no hits in the center.

Knowing how lackadaisical the troops got in the pits, I
asked that my target be brought to me. All five rounds
were in the bull's eye. This is difficult to do with open
sights. I doubt whether I could do it now, even with tel-
escopic sights. I knew then I wanted this gun to go with
me wherever I had to go. Fortunately, I was able to keep
it with me until I was wounded in Germany. I would
readily give $1,000.00 for that gun today.

Unfortunately, not all basic training was fun. We were
required to crawl flat on the ground for 100 yards, under

live machine gun fire, with small explosions going off on all sides. There really was no danger so long as we stayed close to the ground. As odd as it might seem, there was a feeling of compulsion to stand up. Loose barbed wire had been strung overhead to discourage this. One man in our group did, in fact, stand up and was killed.

Probably the most frightening event in training was the gas chamber. We were required to enter one room charged with poisonous mustard gas and another with phosgene. We could not put on the gas mask until we were inside. I really thought I would die before I could get mine on. It seemed to take an eternity. Exposed skin burned immediately. I have no desire to ever do that again.

Not nearly so frightening or disagreeable, but still a matter to be reckoned with, was the day near the end of our Basic Training, when we were told to strip to our shorts because we had to swim across a ten-foot-deep pool of water. I could not swim. In fact, I still can not swim. I kept lagging back as long as I could. Then I confronted the Sergeant. I told him I could not swim and surely would drown if forced to try and cross the water. He asked what hope of survival I had if our troop ship were torpedoed on the way overseas. I asked how many of us he thought could swim across the ocean. He smiled and said, "When this is all over, everyone on this side of the pool must be on the other side." I assured him I could handle that, and simply walked around the pool to the other side. I waved to him and he waved back. Another exercise was successfully completed.

During my stay in Blanding, I had the misfortune to spend the night out in an open field when a full-fledged hurricane passed through, catching us by surprise. Two of us dug a hole deep enough for us to sit in it with our heads below ground level. Even though we had tents with us, the wind would blow them away as fast as we could set them up. We simply huddled together, wrapped the tent around us and sat there all night. By morning the storm was gone. Our hole in the earth was filled with water. Rifle barrels were filled with sand. Where trees had been the day before, nothing was left standing. It was obvious that further training that day was useless. We returned to the barracks and spent the rest of the day getting cleaned up and cleaning our equipment.

Training at Camp Blanding concluded with a 25-mile march, on which I carried a full pack and rifle, as everyone was required to do. Since we were training in the heat of the summer, we were allowed to march at night. We were driven out in the country 25 miles and let off. We had free time in the afternoon awaiting darkness, which we mostly spent in the nearby lakes. While "horsing around," I kicked one of our men. I felt a little pain but thought nothing about it until a little later when I realized there was slight swelling of the right foot. I started the march without telling anyone about it.

Soon the Captain noticed my limp and told me to drop out of the line and wait for the medic's jeep. I insisted on continuing. He knew I could easily have made the trip except for the injured foot. I walked the entire 25 miles anyway. At the end my foot was so swollen the boot had to be cut off. I had broken a bone in my right foot. As it turned out, this was probably a blessing. The men I had trained with arrived in Germany just in time for the "Battle Of The Bulge".

It took three months for my foot to heal. While waiting I was sent to Fort George G. Meade near Baltimore, Maryland. Here I met Johnnie Snesko who introduced me to his cousin, Wanda Mogowski.

Wanda was a tall, beautiful, blonde Polish girl. She had all the qualities necessary to endear one to her. We immediately fell in love. She worked during the day and went to school several nights a week, so our time together was a bit limited. I would go into Baltimore early and see a movie or do something to pass the time until she was out of school. One particular cold evening I selected a theater near her school. I really wasn't interested in the movie, but simply wanted a place to stay warm and wait for her. I sat near the back of the theater and soon fell asleep. Few people were inside, but sometime later I was awakened with someone's hand on my leg. It was very dark inside so it took a few moments for my eyes to adjust to the darkness. I was trying to envision what the beautiful girl next to me looked like. It was then I realized my imaginary goddess was a man, my first introduction to a homosexual. I was so infuriated I picked him up and threw him a couple rows toward the front, right on the backs of others. As I dashed out, I realized I had created quite a commotion. Several of those inside were angrily following me outside. Fortunately, there was a policeman standing just outside the door. In my haste to get out of the theater, I had practically run over him. It was then I learned I had gone into a theater frequented only by homosexuals.

When I left Baltimore, it was clearly understood that when I came back, Wanda and I would pick up where we were forced to leave off. She was Catholic, but by her own admission did not attend church very often and, knowing I was Baptist, was quite willing to change religions.

January 1, 1945, found me standing on the dock in Boston Massachusetts harbor, waiting to board a troop ship. We had no idea of our destination. A band was playing the usual patriotic songs, "The Yanks Are Coming" (and we were), "America The Beautiful", and "God Bless America", among others. "God Bless America" took on a whole new meaning a few weeks later.

Emile A. Fontenot[1], 52nd Armored Infantry Battalion (Company "A"), 60 mm mortar squad also departed the Boston, Massachusetts, harbor January 1, 1945, aboard the General USS Black, a troop ship, which arrived at Le Havre, France on January 15, 1945. He and I were undoubtedly aboard the same ship, though we

Training was finished. Uncle Sam's new recruit was now a soldier.

would not meet for another 55 years. After a couple days at sea we ran into a severe North Atlantic storm, and I felt sure we were going to sink. We were "buttoned down" with huge waves going over the ship. A couple days later we awoke to sunlight and were allowed on deck where the fury of the storm was apparent. The bow of the ship was bent as though it were a piece of tin. Almost everyone except me became seasick. I suppose there is nothing much worse, for many were so ill they wanted to die.

We only got two meals a day. We stood in line to get into the mess hall and then stood to eat. The tables were tall with supporting poles running through the table to hold them in place. As the ship would roll, food not held would slide to the end of the table and off on the floor. You can imagine the mess on the floor. We simply tried to hold our food with one hand and the table with the other. Eating therefore, was a problem. There being nothing more to do, we would return to our spaces. Mine was near or just below water level with the "bunk"

---

[1] Notes from my conversation with Emile can be found in the Appendix.

next to the ship's hull. A German submarine followed us for quite a way, so we were in and out of the bunk a lot. We quickly scrambled for the life jackets when a depth charge was set off and the hull of the ship would move in and out. We were never sure at first whether an explostion meant that we had set off a depth charge, or if we were under attack.

During the late afternoon of January 15, 1945, our ship docked at Le Havre, France. It was bitter cold outside, and snow was piled high all around the dock. We were told exactly when to expect to disembark and to wear all the warm clothes we could get on. Just before scheduled departure we put on long underwear, with some men donning two pairs. By the time we actually left the ship, some four hours later, we were all wet with perspiration. Walking onto the cold dock felt rather like wrapping a blanket of ice around me.

As we walked along single file we were allowed to pick up a cup of hot coffee and a donut as we passed the Salvation Army booth. What a welcome sight they were. I feel the need to point out, as I think most servicemen will attest, the Salvation Army was in evidence often, but not once did I see the American Red Cross anywhere in Europe.

We immediately boarded a train that had backed up to the dock. This train had no heat and no bathroom. In fact, it didn't even have seats. We crowded into boxcars so tight we could barely sit down. This was to our advantage in a way. We could keep a bit warmer. When I looked up I could see stars through holes in the roof from its having been strafed by aircraft. When the train began to move, slow as it was at times, we got even colder. Wind, whipping through the cracks in the walls and holes in the roof, was fierce. During the early hours of the morning the cold seemed almost unbearable. The train stopped often and sometimes remained in place for fairly lengthy periods. On one occasion it stopped in a railway switchyard. One of the men on our car, a rather enterprising soul, got off the train with a couple of companions and disappeared in the railway yard. Soon they returned carrying a small round stove with flue attached and with fire still in it. We were told they had gone into a small shack occupied by a railway employee and taken the stove. This made the place a bit more tolerable. We could take turns warming near the stove. The biggest problem was fuel. Every time the train stopped we would jump off in search of anything that would burn. Many on the train became ill, and some even got pneumonia. I survived with no ill effects. I don't know how long we were on the train, but I believe it was one or two days.

The nights were cold and miserable, but the days were even worse. Every noise overhead brought us to our feet out of fear it was a German airplane. Being trapped inside was worse than being outside where we might be able to do something.

Finally we arrived at a staging area located near Metz, France, and very near the German border. We were housed in what had once been a very large warehouse. It was fairly well heated and had army cots to sleep on. This was, as a matter of fact, the last bed I would sleep on until March 15, 1945, except for one night at a home in Luxembourg.

We were free to spend most of our time doing whatever we wanted while being processed and assigned to a unit. It was here I became a part of Company "A", 52nd Armored Infantry Battalion. Also, it was here I was introduced to real war. Nearby was an area set aside for those killed in combat. The deceased were brought in by truck and laid side by side on the ground. Personal possessions would be removed from their pockets and placed on their chests. As I went down the line I came to a handsome young soldier, lying as if asleep with a faint smile on his face. He had been shot squarely between the eyes. If I see him in Heaven I will recognize him.

The trucks bringing in the dead were stake bed with bodies simply placed inside. Since most bodies were frozen they could not be placed very neatly, but I could tell which truck bore the Germans because they were tossed in rather "helter-skelter". The trucks with German bodies would back up to a large, deep, trench, and dump the bodies, which were promptly covered with dirt by a bulldozer.

Nearby was a portion of the Maginot Line. I went inside it a couple of times. It was rather like a subway with tracks on two or three levels. It was lighted and very clean. One end of the line was under our control while the other was under the control of the Germans.

Information was developed that Germans were planning to come through the line and attack us at some point. Their exit was believed to be the one nearest our barracks. It was hidden in a recess in the hillside and practically covered over by small trees and bushes. Since I was trained to use a bazooka, I was assigned the task of attacking the door. As we approached we could hear sounds coming from inside. I fired one round into the door. The bazooka projectile made a hole about the size of a pencil but it passed through at such high speed it literally melted the metal and sprayed the backside with bits of steel. I don't know how many German soldiers were killed, but three or four were left there. We could hear others running toward the German end of the line.

Shortly before leaving Metz, it fell my lot to walk guard duty one night. Guards were placed on all four sides of the building. Two men were assigned a given wall. Each would start from one end and slowly proceed toward the other end, meeting in the middle. It was very dark on this particular night. When we approached each other we would exchange the password. Anyone unable to give the password instantly was to be shot. Questions would be asked later. A couple of hours after dark and owl began hooting up the hill toward the Maginot Line. A chill ran up my back. Being from the farm, I knew that the owl did not sound right. I backed against the wall, listening for the slightest sound. I inched my way along the wall hoping I was ready for anything that might happen. Soon I realized I should have met my partner. I continued on a short distance and stumbled on his body. He had been garroted. By now the "owl" was down the hill from us. Looking out across the valley and in the direction of a nearby village we could see a light blinking periodically. Soon after the source of the light was located – a German SS Trooper showed up, covered with blood. He was executed forthwith. Following this episode, the doors to the Maginot Line were welded shut.

Emile recalled the cold, miserable train ride to a barracks which was located near Metz, France. He also recalled that one of our sentries at the barracks was killed by a German soldier who had come through the Maginot line near us.

The Journal for the 52nd Armored Infantry Division, previously classified "Secret", but now declassified, for the month of January, 1945, reflects the following: "This unit suffered heavy losses of men and equipment in the vicinity of Bastogne, Belgium during December, 1944. It was now necessary to reconstitute the division. It was found necessary to give the men returning from Bastogne several days of rest and medical attention as nearly all of them had digestive and foot ailments caused by their physical hardships during the previous month. Initially the Battalion was billeted at Saulces Monclin, France. With the arrival of many replacements, it was necessary to move Company "A" to Vic of Lucqay, France on January 7, 1945. The Battalion next moved to

Boulage on January 12, 1945; and on January 16, 1945, Company "A" was moved to Vic Elzange." I believe I joined Company "A" as a replacement on January 17, 1945. According to this report, the month of January was used to re-equip and re-train the unit.

I well recall one training session in which we were introduced to a new type explosive. It was pliable and could be made into almost any shape with the hands. One had only to shape it according to the needs of the moment, place a blasting cap and a fuse in it, light the fuse and maintain a safe distance from the explosion. The instructor drove a steel pipe in the ground, stuffed it full of the explosive and activated it. The company was seated on the hillside during this demonstration. After the pipe bomb was ignited, there was a loud scream from one of our men. A piece of the pipe had hit him in the groin. The injury, while certainly very painful, was not life-threatening. This soldier was only a few feet from where I sat.

Merle E. Thomas[1] (not related to me), Company A, 2nd rifle platoon, also recalled this same training session in France.

The statistical data section of the above report, for the month of January reflects no American personnel killed or wounded, no contact with the enemy and no Prisoners of War taken. I presume there were some things that simply were not mentioned, i.e., the Germans killed inside the Maginot Line, the German who killed our guard at the barracks. I was there on each of these occasions, so I know they happened.

I do not recall how long we were billeted in Vic Elzange. I thought it was only a short time but records reflect that we moved out February 23, 1945. I well recall the day.

---

[1] Notes from my conversation with Merle can be found in the Appendix.

Just before dark we were told to get all the ammunition and hand grenades we could carry and be ready to move out on demand. We boarded half-tracks and drove with lights out for an extended time. The further we went the brighter the sky became. Artillery lit up the sky rather like a Fourth of July fireworks display.

We would move forward a few hundred yards and then sit without explanation, sometimes for long periods of time. By the time it was daylight our artillery was firing over us. We knew the enemy had to be nearby. Occasionally a shell would come from the enemy side. By now rifle fire could be heard at the head of the column. It would quiet down and we would move again. Just as we pulled into a small village, gunfire erupted up ahead and we stopped. The street was so narrow and the buildings so close I could reach out and touch them. When we stopped, not a person was in sight. Moments later faces began to appear in the windows. Most were young, pretty females. They began climbing out of the second floor windows and onto our half-tracks hugging and kissing "the liberators". Unfortunately, we had to move on right away, so all we got out of this was some bread and wine they tossed to us as we pulled away. At any rate, the bread was warm and very tasty.

Up ahead was evidence of the gunfire. A German truck had been caught out in the open and was now disabled and beginning to burn. The driver of the truck was lying on the tailgate of his truck still alive, but badly wounded. A bullet had creased his abdomen, opening his body as though it had been done surgically. One of our medics was working with him as though he was one of our own and said he probably would survive.

Where we went from here I do not recall. This may well have been one of our night training sessions mentioned in the Battalion reports. I do not recall ever returning to a barracks anywhere. I do recall being in Luxembourg after we had been out several days. Here we were given the weekend off. Many natives in the nearby town opened their homes to the American soldiers. Two of us were invited to spend the night with a local elderly couple. Their home was very neat and well furnished. I remember wondering why the smell of a barnyard was so strong at times. Then I learned they housed their farm animals in a barn separated only by a wall common with their dwelling.

Sunday morning found the four of us sitting in the breakfast area. They were reading and we were writing letters home. In mid-morning a very pretty young woman arrived. Immediately, the two of us attempted to communicate with her. She could neither speak nor understand English, so we spent the rest of the day writing our letters and sneaking a glance at her. Thinking that neither she nor the couple could understand us, we were fairly "loose" with GI talk. About four o'clock she had to leave. She walked around to the back of my chair, put her hands on my shoulder and in the most beautiful English I had ever heard said, "Will you walk me home?" I was both shocked and embarrassed, but determined not to miss an opportunity like this.

I assumed from what she told me that she lived near the other side of this little town. We walked across town then out into the countryside, some two or three miles. I began seeing hob-nail boot prints in the earth and knew that German soldiers had been there recently. Soon we approached a little house out in the middle of "nowhere". This was her home. When we were within a few yards of the house I heard sounds from inside. She assured me she wasn't expecting anyone, but admitted for the first time that she was in fact, married to a German soldier whom she had not heard from in a long time and presumed him dead. I wasn't about to enter that house. I told her I would wait outside and if I should come in she must come out and tell me. As soon as she was inside I heard a loud argument, then sounds like cooking utensils banging together. She did not come out. Even though I could still hear voices inside, I left to return to my unit in town. Somehow I missed our trail going back and by the time I arrived in the town it was dark. Much to my surprise, I was challenged by a guard outpost. It was then I remembered I did not know the password for the day. I poured out all the good English I knew, gave the password for the day before, told where I had been and why and lay down in the ditch before I was shot. Fortunately, I had encountered an understanding guard. We cleared it up promptly, and I swore then I would never venture out again without first getting the proper password. It was well known at this point that the Germans were putting on American uniforms and attempting to infiltrate our units, so I could not fault the guards.

According to the Journal for the 52nd Armored Infantry, for the month of February, 1945, our Battalion moved out of Vic Elzange, France on February 23rd and arrived in Spirmont, Belgium that same day. On February 24th at 4:30 PM we arrived in Lince, Belgium and went in search of billets. On February 27th at 8:50 PM we were placed on a four-hour alert. On February 28, 1945, all Company Commanders were called to meet. At 4:00 PM that day we left Sprimont, Belgium, en route to Kornelimunster, Germany. We arrived in Kornelimunster at 11:05 PM that day. According to the Statistical Data of this report, there was no contact with the enemy and no American soldiers were killed or wounded during the month of February.

I vividly recall passing through Liege, Belgium and Aachen, Germany. I never saw such destruction anywhere that compared to Aachen. I do not think a single building was intact. We could only get through by following a bulldozer. While stopped waiting for the bulldozer to clear away mountains of bricks and broken buildings, I noticed a young woman stoop and enter an opening alongside the wall of a collapsed building. The building had collapsed in such a way the roof had fallen a few feet from the base of the building and then leaned against the side of the building.

This woman had established a home there for herself and two very small children. She had hung quilts over the open ends and built a fire inside. It appeared fairly cozy, but remember that snow covered everything. I have no idea where she found food and water, except that water could have come from melting snow. Needless to say, she could not run down to the local market. It, too, had been destroyed. Except for this woman, I did not see another person in Aachen. I believe I remember correctly that Aachen was one of the most heavily bombed German cities throughout the war and was considered totally destroyed.

The soldier coming face to face with the enemy is often faced with situations in which there is no good answer. I do not remember our exact location, but we were endeavoring to capture a small German town. We were fighting house to house. A few yards in front of us, we could occasionally see a German rifle or a hand and forearm extending from behind a building. As we contemplated our next move, I saw just the front edge of a German Soldier's helmet extend past a building. Then a hand appeared and placed a grenade in the hands of a young German boy, six to eight years of age. The boy was then pointed in our direction. As he started running toward us, it was decision time. If I had tried to shoot the grenade out of his hands, the explosion would surely have killed him. If he were allowed to advance any further, we would be killed momentarily. In situations like that, a person does what he has to do. I was spared the responsibility of this awesome decision when someone near me fired. The moment the grenade exploded the German soldiers, who thought the boy had delivered the grenade all the way to us, charged into the street. The battle for that town was over very quickly.

One sunny afternoon we were strung out single file walking along a hilltop when a German fighter plane came over the hill and began strafing us. We scattered like chickens, every man for himself. I jumped into a ravine and crawled under the overhang just before the plane made a second pass right over my head. I could feel the impact of the bullets in the dirt above me. He left just as soon as he had come thinking, I surmise, he had better get away while he could. We immediately got back in file and continued our march. If you haven't heard a few hundred men singing "God Bless America" from a hilltop in Germany, knowing that soon some of them would die, you can not know the full meaning of this song.

Mail delivery started at the rear of the column and was passed forward. We took ours and passed the rest along. It was while walking along the aforementioned hill I received a letter that my Grandfather "Pappy" Thomas had died. I remember mentioning this to my commanding officer and he said that I probably could be relieved of duty to go home to his funeral. I pointed out he would have been buried before I got there. He died February 17, 1945. I'm not sure what I would have done had I known of his death a day or two earlier, but suspect I still would have stayed where I was.

At times, rest and periods of sleep lasted no more than a few minutes. The body can reach the point where a person can fall asleep almost immediately taking advantage of even brief periods of potential rest. One afternoon, following a lull in the fighting, we sat down on the side of a rather steep hill. I was so tired I lay down on my back in a shallow ditch. When I awoke, rain was falling on my face and it had been raining long enough that water was running down the ditch where I lay. You are pretty tired when water in the face does not awaken you immediately.

It was a real treat when a field kitchen came along. This happened only two or three times from the time I left the barracks in Vic Elzange, France until March 14th when I was wounded. I recall one particular visit by the "chow wagon". Snow covered the ground and we had not seen the wagon for several days. The fragrance of the hot food and the steam coming from inside was delightful. When I finally reached the serving area, all that was left was spinach and bread. I am not especially fond of spinach, but it tasted good that day.

Since we were constantly on the move sleeping bags carried by trucks rarely caught up to us. One cold, snowy night they arrived just as we came upon a large barn with some hay in it. I crawled inside the bag with clothes and shoes on just in case we might have to get out in a hurry. We never zipped them all the way up. During the night I awoke, realizing that something which did not belong there was in the bag with me. My first thought, heavy with sleep, was that it must be a snake. Then I realized it was too cold for snakes to be out. Fishing around in the bag I caught the culprit, a small rabbit.

It appeared to me the German soldiers did not especially like to fight at night, so we moved at night and got set up ready to attack at dawn. I found that many Germans had their wives or girlfriends with them. It was not at all uncommon to hear them laughing and talking at night, and playing the portable phonograph. At that time, Marlene Dietrich had just made a very popular version of "Lili Marlene". The Germans all seemed to have a copy of this record. Early one evening, I heard "Lili Marlene" wafting across an open field. I crawled toward the sound. As I got closer I could see a small tent over a hole in the ground. Visible under the edge of the tent was a German soldier. I raised my gun, took aim on a button in the center of his chest and was about to squeeze the trigger when I saw a female in there with him. It appeared she was preparing food. I could not kill that man while this woman, quite possibly his wife, looked on. I simply crawled back to my place and let him live at least one more night. What happened to him subsequently, I do not know.

I think it was now sometime in February 1945. I believe we were somewhere near Rheinbach, Germany. After a day of intermittent skirmishes, we took control of a small village, just as it was getting dark. A cold rain, mixed with sleet and snow, was falling. We were wet and cold and felt secure enough to get out of the weather, dry out, and get a little rest.

It looked as though it might have been a mining town with small houses dotting the hillside. My "blood brother" was a soldier from Minnesota named James Waggoner. We selected a small, neat white house and walked in. Almost everyone, especially those who had any experience in combat, teamed up with a trusted friend, a "blood brother", for those occasions when we were in close combat with the enemy. In order to protect one's backside, it was necessary at times to fight with our backs together. As long as we felt our "blood brother," there was a sense of security. We did a room-by-room search, believing at first that it was not occupied. In the kitchen, the last room we came to, huddled around a small coke-burning stove, was an older woman, her husband, and a young woman we learned was their daughter. Waggoner could speak some German.

What a shock it must have been for them when two dirty, unshaven American soldiers came through the door with guns drawn. They sat motionless and speechless, with fear evident on their faces. With the interchange of the few words of German we knew, they soon relaxed a bit. They seemed no threat to us, yet we were still alert to the possibility they might not be too glad we were there.

James took a seat in the corner of the room, rifle across his legs prepared to sleep a while. I was to remain awake and on guard. It wasn't long until the young woman became restless and wanted to leave the room. Since I had no idea where she wanted to go or why she wanted to leave, I would not let her leave without one of us going along. When she could no longer bear it she led me to a small door along the wall of an unfurnished room. I believed it was a closet but there was no way for me to be certain. She reached for the doorknob. I stopped her, took the safety off my rifle and yanked the door open. It was in fact a small closet with a few garments hanging and some boxes on the floor. She looked at me then at the closet floor. I motioned her toward the closet still wondering what she was concerned about. She knelt on the floor, picked up a small cardboard box and held it close to her breast. Still kneeling, she looked up at me with the most pleading expression one can imagine. It was then I realized the box held her newborn child. We learned later that German soldiers fleeing town in front of us told the populace the Americans would kill all the children and old people and would rape all the young women.

Soon it was apparent they felt safe, as did we. The mother asked if there was anything she could do for us. We each had only two pairs of socks, one pair on our feet and the other in our helmet where body heat would dry them. We asked if she would wash our socks. She did and dried them in the oven of the stove. Near daybreak, the mother created a bit of a stir when she climbed on a chair and retrieved a metal container from the rear of the cabinet. Inside were a number of smaller boxes nestled one inside the other. The smallest one, perhaps a half-cup in size, contained one of their most precious commodities, coffee. We enjoyed our first cup of hot coffee

in a couple of months. Before we left, James and I emptied our rations and replenished their coffee. They now
had more coffee than when we arrived. You have never
seen three more surprised and pleased people.

Morning came and it was time to get back to the war.
With tears streaming down their faces, the mother,
father, and daughter hugged and kissed us as we left.

Knowing what I know now, it was on the morning of
March 7, 1945, that we entered the town of Westum,
Germany, not far from the Rhine River. Much to our
surprise, we were told to "fall out" and get some rest. I
entered a house alongside the street and found it unoccu-
pied. It was a beautiful home. I lay down on the biggest
most comfortable bed I had ever been on in my life. I
had hardly stretched out when a jeep going up and down
the steet with a bull horn blaring, ordered us back on the
street. From all the excitement, it was apparent that
something important was about to take place. Officers
and NonComs were running about shouting orders in
every direction.

The good news was that the bridge over the Rhine River
at Remagen was intact. What a break it would be to
walk over that river. No one questioned the need to get
there as quickly as possible. We were not far from the
bridge, maybe four or five miles as I recall. We started
out running a while then jogging. As we approached, we
could hear rifle fire and knew that contact had been
made. The intense fighting was over. Snipers were still
around. One was firing on us from the steeple of a
nearby church. One of our tanks shot the top off the
steeple and all was quiet.

The Bridge at Remagen was built in the years 1916 to
1918. It was a double-track railway bridge built to create
a direct connection between the Ahr route and the railway network east of the Rhine. It was named after

General Ludendorff, then the First Quartermaster General of the German Army. Foot paths were built on both side of the bridge to facilitate the passing of marching troops. Access ramps had been constructed on both ends so it could be used for vehicles. The bridge was 1,066 feet in length and high enough to allow river traffic to pass safely beneath it. The river flows rapidly to the north at the rate of approximately seven feet per second.

The bridge at Regmagen over the Rhine River

The bridge was captured the afternoon of March 7, 1945, by Company "A", 27th Mechanized Infantry Battalion under the command of 2nd Lieutenant Karl H. Timmerman and one platoon of Company "A", 14th Tank Battalion under the command of 2nd Lieutenant John Grimball.

I clearly recall arriving in Remagen on March 7, 1945, while it was still daylight and believe we were among the first units to get there. Being as near Remagen as we were when the bridge was captured supports this belief.

You might wonder why we did not cross the bridge immediately. This was undoubtedly due to the need for basic planning which had to be done on the spot. Where would each unit go once on the other side? What would their responsibility be? What was the condition of the bridge? Then there were the prospects of a massive counter attack by the Germans. If the bridge didn't stand long enough to get substantial forces across, the enemy would surely annihilate those that managed to get across.

By the time crossings began, around 3:00 AM March 8, 1945, the town of Remagen was described as a huge traffic jam caused by all the units converging on the city and waiting to cross the River. Company "A", 52nd Armored Infantry crossed during the early morning hours of March 8, 1945. This was the first Battalion of enemy troops to cross the Rhine River since Napoleon crossed in the 1800's.

It was a very dark night and, needless to say, there were no lights to show the way. Some of the bridge floor was missing, making it necessary at times to jump over a rather wide empty space. Anyone falling through surely would have drowned in the cold water. Once on the East side of the river we turned north, went through the town of Erpeler Ley and up on top of the hill overlooking the bridge and the town of Remagen. We were to protect against a German counter attack.

We spent much of the rest of the night of March 7-8th "digging in". We began taking artillery fire mostly from overhead bursts that rained shrapnel down on us. Waggoner and I continued digging deeper then back under the earth. A shell landed very near, causing the earth to cave in on top off us. We dared not get out, so we sat there the rest of the night with the earth resting on our heads and shoulders. The wisdom of this was apparent in daylight. Where there was grass when we arrived, the ground was now chewed up as though it had been tilled.

The morning of March 8, 1945, dawned beautifully. The sky was blue and the sun was out. As we emerged from our "new home," we immediately came under fire from the enemy, who was firing at us from railroad box cars they had moved in during the night. To me their efforts appeared utterly stupid, the equivalent of suicide. From our vantage point high on the hill we could easily pick them off, one at a time.

Looking back down on the bridge from Erpeler Ley.
Photo courtesy of the National Archive.

We spent the day being alert to a counter attack and diving into our fox holes when artillery came in. A great deal of time was spent watching the aerial show as German planes tried to knock out the bridge. The hill overlooking the Bridge was so tall and the face so sheer it obscured the view by enemy planes as they approached from the East. They had no way of knowing that during the night American Forces had pushed every piece of armament they could over the bridge. Among this Force were trucks mounted with anti-aircraft guns parked bumper to bumper under the hill. The first three German planes that came over were met by a wall of bullets. All three were falling at the same time.

I did not want to spend another night with shrapnel raining down on us, so we decided to put a top on our fox hole. I volunteered to go into the nearby woods in search of something to support the earth over our heads. Needing both arms to carry any logs I might find, Waggoner agreed to sit guard at our foxhole. I wasn't having much luck finding what I needed and would check frequently to see that Waggoner was still in place. Then, I heard what I thought was a low whistle. I looked around and saw no one. Waggoner, was still in place with his rifle across his legs. Soon I heard the whistle again, much closer this time. I turned and was face to face with three German soldiers all decked out in full battle gear, grenades hanging all over their chests. Two of them held a rifle and the third a light machine gun, all pointed directly at my stomach. I felt at the time I could have touched the spots where I would be shot. I truly felt the hair on my head raise my helmet. I managed a look at Waggoner and he was not there. It probably saved my life. Had shooting started, I surely would have been killed by one side or the other.

The German soldiers were trying to communicate with me. I couldn't understand a word they were saying. I gave them every word of German I knew with no apparent success. All the while I was backing slowly away intending, if possible, to reach the edge of a nearby deep ravine and roll off into it. For reasons I still cannot explain, I reached inside my coat for a trench knife. Undoubtedly they thought I was reaching for a gun. All three literally rammed the barrels off their guns into the earth and surrendered. With their guns standing alone in the earth and knife in hand, I marched my three prisoners up the hill and turned them over to Waggoner, just before my knees buckled. This was the only time I ever had such a feeling and believe it was because I felt so vulnerable without my rifle. I swore then I would never again be separated from it even for a moment.

Waggoner returned shortly and told me he had turned the prisoners over to the Military Police and while doing so learned that all three had appeared for the purpose of surrendering. They claimed they had been forced into service the previous day and did not even know how to fire their weapons. One was a house painter and the other two were carpenters. Battalion reports reflect that on March 8, 1945, the "52nd" took three (3) prisoners at 3:00 PM and turned them over to the "PWE" (Prisoners of War Exchange). This time would coincide with the aforementioned incident.

Just before dark a German spotter plane came over. We presumed he was checking to see if we were still at the same place as the night before. We expected artillery fire and it came during the night. The following morning, a spotter plane came over again. We presumed he came to check on the damage they had done. This was his last trip. During the night, one of our tanks had pulled under a tree atop the hill and took out the plane with machine gun fire. The hill shook with our cheers.

I do not recall how long we remained in this position. Battalion reports reflect that on March 9, 1945, at 11:25 AM, orders were given to prepare to move. I well recall the order being explicit, in that we should be well-armed with all the ammunition and grenades we could carry, and we were told to be ready to move out within 20 minutes. As usual, we were not told where we were going or what our objective was. We walked back to the bridge and then South along the East side of the Rhine River.

Along the way we acquired a new Second Lieutenant just as we approached an intersection of two roads. Being at the head of the column I sat with him and the Sergeant as they consulted a map trying to ascertain where we were and where we were to go. The Lieutenant made a decision. I knew he was wrong, as did the Sergeant, and we told him so. We lost the argument and on command started down a narrow gravel road the way the Lieutenant wanted to go. After several miles the road ended abruptly at the edge of a field. By now it was dark and also raining torrentially. No one knew where we were. Even the Lieutenant admitted he was lost.

I volunteered to lead a three-man patrol in an effort to locate the enemy or find a distinguishing landmark. No one wanted to go with me. Finally, two men were selected over their objection. Both were wearing the old "slicker" type raincoats, as was I. I removed mine and asked that they do likewise, pointing out the coats would make far too much noise going through the trees and bushes. They refused to go without them and I relented because of the heavy rain, feeling the rain would drown out the noise. We were standing under a huge oak tree and agreed that if we were separated, that would be our landmark and meeting place. It was so dark I could barely see the outline of the tree against the night sky.

We started, working our way down a steep, rocky hill covered with head-high bushes similar to what we call scrub oak. Eventually, we reached the bottom of the hill and found ourselves walking along a small, rocky stream bed.

As we walked along the stream bed, now with little water in it, I could hear sounds in the distance. As we drew nearer to the sound, I realized someone was digging in rock or gravel. Getting even closer, I could see German soldiers preparing defenses along a railroad track where it entered a tunnel. They had built a fire in the tunnel, which was a great help to us in ascertaining where we were. I had seen the railroad tracks and the tunnel on the map we had looked at earlier and knew exactly where we were, seven miles in the wrong direction and now behind the German lines. Armed with this information, we started back. The almost dry stream bed was now a raging torrent. Water was waist deep on me and I am six feet three inches tall. The current made getting across the stream and back to our unit very difficult. We had just gotten across when one or our men, shaking from the cold, lit a cigarette before I could stop him. I knew the Germans could see it, so I started up the hill as fast as I could. It was steep and very slick. I would often slide down about as far and I had gone up. My two colleagues trying to come up behind me with their raincoats dragging on every bush made a good target for the enemy. They opened fire with a machine gun. I could hear the bullets hitting near me and could feel the impact just below me. Soon I realized both colleagues were silent. They were both killed.

Back on top of the hill I had no trouble convincing the Lieutenant where we were. Rather than try to make our way out in the darkness, we felt it advisable to dig in where we were. Next day dawned beautifully. The clouds were gone and the sun was out. We realized early that Germans were about, but had no idea how many there were. It was decided that we would take a chance. Word was passed to fix bayonets and on signal raise them above the hole and come out fighting. The sun striking more than two hundred shiny bayonets was quite a sight. The Germans apparently thought so, and most ran. Those who didn't were killed during a brief skirmish. The one thing we could not handle way back there was prisoners.

Just as expected, getting out was not nearly as easy as going in. We presumed the enemy would regroup and be after us shortly. To me it seemed more risky going out on the road. I presumed they would be waiting for us. So, I elected to go cross-country, feeling I knew a shorter way out. At first I was pretty much alone, but then realized that most of the company was following me. We were just about to the top of the hill and momentary safety when a German tank on the opposite hill opened up on us with an 88 MM cannon. The shell exploded below us and we got over the hill without any casualties, so far as I am aware.

Pausing for a short rest, I stood watching three of our Mustangs in a dogfight with three German Messerschmidts. We all cheered as the last German plane fell and our Mustangs flew away. Just as the fight was over, having stood in the same spot for several minutes, I took one step forward. In mid stride I heard a thud and felt a fierce tug on the heel of my right boot. A .50 caliber projectile had hit the heel of my right boot, taking out a chunk of rubber. Had I not moved when I did I would undoubtedly have been hit in the upper body. Once again, God was looking out for me.

As I approached the intersection where we had been the day before, I saw the Lieutenant standing there. One of our Sergeants who had survived the Battle of the Bulge was in a heated argument with the Lieutenant, asking him some very pointed questions about how he first refused to listen and got us lost – and then happened to be the first one out leaving our two dead comrades behind. The Lieutenant was citing the articles of War and the code of Military discipline, but was obviously losing the argument to the Sergeant's .45 automatic. We all walked away. I never saw the Lieutenant again. The Sergeant was killed a few days later.

Emile and Merle both recall being ordered by our Lieutenant down a wrong road and in behind the German lines on a very wet, cold night. Emile knew that a three-man patrol had gone out in an effort to determine our location. He knew that contact had been made with the enemy, and that two members of the patrol had been killed. He had no idea that I was the surviving member. Merle, likewise recalled this event. He and Emile both remember that our Second Lieutenant

90

was transferred because of this mistake, and that the Lieutenant was killed soon thereafter.

The After-Action Report for March 11, 1945, reflects that Lt. Edward Bills was relieved of command of Company "A" on that day, and assigned to Company "C". Lieutenant Bills was killed by enemy fire at 2:15 PM on March 11, 1945. [Excerpts from the full report that pertain to Company "A" may be found in the Appendix.]

During the night of March 12-13th we walked all or most of the night. Just before daybreak, we passed through a densely wooded area along a gravel road. American infantry was situated in the woods on both sides of the road. It was then I learned we had been called to attempt to take control of the Autobahn Highway, Germany's military lifeline, near the town of Kalenborn. The infantry chided us as we passed through, tipping us off as to what was in store. They had tried without success for three or four days to move forward, and were driven back each time. On paper, it was logical to send us since we were an armored unit, except for the fact we had no armor with us at the time.

I have since learned that on March 13th, 1945, just before dawn, we were approaching Kretzhaus, a suburb of Kalenborn. Fortunately, I was at the head of the column, which was not a bad place to be. Here I learned first-hand what was going on and what was expected. Just as it was barely light enough to see the outline of buildings, we stopped at the edge of the forest. In front of us, and nearest to us, was a large sawmill operation spread out on both sides of the roadway. Beyond that and approximately 100 yards on our left side of the roadway was a huge pile of crushed stone 20 or 30 feet high and spread out 60 or 70 feet across at the base. Directly beyond that was the first house on the left side of the road, with the first house on the right being one lot further away. Beyond these two houses were others lined up on both sides of the road. Up ahead, cars could be seen going in both directions. Another road intersected on our left, forming a triangle covered with tall pine trees. Being visible to the enemy, we moved into this triangle[a]. As it became daylight and seeing how vulnerable we were, I took my squad and made a dash to a shed[2] to our left. Barely had we reached the shed when a mortar landed precisely where we had stood minutes before. Bodies were hurled into the air, some landing in the treetops. The battle of the day had begun.

I moved, with my squad following, toward the pile of crushed rock[3], barely in time to see the shed blown to splinters. The ground was too hard to dig, so I started pulling the crushed stone down forming a depression rather like a bathtub. Unfortunately, other members of my squad stopped a bit short of the rock pile and moments later took a direct hit, killing all of them. I heard a "Screaming meemie", a German shell that made a screaming sound as it approached, coming toward us. I dived into my spot. The explosion literally covered me with dirt and debris. I could not hear for several minutes. This bomb[4] blew a large hole in the earth, flinging our men away from the center like spokes of a wheel. Here I lost a friend, Wayne Parkey, from Knoxville, Tennessee. Wayne was a "city boy" and never quite learned the rudiments of self-preservation. Often I have thought that if only I had insisted he come closer to me at the rock pile, he might be alive today. I quickly returned to my spot next to the crushed rock. Very heavy fire was now coming in, but going over my head into the bulk of our forces and into the woods we had just come through. I soon realized there was a machine gun to my left[5] and every time it chattered a man fell. He was taking a terrible toll.

---

[a] **See the maps on pp. 109-111 for locations where numbered.**

I crawled to the edge of the rock pile hoping I could see the machine gun and take it out. I believed it was in a clump of trees ahead and to my left, but I couldn't see it. I didn't see a muzzle blast and knew it was sheer suicide to try and cross the open area between us. Random shots fired into the trees brought no results. I moved to the other end of the rock pile, next to the roadway intending to go around and maybe in behind the machine gun. A very cautious look, at ground level, found me looking squarely into the barrel of a Panzer tank[6], which had pulled up behind the first house on the right side of the street. The tank was well hidden under a large evergreen tree with just the barrel of the 88 MM gun sticking out. The gun suddenly moved in my direction. We had reports the Germans were running short of ammunition and I doubted they would waste an 88MM on one man. Still, I rather expected it might happen, since they knew they were fighting a losing battle. So I crawled to the other end of the rock pile, still hoping to spot the machine gun. This went on, back and forth, until early to mid afternoon. Not one friendly soldier had made it to where I was, except for a newly assigned 2nd Lieutenant. His bright, clean clothes looked newly-issued, as if he had just stepped out of headquarters far from the front. He came up along side me and immediately started climbing up the rock pile. I caught his left foot, endeavoring to pull him down, screaming at him that it was lunacy to climb up there. He kicked free and continued to the top. Almost immediately a large caliber shell hit him, severing his left leg at the hip. He was dead when he hit bottom. What he expected to accomplish under the circumstances, I do not know.

An American tank[7] came up the road and stopped alongside me. I tried to point out the German tank across the street, but they either didn't see me or chose to ignore the warning. It probably would not have made any difference what they did because almost immediately the "88" fired, shooting completely through the turret of our tank. No one survived. A second tank[8] pulled up behind the now disabled one. Another shot from the "88" went through the turret of both tanks. The first one hit now had four large, round holes in it, two entrance and two exits. Both tanks were burning so furiously I had to move away to avoid the heat. A third tank, seeing the fate of the other two, started to back away when it was hit. One man got out of it with a hand missing.

Emile told me that he had appropriated an unused fox-hole to the right of the roadway and a few yards to the right and rear of my starting position. He could see down the road leading through Kretzhaus. He saw a small shed off to his left, and a large pile of crushed rock up ahead on the left side of the road. Three US Tank Destroyers came up the road, and as they passed, three members of Emile's squad got in behind the destroyers and advanced with them. Just as the destroyers got to the edge of the rock pile, a German tank, hidden under a tree and alongside the first house on the right side of the street fired, knocking out the destroyers killing all three of the men behind the destroyers. A third U.S. Tank Destroyer came up along side the two that had been destroyed and it suffered the same fate. Only one man got out of the three destroyers and he was missing a hand. Soon thereafter, the German tank backed away.

At this point in my life my vision was very acute. While the Panzer was busy with our tanks I was firing at the Panzer, hoping to put a bullet in the slit the driver looked out of. I could see gray spots where my bullets were hitting, all very close to the "slit". Whether I got one inside I do not know but watched as the Panzer backed away and left.

The machine gun continued its chatter of death. I felt I now had a chance to take it out with the Panzer gone. I crawled into the ditch[10] alongside the road, which was almost full of water with pieces of ice and debris floating on top. I must have gotten wet but don't remember being cold. As I approached the side of the house, I could see a door at the rear of the building. I also saw a basement window I knew I had to pass. Basements were inherently dangerous. I ran as fast as was humanly possible and as I vaulted over the window, I remember feeling I was floating over in slow motion. I immediately entered the doorway and up to the second level. Looking out the window I could see the machine gunner. Three large rocks, probably 3 feet high formed a perfect little fort. It was obvious why my random shots had not reached him. When my gun barrel broke the window-pane he turned toward me but it was too late[11]. With him out of the way and the tank gone, things quieted down a bit. Still, bullets were coming through the walls of the house leaving holes of all sizes. A search of the upper level revealed no one.

Before opening the door to the basement[12] I held a grenade in my left hand and put the safety pin in my mouth. With the rifle in my right hand I kicked open the door. All I could see were the backs of German soldiers all straining to look out of the small basement window. What fight they had in them, if any, was gone. All raised their hands. When I went down inside the basement I found nine German soldiers. On command, they went up the stairs and toward our forces as I had ordered.

Still inside were three civilians, an adult man, his wife, I presumed, and a young woman, eighteen or twenty years old. With a floor covered with the German weapons, I did not want to test their loyalty by turning my back on them to exit the stairs. Although I regretted making them go outside in the hell that was in progress, I felt I had no choice. The two women readily started up the stairs. The man refused to go at first, saying in broken English, "You will have to shoot me first". His shirt had ridden up a bit in the back, and his over-sized pants were hanging a bit low. When I pricked the top of his bare buttocks with a very sharp knife, he quickly changed his mind, and went up the stairs two-at-a-time.

Throughout the day the firing was so intense there was an almost constant roar. The bombs falling nearby would for an instant, drown out the rest. It was usually impossible to ascertain which side was firing. I could look towards the rear and see almost total devastation. Ahead there was no obvious damage. Where was our artillery?

Emile recalls that Company "B" was off to his left, and a German machine gun was cutting them to pieces. Emile was told that this one machine gun almost totally decimated Company "B". Then the machine gun went silent. Emile didn't know at the time if the gunman had been killed, or simply had pulled back. While still in the foxhole, Emile saw "a bunch" of German prisoners running down the road toward the American positions.

At this point Emile moved out to his left, going between the shed and the rock pile. An American radioman in front of him was running bent over, nearly horizontally at the hips. A large German gun fired on the radioman, completely decapitating him. Nonetheless, the mortally wounded man continued to run several steps before falling.

An enemy machine gun was firing somewhere further up the street. I exited the house on the side opposite my entry[13]. Seeing how totally vulnerable I was I crossed the street diagonally to the first house on our right side of the street. Running as fast as I possibly could, I heard machine gun fire hitting the mud. I glanced under my left arm, which was about shoulder high, and could see the bullets hitting the mud less than a foot from me[14].

Upon entering this second house, I found myself in a room full of shelving, each of which was filled with canned food. I saw an elderly female standing at the opposite end of the room holding a large German Shepard dog. She spoke to the dog and he attacked me. I killed the dog and went in search of the woman, not intending to harm her, but with every intention of scaring the hell out of her. I searched this house from roof to the ground and never found her. While on the second floor I looked across at the adjacent house and there on the roof was a pile of empty shell casings. I presumed this was where the machine gun that fired on me had been. Again I realized I was totally alone. Except for the Lieutenant who was killed earlier, I had not seen another able-bodied American soldier since early morning. It was now getting well into the afternoon and I decided the prudent thing was to retreat a bit and make contact with our forces. I subsequently learned, as I will mention later, that most of my company had been killed, which explains why I was alone.

Back at the first house I found three or four Americans who had charge of a wounded SS Trooper. I do believe this was the meanest-looking, most arrogant, uncooperative man I have even seen. Although obviously in need of medical attention, he refused to let anyone touch him. In spite of his condition and the fact he was outnumbered, he grabbed a pistol from one of our men, obviously intent on killing to the very end. The end for him was right then.

Emile remembers going around behind the first house on the left side of the street (the one I had first entered) and saw three or four American soldiers standing near a wounded German soldier. When the German attempted to grab a sergeant's .45 automatic pistol, someone in the group had to kill him. Emile was surprised to learn that I was one of the American contingent.

97

Emile continued across the street and in behind where the German tank had been. To his surprise, the tank had backed up only a short distance, and was stopped with its hatch open. Voices could be heard coming from inside. Someone dropped a grenade down the hatch and destroyed the tank and those in it. As far as Emile knows, only three men in his squad survived this battle.

I shall never know, of course, but one can only wonder if I did, in fact, put a rifle round inside the tank, injuring or killing the driver, and that this was why the tank moved back only a short distance. Emile said that he had seen that happen before, and concluded that this was probably what had happened in this case as well. Merle's squad was sent about a hundred yards north of my position and did not pass through the sawmill.

The area to our rear was one of total devastation. The evergreen trees that been so green and beautiful that morning were now nothing but broken limbs and splintered tree trunks. Bodies of our men could be seen lying all about.

Firing had quieted down considerably. Soon, it would be dark. With the help of another soldier we dragged railroad cross ties from the saw mill yard as near to the German traffic as possible and built a small "fort". We stacked the ties about two or three feet high, leaving the end toward the enemy open. We covered the top with cross ties. Somewhere we found a bazooka with a couple rounds of ammunition and "set up shop" to knock out the first enemy vehicle that came near enough. The evening was very quiet, with only an occasional artillery shell coming in. It was my turn to rest while my comrade sat guard. I lay on the ground with my head at the closed end of the shelter. Sometime after midnight, an artillery shell exploded directly over us[17]. I was awakened with such a jolt I bumped my head against the top of the shelter. My first thought was that some very strong force had yanked my left leg. I had no feeling in the leg, neither did I have any pain. It was so dark I couldn't see a thing, but I knew something was wrong. Putting both hands around my upper left thigh, I started down my leg. When I reached the ankle, I could feel warmth and what I was sure was blood.

When I had gone to sleep I stretched out full length and my foot had extended out past the roof of our shelter. A piece of shrapnel severed the left achilles tendon with smaller pieces imbedded in other parts of the ankle. Some are still there. Why it did not sever the leg bone I do not know because the top of my boot was no longer attached to the bottom. The foot was still there but I could not move it.

When my comrade (whose name I do not know) realized I was hit he got out of the shelter calling for a medic. When last I saw him he was wandering about in the dark, seemingly hysterical. Soon a medical corpsman showed up. Where he came from I do not know. He examined me as best he could in the dark. We didn't dare turn on a light. With his help we made it back to the basement of the first house I had entered. The basement was now a command post.

The medic covered my ankle and foot with sulfanilamide powder, standard treatment of the day, and wrapped it in a heavy bandage. I lay down on the concrete floor, elevated my foot on one of the shelves, and was asleep almost immediately. Sometime later, while it was still dark, I awoke and realized my head was no longer on the concrete floor but was now resting on something warm and soft. The young woman whom I had forced to leave the house earlier had returned and was holding my head in her lap. The two adults there earlier had also returned.

The enemy resumed heavy shelling at daybreak. It was so intense the medics refused to come to take me out. Finally, some time after noon, word came over the radio to have me ready at a precise moment, so precise we synchronized our watches. The ambulance, a jeep with litters built onto it, would come in, turn around and leave, with or without me. To my surprise, none of our men in the basement wanted to help me get outside and on the jeep. Moments before the jeep was to arrive I went out side with the help of the young woman. With shells falling all around she stayed with me until I was picked up.

The ambulance came up the road at a high rate of speed, sliding to a stop and into his turn. I jumped onto the passenger seat and we took off as fast as he could go. We headed along the road I had walked in on the previous day. There was nothing but total devastation as far as I could see. Foxholes dotted the entire area. Bodies were lying everywhere in the most grotesque positions. I could hear calls for help from almost all directions. It seemed especially sad to go past them, but shells were falling everywhere. Over the din of explosions, the driver explained he had been told to come for me only and "then to get the hell out of there". It was March 14, 1945. Soon I would safely be out of "Hell's Corner".

All those behind me caught the brunt of what was described by General Eisenhower as probably the most concentrated artillery bombardment laid down by the Germans during the entire war. These men didn't even get to see their enemy. Again I was at the right place at the right time.

We had gone only a short distance when I saw an injured soldier lying in the ditch near the road. His arms were outstretched pleading with us not to leave him. I asked the driver to stop. He refused at first, then slid to a stop backed up with wheels spinning and stopped alongside the man. The injured man stood up and limped to the jeep. The driver took off before he could get aboard so I simply reached out, caught him around the waist and pulled him on top of me. Only then did I realize his right foot had been severed at the ankle. He had walked to the jeep on the open wound. Hanging on as best we could with the jeep "flying down the rough road" we managed to wrap his foot in a bandage in an effort to stop the bleeding. The injured man repeated, over and over, "thank you, thank you for stopping." The medic said he had never seen such carnage.

We were taken to a shed just behind the lines. Two doctors were working feverishly over the wounded. They were attempting to clean gunpowder out of the open abdomen of one of our men. The man was in shock and they were working without anesthesia. They closed him and felt he would live. When my turn came, one doctor told the other to amputate my left foot. I objected so strenuously that they passed me along to the rear. Besides, they were swamped with mortally wounded coming in all the time.

My next recollection is of lying in a row of wounded on the floor of Orly Airport, in Paris, France. Here the wounded, now on stretchers, were placed side-by-side in rows across the wide expanse of the airport passenger area. All of us were awaiting evacuation to a hospital, hopefully in the United States. A nurse moved down each row, one man at a time, establishing identity and nature of wounds.

When the nurse got to me she asked the routine, "Where are you wounded?" I told her it was my left ankle. She asked if I could stand with her help and when I did she asked again, "Is that all?" referring to my ankle. I told her I thought so. She began removing my field jacket then my shirt and finally even the top of my long underwear before she was convinced my wounds were confined to my left ankle. She then held up my muddy, torn jacket. The left side of the body of the jacket just above the waist and the inside of the left sleeve had been shot away. My first thought was that this happened when I was running across the street in Kretzhaus and the machine gun was firing at me. Only God could have directed bullets through there with out one hitting me.

The nurse took somewhat longer with me than others. She helped me to the bathroom and asked that I look at myself in the mirror. I saw a face with almost two month's growth of beard and long matted hair that had not been washed for a long time. Through this peered two eyes, fixed in a wide-eyed look, a classic case of "battle stare". She tried to shave me but the razor kept clogging up. Finally she cut what she could with scissors and then shaved the rest. She washed my head in the sink. What a delightful feeling it was to have that part of me clean again!

With her help I was able to send a short letter home, telling my Mama and Dad I had been wounded, "but not too bad." I offered no other information at the time. Everyone at home knew that when Western Union approached the house it meant bad news. I was pleased to learn that my letter got home before Western Union arrived. As expected, the telegram suggested my injuries were worse than they really were.

When it came my turn for evacuation, all the airplanes destined for the United States that day were filled so I was taken to a hospital in Bournemouth, England. This hospital was a complete facility. The doctors had time to proceed deliberately. Since the Achilles tendon had been severed, it had to be overlapped a bit to make it reattach. As it was explained to me, this tendon is rather like a window shade. Cut it loose and it rolls up. The Doctor also explained to me that even if he were successful in repairing it I would always have to wear a shoe with a high built-up heel, since I would never be able to put my foot flat on the floor again.

The first two surgical attempts were failures. When the cast was removed and I put even slight pressure on the foot, the tendon came loose again. After the second attempt I was told to soak my foot in warm water. The skin graft promptly came off. After the third attempt I was prevented from putting any weight on the foot for several days and told to stay clear of water. As soon as I thought the skin graft was sufficiently healed I would slip into the bathroom after everyone else had gone to sleep and sit for hours with my foot in warm water. At first, I could flex my foot very little. Gradually, I could do more. It became apparent I was on the right path. Soon I was able to stand on that leg without everything coming apart. With endless hours of flexing and walking about, progress was very apparent. The nurses were aware of my progress and protected me from being discovered by the Officer of The Day, when he made his routine bed checks. This same foot has carried me around ever since, even through a 26-year career as a Special Agent of the Federal Bureau of Investigation.

While I was in the hospital in England two Army Officers came to my bed. They told me that all but twenty-three men of Company "A" had been killed and as a Private First Class, I was the senior surviving officer. They said they had checked my I.Q. and it was of sufficient level they were offering me a Battlefield Commission as a Second Lieutenant. I asked what the future held for me if I accepted. They said that as soon as I had sufficiently recovered I would be sent to an Officers Candidate School somewhere in France and upon completion of that I undoubtedly would be sent to the Far East. I politely declined their offer.

Germany surrendered May 7, 1945. On May 23, I departed Bournemouth, England aboard a troop ship.

103

The war with Japan was still in "full swing" so we were told nothing about our destination.

This ship was very much like the one that had taken me to Europe earlier in the year, but my accommodations now were very different. The wounded soldiers now occupied officers' quarters. Officers were housed with enlisted men, but no one complained. We were all on our way home. The wounded were served three meals a day on white table cloths. All the others got two meals a day and ate standing up. The trip took ten days. There was little to do except listen to the rythmic vibrations of the ship's engines and ponder my future. Would Wanda still love me? What could I do to support a family? How would I be received at home? I still walked with the aid of crutches. My prognosis was still in doubt.

June 3, 1945 was a beautiful day. The sky was blue. The sun was shining. Suddenly the ship seemd to vibrate from cheers of the passengers, starting at the bow and progressing towards the stern. It was then I looked out and saw the Statue of Liberty gently floating past. I was home.

Welcomed home by "Lady Liberty"

The ship docked at the Brooklyn Naval Yards. The wounded were the first to disembark. We were not allowed to walk off even if we could have. We were carried on stretchers to waiting ambulances. A wounded man next to me asked to be lowered to the ground so he could kiss the earth. That is what this great Nation can mean to you, especially when you have looked death in the face.

There was an enormous crowd of people on the dock, mostly young women. They swarmed about us, hugging and kissing us as we were placed in the ambulances.

I was taken to Halloren General Hospital, Long Island, New York for a few days, then to a hospital in Augusta, Georgia. My condition soon improved to the point that I could walk with a cane and was allowed passes to go home virtually whenever I chose.

I shall always remember the first time I went home. When I last saw my mother, in the fall of 1944, her hair was black. As I approached the house, I could hardly recognize her. Her hair was snow white and she was very thin. The strain on her was obvious.

I received an honorable discharge, for medical reasons, on September 21, 1945. The previous 15 months had seemed an eternity. In spite of all that had happened, all the days and nights in the rain and snow, I had not even had a cold. I now weighed 175 pounds.

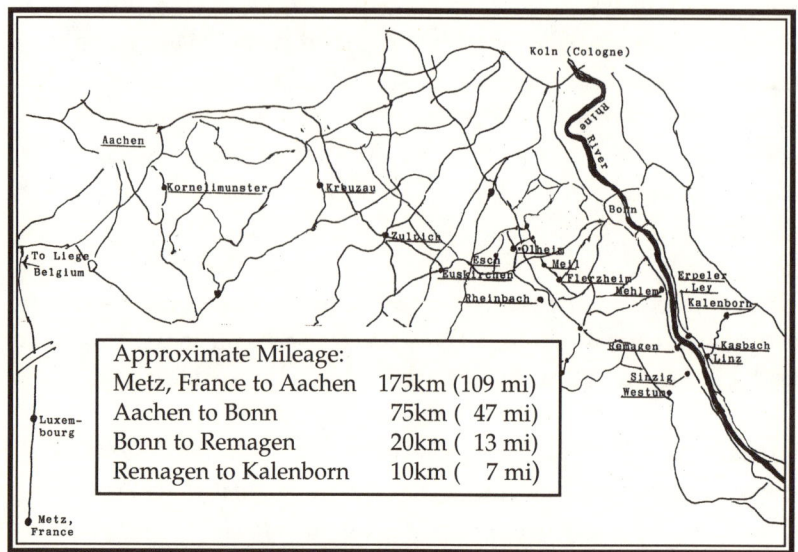

Approximate Mileage:
Metz, France to Aachen   175km (109 mi)
Aachen to Bonn   75km (47 mi)
Bonn to Remagen   20km (13 mi)
Remagen to Kalenborn   10km (7 mi)

__Map 1__ - Battle route from February 28 - March 13, 1945

Battle Route - Feb 28 - March 13, 1945

Time	Date	Location
	02/28	Kornelimunster, Germany
09:30 PM	02/28	Kreuzau
	03/03	Zulpich
12:20 AM	03/04	Geil
11:00 AM		Rovenvich
03:49 PM		Oberelivenich
01:00 AM	03/05	Woscheim
02:40 AM		Euskirchen (Billeted)
08:35 AM	03/06	To Esch
01:35 PM		Esch
02:50 PM		Ollheim
03:50 PM		Miel
05:20 PM		Flerzheim
08:45 PM		Mehlem
12:20 AM	03/07	2 hours rest
01:00 PM		Gimmigen, Heppingen, Westum
03:50 AM	03/08	Crossed Rhine River @ Remagen
04:15 AM		Erpler Ley
11:25 AM	03/09	Kasbach
01:30 PM	03/10	Hill 363
05:30 PM	03/12	To Kallenborn
05:00 AM	03/13	Battle of the Sawmill begins

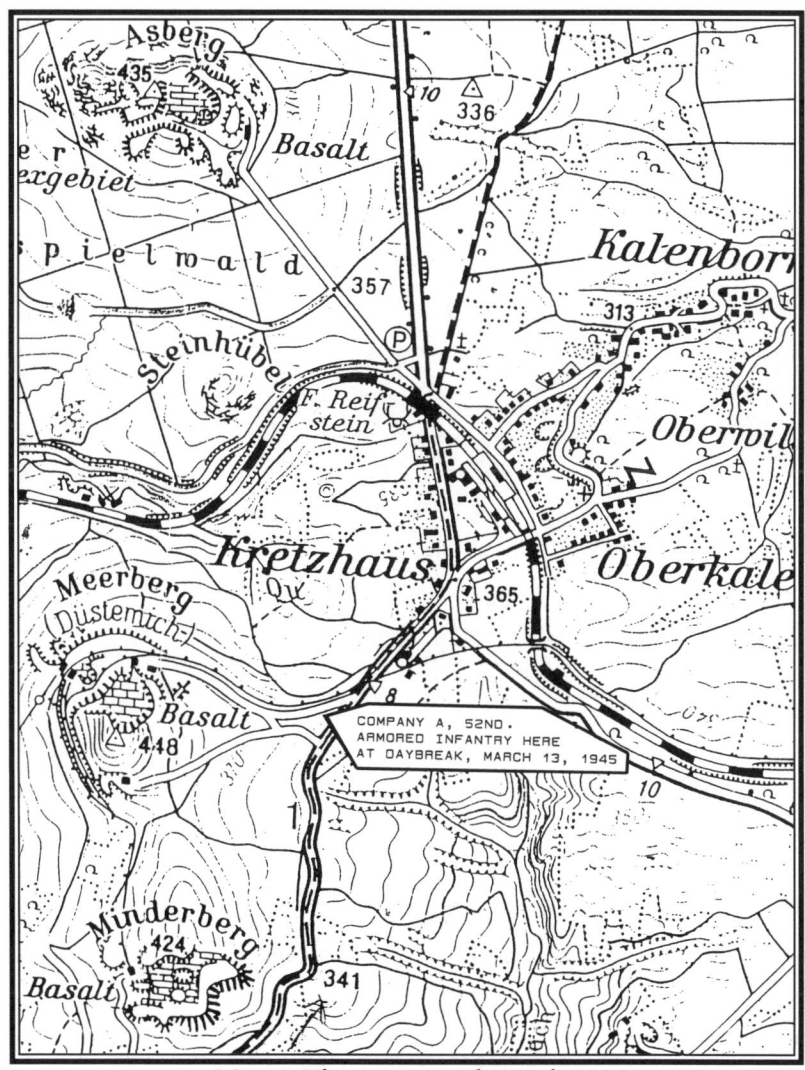

Map 2. The area around Kretzhaus

107

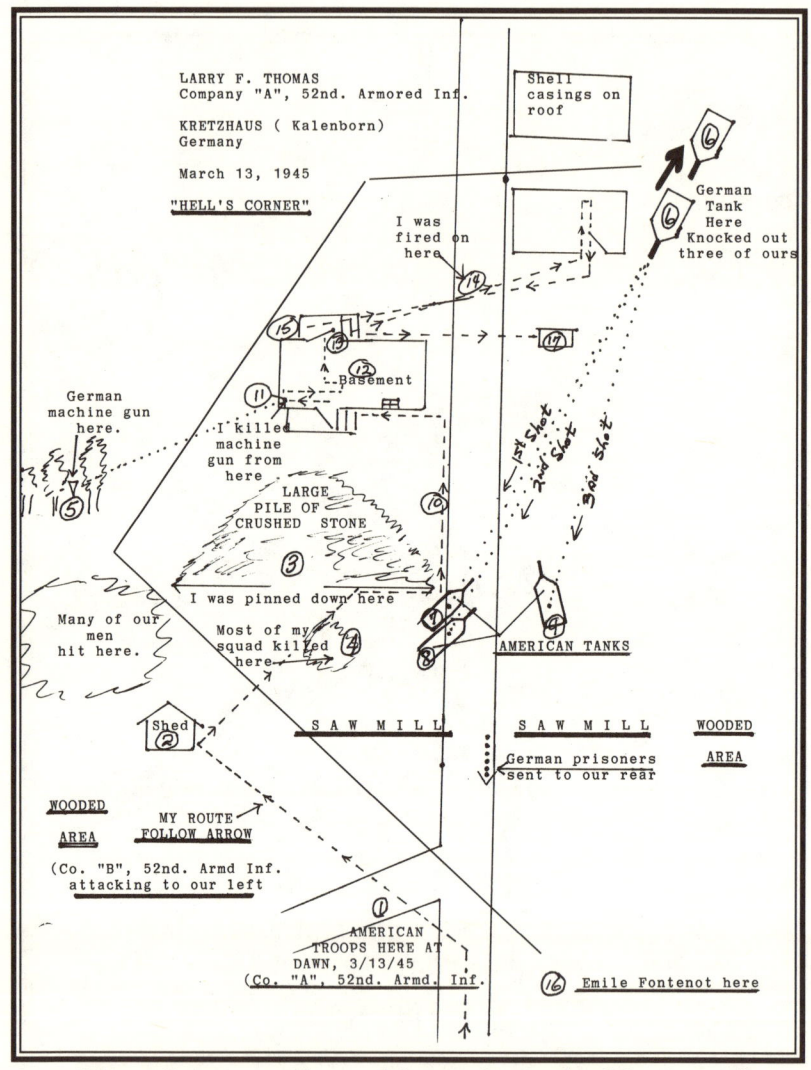

Map 3. Locations referenced during the Battle of the Sawmill.

OBSERVATIONS

Throughout the years I had endeavored to remember and record all the things I did and all that happened to me from the time I arrived in Le Havre, France until I was wounded on March 14, 1945. From the very beginning I have been frustrated by the fact that I cannot recall some days, while other days and events are very clear. I now know that I was in battles I do not recall. I can only conclude that one can be under such stress and so deprived of rest and sleep that the brain simply shuts out some things to prevent the body from collapse.

I know the weather in January, February and March, 1945 was not good. I well remember marching in snow storms and the night we spent in the barn with several inches of snow on the ground, but I do not recall what we did the day we entered the barn or the day we left.

The night I led a patrol to determine our position I know it rained torrentially and I waded through water up to my waist, but I do not recall feeling cold. This was true on March 13, 1945, when I crawled along a ditch almost full of water with ice floating in it. Even then I do not recall being wet or cold. Surely I was both. I can only think that the pressures of combat overpowered bodily discomforts and by the time I could relax, my clothing would have dried. I was fortunate in having been issued the then-new shoe pacs, with rubber bottoms and leather tops. I don't recall my feet ever feeling cold.

From the time we left our barracks near Metz, France until I was hospitalized I did not bathe, did not change clothes, did not shave although I endeavored to one time in a cold stream, and had only one hot meal. If my memory serves me well I had a sleeping bag only one night. My outer jacket was poorly insulated but I was fortunate to find one on a dead soldier that was a newer issue than mine and was quite well insulated. I cannot explain how I survived the winter weather without suffering some illness, but I did not even have a cold.

Once we left our barracks we were constantly on the move except for the weekend break in Luxembourg. It is abundantly clear from the "After Action Reports" that once we had the extreme pressure on the German forces, it was prudent to maintain it. Our objective was to prevent them from having time to build defensive positions. You will note that only once from March 1, 1945, until March 14, 1945, is there a notation of our forces being allowed to rest. This was on March 5th when were told to get a couple hours of rest. We continued our attacks throughout the days and nights. We had only brief periods to rest, often as little as 15 minutes, while we were waiting to move on.

Why (or how) I survived while so many were killed I do not know, except that it was not my time to go. If what I did contributed to my survival it was due to the fact that I was a proficient hunter and knew the value of stealth and concealment. I also had exceptionally good eyesight. I THANK GOD FOR MY SURVIVAL. THE CREDIT IS HIS.

I am a bit disturbed by the fact that my memory in specific instances is in conflict with the official record. For example, I clearly recall the instance at the barracks near Metz, France when one of our guards was killed. The official record for January and February reflects no American casualties. Also, after this happened, I fired a bazooka round through a steel door of the Maginot line, killing German soldiers, yet the reports for January and February reflect no contact with the enemy. I have chosen, however, not to compromise my clear recollections.

REMAGEN, GERMANY 1998

When the Ludendorff Bridge at Remagen was built in 1916-1918, the people of Remagen objected to it. Since it was built primarily for military purposes, they felt that in time it would surely bring the ills of war to their town. Once it was destroyed they had no intention of allowing it to be rebuilt. At one point authorities intended to remove the two pairs of large bridge towers still standing, one pair on the West bank and the other on the East along with all vestiges, as if to say the bridge never existed. The then mayor of Remagen, Hans Peter Kurten, struggled to turn the towers into a museum.

Today "Friedensmuseum" stands as a monument to peace with the flags of the United States and Germany flying high atop the Bridge Towers in Remagen. Kurt Kleemann, a gentle, very pleasant man who speaks five languages, currently serves as curator.

Accompanied by my wife Lillimae, I arrived in Remagen on May 14, 1998. After getting settled in our hotel we picked up our rental BMW automobile, hoping to spend a day or two in search of where I had been in 1945.

First, we ventured out to Friedensmuseum. While preparing to pay for admission, I commented I was last here on March 7, 1945. Hearing this, the attendant advised us that we were special guests. This was my first, but not the last time I was welcomed to Germany as a former member of the United States Military, for "helping make us free". After touring the Museum we drove to the office of Mr. Kleemann, who was expecting us.

Mr. Kleemann was proficient in English and extremely knowledgeable of events of World War II, especially in the Remagen area. After a period of getting acquainted and upon learning of my unit affiliation, Mr. Kleemann asked if I was willing to record my recollections of participation in World War II on tape. When I finished, some three or four hours later, I learned that Mr. Kleemann, who had been almost totally quiet, was more knowledgeable of the activities of Company A, 52nd Armored Infantry than I. He told me of battles that I must have participated in, though I do not recall them.

Mr. Kleemann, then gave me a copy of the now declassified report of Company A for the month of March, 1945. I received it with great anticipation, hoping it would provide details of exactly where I had been and what we had done.

It was clear that my recollections did not agree, in several instances, with the report. I had to pause, facing the conflict between the report and my memory. I expressed my concern over this to Mr. Kleemann, telling him that above all else I wanted to be correct in what I said.

His reply was quick in coming, "Stick with your memory. I would question the accuracy of reports much quicker than the memory of the combatants." He pointed out that he had talked with many veterans and found their memories very accurate, but not necessarily in agreement with the Army's reports.

After finishing the recording session, I told Kleemann I had rented a car, had already ventured out of Remagen a bit, and noticed an absence of road signs and doubted I could ever find my way to where I hoped to go. He agreed I was probably correct, especially in the smaller towns which are almost void of road signs. I asked if he could possibly go with us the following day. He hesitated, saying he had not driven since his involvement in a serious wreck. I pleaded, explaining I would drive if only he would direct me. The next day he showed up at our hotel as agreed. He took one look at the shiny BMW and reasoned he would give it a try. We had not gone far

112

before he announced, "This little ball of fire is pretty OK", and he continued to drive.

We drove South out of Remagen to the ferry and took it across the Rhine River to Linz, then to Erpeler Ley, which surrounds the twin Bridge Towers still standing on the East side of the river. Kleemann drove to the top of the hill overlooking Remagen. Once on top we found a park-like setting with a large playground covered with grass. At the rear of the playground 200 yards or more from the brink of the hill was a small hotel and restaurant nestled in a thick growth of trees.

I'm looking at the remains of the Remagen bridge I crossed 53 years earlier. My memories of that time come flooding back, and it's as if I was that 20-year-old soldier again. The experience was overwhelming.

As we sat enjoying a cup of Cafe Latte, we talked about the changes since March 8, 1945. I remembered the entire hill was clear of trees and covered with grass and that we had taken up defensive positions a few hundred yards to the rear of where we sat. He said I was absolutely correct in all I recalled. The hill was without trees in 1945 and he knew exactly where our position had been.

We left the hill and traveled East. Kleemann spoke little, saying that if I saw a place that looked familiar I should let him know. Suddenly, I asked him to stop and wanted to know if we were near a town. He didn't answer trying, I'm sure, not to unduly influence me. After a short look around we drove on. A town was just beyond the trees and out of view. He continued to drive slowly without saying a word. He drove along every street in the small town of Kalenborn, going in both directions and then back along the route we had taken coming in.

When we reached the point at which we had stopped on the way in, I told him I thought this was the site of our battle on March 13, 1945. But now 53 years later, there is no sawmill. Trees are where I think the sawmill was, and the house I first entered on March 13th was no longer there. We walked the street in search of this house, but could not locate it. Of course, we considered the possibility that if it is still standing it could have been remodeled, maybe even totally rebuilt. This was on Saturday and no one seemed to be at home.

Where the sawmill had stood there now was a lumber company on the south side of the road. Two or three workers were in the yard. Kleemann spoke to them and learned they were too young to remember World War II, but they did remember hearing that a sawmill was in operation on this site before the lumber yard was here. We left the area ninety percent sure we had located the site of the March 13th battle.

Subsequently, Mr. Kleemann wrote that he had determined we were in Kretzhaus, a suburb of Kalenborn and is certain we were at the exact site of the battle.

Mr. Kleemann, in his letter advised that Jakob Weiler, a German author, has identified and interviewed a German Sergeant Major Adam Hild, who on March 13,

1945 fought from a position not more than 50 yards from my last position.

Also, Weiler is now preparing a book on "A Day 2 Day" account of the last 100 days of the war and has asked permission to include my taped information in his book.

❧   ❧   ❧   ❧

By letter dated February 8, 1999, Mr. Kurt Kleeman of Remagen, Germany, provided the following:

"Translation by Kurt Kleeman, from Jakob Weiler's typoscript. He received Hild's report about 15 years ago.

"Adam Hild from Bad Hersfeld (Germany), was Sergeant, and on March 13, 1945, led company 7 of the Panzer-Grenadier-Regiment 110:

"We were sent to Remagen at top speed. There we had once more fierce fighting. In our position at an edge of a wood, near the houses of Kretzaus (Germany), I had no contact (to friendly troops) nor to my left nor to my right. The 'Amis' (Americans) only could come through the woods. Every morning, with the first light they came up in groups of 20-30 men. "Germans legt die Waffen nieder! (Germans put down your weapons!"), they shouted. We had few MG 42 in our position and welcomed them as soon as they had come up to a distance to throw hand grenades. Soon we could repulse their attacks several times.

"When we had to leave our position, we went back to the houses, where I had prepared a second line. In the evening we made a counterattack and forced the 'Amis' out of their position. This happened during several days.

"In my command post, there was a group of 15 girls from Cologne, who did not want to leave this cellar at any rate.

"Then I took the right side of the road. At the railroad track stood Count Schimmelmann with his tanks. Three of them were in advanced position, because the Americans showed up with 10 or 15 tanks. One of our tanks broke into a house and was trapped there, but it could still fire and shot down everything that came in sight. The 6. Kompanie was to our left in a factory and a Villa. I had a VB [sic - definition unknown] with me, but did not get any help from the artillery. In front of our position, in the woods, there was a lot of ammunition and anti-tank grenades. When the Americans came up in the morning, we fired into the ammunition piles, by that the Americans suffered severe casualties.

"Once five American first aid men appeared to pick up the wounded. One of my first aid men went out and helped them. When the Americans were about to leave, they wanted to take my man as POW with them. I was prepared for that and told my men; "If they take our man with them, then shoot at their heels, so they'll learn to run." So they did. The "Amis" ran like hares.

"I got orders to dig in on the far side of the railway enbankment. We got under heavy fire and the Americans overran our position. We slipped away behind their lines into the woods and eventually found our regiments staff." [End translation]

Note: When Company A, 52nd Armored Infantry passed through the 3rd Battalion, 310th Infantry, near Kretzhaus during the early morning hours of March 13, 1945, they remarked to us that they had tried for 3 or 4 days without success to move forward. This would appear to coincide with Adam Hild's first remarks.

Adam Hild mentions he was on the right side of the road (would have been on my left) and he moved from the woods back to the houses where he had established a "second line".

Then Hild moved back again to the railroad where he "dug in". I was not aware of the existence of a railroad in 1945, but when I returned in 1998 I found the railroad to be just ahead of my position near the intersection of the roadways as shown on my hand-drawn map. This would have placed Hild less than 50 yards from my last position.

~ ~ ~ ~

Nearly 40 years later I received a phone call from the Department of the Army. The person at the other end asked my name, date of birth, social security number, and if I remembered my Army serial number. This seemed an odd request but I gave all the requested information. He said I was entitled to the Bronze Star. I asked if he meant Battle Stars knowing I had received two of those. He said that he was referring to the Bronze Star for Valor and that the order had been issued by the commanding General. The order had been mixed up with some other papers that had been hastily filed at the end of the war and the supporting details were no longer attached. Not until somebody went through the old files at the Pentagon did the order even turn up. I received the medal a few weeks later at a ceremony held at the American Legion Headquarters at Hartsville, Tennessee.

The 52nd Armored Infantry was one of the very few battalions to receive two Presidential Unit Citations.

RETURN HOME

Being out of the army and returning home was wonderful, yet the adjustment was not easy. My nerves were far from settled. Sudden movement and loud noises were likely to make me "hit the dirt" or duck behind the nearest tree. At home it was no problem, but sometimes it was embarrassing when I was elsewhere. I had gone into Hickman one afternoon and was just entering the general store when a passing car backfired. I literally dove through the door, knocking down a woman about to leave the store. It wasn't until I acquired a pistol that I really began to quiet down. I had no desire or intention to harm anyone. It simply gave me a sense of security I didn't have without it. No doubt I would have used it had I been genuinely threatened.

One particular day I had taken Dad's car to Hickman. I went into the drug store to have an ice cream soda. While I was in there, someone came in and told me that one of the local "toughs" was outside stuffing dry leaves into the exhaust pipe of the car. This would prevent it from running. I watched a few moments, then approached the young man and ordered him to stop and to clean every one out while I stood there. His mistake was not realizing that I was not the same person that had left Hickman in June, 1944. I asked what he was doing. I still remember his reply, "Can't you see, you bastard you?" I was livid. It was all I could do to control myself. I pointed the pistol directly at his face. The leaves were out in short order. When he had finished I went back in to finish my soda. He followed me in, bringing a bunch of his buddies. As they approached I said not a word. with an air of authority, I simply laid the pistol on the marble-top table. After a few moments I told them that the old fun and games were over and there would be no more warnings or second chances. They knew what I meant. There was never another incident. One of the group asked the pharmacist to call the sheriff and have me arrested for carrying a pistol. He reminded them that they had started it all and suggested that the smart thing to do was to go home.

❧   ❧   ❧   ❧

Mama and Dad were very much opposed to Wanda Mogowski, and were unhappy when I told them I was going to Baltimore to see her. As painful as it was for both of us, we agreed we probably should "cool it" for a while. Here I was in no condition to work, had little money, and she was Catholic. I was Baptist, which was of equal concern to her mother and family. We agreed that with no harmony on either side it would be difficult to sustain a marriage. We corresponded for several months and then drifted apart. I never saw her again.

❧   ❧   ❧   ❧

Mama, Dad, and I were sitting around the fire late one evening just shortly after I was discharged from the Army. I saw a light reflecting in the mirror that hung over the fireplace. I knew that it had to be coming from the direction of the barn. There was no electricity in the barn, so I knew someone had to be there. As the light flickered on and off I casually got up, trying not to alarm Mama, got the shotgun, and quietly went out the back door towards the barn. As I approached I could hear someone in the corn crib shucking corn. When I got to the doorway of the crib I turned on the flashlight so that it illuminated the end of the gun barrel. Much to my surprise "Uncle" Matt, was there. Knowing that he always carried a pistol, I cautioned him not to reach for it.

He started crying profusely, and said, "Master Thomas, you could shoot me and even if I could I would never do anything to hurt you."

"Uncle Matt, why are you here stealing corn?" I asked. "Because I'm hungry and too 'shamed to ask for it," was the reply. By this time Dad, suspecting something was amiss, had come to the crib. The three of us sat together and shucked and shelled him a bag of corn so he could have it ground into cornmeal. Then we took him to our house and fed him a full meal. Afterwards I took him home in my car.

Uncle Matt wasn't a very productive employee; but even so, we gave him work when he wanted it. When he didn't show up for work, we would check to see if he was ill. He never had a chance to improve his lot. He lived in a one-room shack with a dirt floor, in the poor part of town. His personal hygiene was lacking, but when he needed help we gave it to him.

Shortly after the corn incident I went to work at the Veterans Hospital in Murfreesboro and did not see Uncle Matt very often. On occasions when I would be in for a visit I would go to see him, since he always asked about me. Dad would keep me posted on his condition, assuring me that he was "looking out" for Uncle Matt, making sure as he grew older and more feeble that he had food, warm clothes, and firewood.

Uncle Matt died while I was in New York. Had I known it soon enough I would have come home to bury him. Dad told me that Uncle Matt, in his last words asked for me. In spite of his faults I loved this man. I truly did not know what racial bigotry was until I went to New York and would watch members of the white race move when a black man sat beside them on the subway.

❧   ❧   ❧   ❧

It was obvious that my presence coupled with things like the incident at the general store was getting on my

Dad's nerves. It all came to a head one morning when he told me to get the team of mules and start plowing one of the corn fields. I was hurt that he could be so insensitive. My ankle still swelled every day and turned a dark blue color. I knew that walking in plowed ground was not possible. Besides, I still walked with a cane. Mama was devastated. Dad went on to the field. She sat on the front porch holding me and crying. When she gained her composure she explained that she was worried about him, that he had not been his normal self lately and she felt he must be going through the "change of life." Dad was only 46 years old then and a little young for that. She told me I probably could never work with Dad in harmony, that few people could and that I should endeavor to find some other work I could do. She said that Dad had profited handsomely from our joint efforts before I left for the Army and the farm was now paid for. Going out into this new world was frightening, but I knew I had to do it.

I had saved a little money while in the army. I took some of it and bought my own car, a 1939 Plymouth, the worst vehicle that ever was made, I think. Fortunately, my uncle Lloyd Thomas was employed at the Veterans Administration Hospital in Murfreesboro, Tennessee. He was able to arrange employment for me there. He also provided an affordable place for me to live. I started to work at the VA hospital in the fall of 1945 as a "doctor's assistant." My responsibilities were to serve as a security guard for the doctor. This hospital at that time was primarily psychiatric. Most of the patients were or could be violent. Dr. White, to whom I was assigned, was a very small man and definitely needed protection when he went on the wards to make routine rounds. It was not at all uncommon for me to have to restrain a patient. By now I weighed 204 pounds, the most I had ever weighed. My size should have been enough to discourage most assaults on the doctor; but some patients, all veterans, were in such a mentally disturbed condition they were beyond being able to reason.

The VA hospital collaborated with Erlanger Hospital in Chattanooga, Tennessee, and Vanderbilt University in Nashville, Tennessee, both teaching institutions. They periodically would send a group of nurse trainees to Murfreesboro for a period of psychiatric training. WHAT A PLACE FOR AN UNMARRIED 21-YEAR-OLD MAN TO BE! It was here I met Nina Irene Gray, a Vanderbilt student nurse from Shreveport, LA. She was the prettiest, sweetest, most considerate woman I had ever met. She was my "Yellow Rose of Texas". My world started turning around immediately. Soon Nina returned to Vanderbilt and I started commuting to Nashville as often as she would let me come. It was love at first sight for me, but I had a bit of convincing to do in order to bring her around.

Nina Irene Gray

The difference in our backgrounds was apparent. She was "the city girl," mannerly, well-spoken, and polished. I was "the country bumpkin," lacking in social graces and often reverting to butchering the English language. I knew English grammar, but it just seemed easier at home to use "ain't", "over yonder" and similar local terms. Nina was already in her second college working toward her Bachelor of Science degree and I was looking at a high school diploma with no prospects for any particular profession or field of endeavor. I knew for sure I did not want to be a farmer, nor did I want to lose Nina. As we got more serious about one

122

another, Nina very delicately told me one day that I should think about going to college. I had no money and knew that Dad would not finance a college education. That had already been ruled out.

I began checking around and found out that Cumberland University Law School, then located at Lebanon, Tennessee, was offering its last class under an accelerated curriculum. This appeared ideal. I could get the degree and be near Nina. I had already ascertained that Vanderbilt would not take me, since I had not studied

pre-law. Besides, Vanderbilt would take four years and I could get a degree in three years at Cumberland by going straight through taking no summer vacation. This meant I would graduate just

Cumberland University Law School, 1947

about the time Nina finished at Vanderbilt. As our relationship progressed, Nina told me she had promised her mother that she would finish college before she married and she planned to honor that promise.

As it turned out, Cumberland was an excellent choice. I enjoyed the course of study and found out I could make the grade rather easily and still spend a lot of time with Nina. Because I was a disabled veteran, all my expenses at school were paid and in addition I received $125.00 per month in disability benefits. That was all the money I needed at the time.

Larry Ford Thomas, 1947

I still had one problem, however. I had not yet convinced Nina I was the man for her. If I had, she did not let me know it. On one occasion I arrived at Mary Kirkland Hall, her residence on the Vanderbilt Campus, only to find out she had another date. In fact, it turned out she had a second later date. The Thomas persistence showed through and I waited until she came in from the first date. We went out for "just a few minutes" and it turned into a date for the rest of our lives — almost.

Nina Irene Gray in Centennial Park, 1947

That summer Nina went to Shreveport for a summer vacation. I wrote to her every day and got a letter from her every day for a while. Then it was every other day and toward the end of summer I hardly heard from her at all. Fortunately, I knew when she was to return to Nashville for the fall term and simply showed up at the airport to meet her.

The reason the letters had stopped was apparent. She was wearing an engagement ring that would knock your eyes out. I really didn't quite know what to do or what direction to take. But I was here and he was there, so I decided to stay in close. As it turned out, this new love of hers was a real swashbuckling Don Juan that had literally swept her off her feet. Besides, he was quite a bit older than she. She had already expressed her fondness for men older than herself. I reminded her that I was older than she by one year. She sent the ring back within two weeks and said she never heard from him again.

Nina's schedule from time to time changed when she had to start doing shift work at the hospital, so it often interfered with our being together. Frequently, our time together was limited to just an hour or two at the end of her shift and before she had to be inside the dormitory. Curfew was 11:00 PM and doors were locked. It was bad when a student got locked out and had to plead to get back in.

Sweethearts outside
the dormitory

On First Street on the way out of Nashville toward Lebanon, there was a restaurant called Malone's that stayed open all night. I was unusually tired and sleepy one night after leaving Nina and stopped to get coffee. Waiting there and trying to get a ride eastbound on Highway 70 was a young, good-looking sailor who said he had just been discharged and was trying to get home somewhere in the eastern part of the US. At that time helping a hitchhiker, especially someone in the military service, was the thing to do. So I offered the sailor a ride. As it turned out one of the smartest things I ever did was to put my pistol inside my waist band before he got in.

I was driving a "sharp" 1943 Oldsmobile, which Nina and I had bought together getting ready for our impending marriage. Before long my passenger began asking far too many ques-

125

tions about the car, noting it was one of the new ones with an automatic transmission. When he asked about the tires I expected trouble. We were seven or eight miles out of Lebanon when I heard a "click". I turned my head toward him and immediately ran into a switch-blade knife touching my neck. He told me to stop the car and get out, and that I would not be harmed. I knew I was not going to let him take this car, most especially since Nina had contributed toward the purchase of it. I professed to be looking for a wide shoulder and was in fact searching for just the right place to stop. Just before the car actually stopped rolling I put the gear in "park" opened my door, and stepped out. The car's jerking to a stop threw my passenger about a bit. Before he could recover I had the pistol in his face. I can still see the fear on his face. His wide open eyes looked like fried eggs. He started pleading with the "I wasn't going to hurt you" routine. I got him out of the car and over the nearby fence, which had a strand of barbed wire on top. I tossed his duffel bag and other things, except for his knife and identification, over the fence and drove on toward Lebanon. He was still protesting as I got beyond hearing range.

It seemed that the Lebanon Police always waited for me at the City Limits. I hoped they would be there this night and they were. I told them what had happened, gave them the knife and identification and was told to go to the police station and wait for them. In just a few minutes they came in with the sailor, whom they had found walking along the road. It was decided the best thing to do was to turn him over to the military police.

A NEW THOMAS FAMILY

I completed Law School with an LL.B. degree in December, 1947. Nina finished at Vanderbilt in January, 1948. Our wedding was set for Saturday, March 27, the Saturday before Easter Sunday. The next three months were busy for both of us, but much more so for her. In addition to making the wedding plans, she had to take the Tennessee State Board examinations in order to be licensed as a Registered Nurse.

I still did not have employment, partly because I really did not know what I wanted to do, nor had I taken the Tennessee State Bar examination. The Bar examination was only given twice each year. The next exam was scheduled in April, while we were on our honeymoon.

My closest friend and roommate in college, George W. "Dick" Mullins Jr., intended to practice law in his home town of Murfreesboro, Tennessee, and wanted me to join him. Both of us knew that my strong point in moot court exercises in law school was not courtroom trial activities. My professor, the renowned Judge Sam B. Gilbreath, was also a personal friend. He said I excelled in research and the writing of briefs and related legal documents, and suggested I consider a corporate law practice. A license to practice was not a prerequisite for this field, but it certainly was an asset. I intended to take the Bar exam when it was offered in the fall of 1948, but by then I was established in Kentucky and never returned to take it. "Dick" Mullins, did open a law practice in Murfreesboro, but in a rather short time moved to Atlanta, Georgia and affiliated himself with a large insurance company.

Wedding Day
March 27, 1948

Nina and I were married March 27, 1948, in Shreveport, Louisiana, by Bishop Dana Dawson, of the First Methodist Church located on Texas Avenue. I had saved a little money, and Nina had some, so we decided to honeymoon in Cuba. Cuba, at that time, was considered a vacation paradise rather like Las Vegas, Nevada is today. We were to take a ship out of New Orleans, and had gotten to Jackson, Mississippi, when there was a political upheaval in Cuba, making it undesirable to go there. We settled for a tour of Mississippi.

In Jackson, Mississippi, we found a very nice, cozy motel with a kitchenette. Motels in those days were few and far between and often were not the type of place where one wanted to stay. Most travelers stayed in Hotels. One evening, Nina expressed her desire for some calf's liver, which she dearly loved throughout her entire life. I went out looking for it without having asked how much I should get. To be sure I had enough, I bought two pounds, one for each of us, only to learn I had enough for at least five or six people.

It was time to start thinking about settling down somewhere. We didn't even have a place to live. So we headed back to Nashville, knowing that Nina could always get a nursing job while I looked around further. We located a furnished apartment somewhere in Nashville. I have no idea where it was located but I do recall that the landlady was a Mrs. Davidson. She was very intrusive and complained constantly if we were around the apartment during the day. We presumed she was concerned about the utility bill. It soon became apparent that this was not going to work out. So we simply left and went to Hickman and stayed with Mama and Dad for a few days.

Dick Mullins learned that John Overton, an attorney in Knoxville, Tennessee, was searching for a law-trained partner to open an insurance adjusting office in Somerset, Kentucky. In mid-1948, John Overton and I formed a partnership - Overton and Company. I would handle investigations and claims in Kentucky. He had established contacts with several large insurance companies and would work out of Knoxville. There was work to be done immediately.

This would later prove an invaluable experience and was instrumental in determining my future pursuit. There were many interesting and challenging cases to handle. I often found myself working with local police agencies in common pursuits. While investigating one particular case, I learned the police were looking for the same man I was. He was a fugitive and had been hiding from them. Contacts with this subject's family made them realize that I potentially offered money, so they were inclined to cooperate. They agreed to a meeting between the fugitive and me. We meet in a hay barn in a desolate corner of southern Kentucky. I told the police and they agreed to move in immediately after I had finished, making it look like they had followed me there. It worked to perfection with me getting what appeared to be arrested. The fugitive's family never learned the truth.

～ ～ ～ ～

Another case took me deep into the woods along the Cumberland River in Southern Kentucky. A truck which my company insured had reportedly been destroyed by fire along a given road. When I contacted the US Post Office Rural Mail carrier seeking directions, he told me where the truck was located, but said my car could not get there. Little did I know why. Furthermore, he did not think it advisable for me to go there alone, even if I could get over the road. As it turned out, the carrier owned the land where the truck was located. We agreed on a time he would take me to the truck using his army jeep. He asked if I had a pistol. I told him I did and he said, "Bring it along. You won't have to use it, but you still need it." At the appointed time we met and started along the road. We traveled only a short distance when I saw a man standing in the tall trees atop a hill above us silhouetted against the skyline. He was holding a shotgun. My driver waved to him. He waved back and we continued on. This was repeated a second time along the way.

Then we suddenly arrived at a location where several men were busily engaged in the making of moonshine whiskey. It was explained to me that we had already passed two other stills in operation. One of the men approached my driver. The driver told him who I was, why I was there, and who I wanted to see. Almost immediately a young man came up to my side of the jeep. At first he was only superficially cooperative and was rather difficult to deal with. I saw him look down at the pistol partially hanging out of my right front pants pocket. His demeanor changed immediately to one of utter cooperation. Before I left he admitted that he had taken the truck to North Carolina and brought back a large load of peaches. Before he could get back with them they began to ferment and spoil, so he decided they were only good to make peach brandy. After unloading the truck and while trying to turn it around, it turned over on the hillside. After it rolled over a time or two it was beyond repair, and even though it was a new truck, he simply set it afire rather than trying to get it out. Needless to say, we paid him nothing. The insurance company was especially appreciative. They even sent me a bonus along with my payment. On the way out, my driver pointed out the impact my pistol had on the man and advanced the opinion that had I not taken it things would have been completely different. I'm sure he knew.

❦   ❦   ❦   ❦

Other cases were equally interesting. I avoided going to eastern Kentucky if at all possible, but sometimes I had to do it. In Kentucky it was the law, and I think it still is, that anyone could carry a pistol legally so long as any part of it was visible to the public. The barrel sticking out of the bottom of a holster qualified. When I went to Eastern Kentucky so did the revolver, a .38 caliber Smith and Wesson side loader.

I was to be gone a day or two, so Nina decided to go with me. We arrived in Hazard, Kentucky, and found ourselves unable to do anything until the next day. We checked into the Daniel Boone Hotel. It is my personal opinion that Daniel Boone probably stayed there when he went through the first time. The bathroom serving our room was down the hall. The fire escape was a grass rope coiled up in a heap with one end tied to the radiator. One electric light bulb hung from the ceiling and it was turned on and off with a pull chain with a string tied to it. The bed stood squarely in the middle of the room. The sheets were spotlessly clean and had been ironed.

The next morning we were up early, hoping to get my work done quickly and go home. We drove out of Hazard along what I believe is the only straight stretch of road in that part of the state. It was drizzling rain. Up ahead was a car moving very slowly. Suddenly I realized he had stopped squarely in the middle of the right lane. With the road open ahead I started around. It was then I realized why he had stopped. An old man, stooped from the waist and hobbling on a cane, walked out of the weeds onto the highway directly into the path

131

of my automobile. I could not possibly stop without hitting him. I elected instead to steer into the rear of the stopped car.

I knocked this car several yards down the road. The trunk lid flew open. Inside were all the gallon jugs of moonshine whiskey he could get in there. Not one was broken. The driver was very apologetic, acknowledging that he had stopped adjacent to a sign that said, "No stopping on the roadway." He said he would repair my car and told me to take it to the local Oldsmobile dealer and he would be down there just as soon as he could.

The entire front end of my car was knocked out. Water from the radiator spewed in all directions. Nina often told that when we hit, she was thrown up under the dash, spraining her ankle. Instead of looking after her, I jumped out to check on the car first. I think maybe she was right.

I had the car taken to the Oldsmobile garage, asking that they repair it so it could be driven to Somerset. I waited for the driver of the other car. I haven't seen him yet. The sheriff suggested I go home and forget it. He pointed out that the brother of the driver was the local judge before whom my case would appear. I didn't finish my investigation and refused, thereafter, to go to that area. Every man I saw while I was there had a gun in his pocket. At that time there were 23 murder trials on the docket in Hazard County.

I was kept busy with all the work I could handle. There was a constant flow of cases. I was pleased to learn some forty years later that Overton and Company is still operating.

~ ~ ~ ~

I had become friends with Dr. Jack Harris, a dentist with offices in Somerset. He came to me with the proposition that seven local doctors were in the early stages of forming a medical clinic and needed a business manager. At first I declined, but as we talked further the challenge became irresistible.

They were preparing to construct a new, totally modern building housing their offices, a pharmacy, laboratory, and X-ray facilities. This building would include all that was needed to practice the best medicine known at the time. Their first priority was to form an organization to carry on the business. Initially, they considered only a partnership. It was easy to convince them of the weakness of doing business this way. Since I was friendly with a prominent local attorney who had a complete legal library, I started researching the possibility of forming a corporation, which at the time would offer tremendous tax advantages.

It did not take long to determine that the Commonwealth of Kentucky had no law preventing a corporation being formed "to practice medicine." Initially we incurred the wrath of the American Medical Association on the premise that a corporation, although an entity under the law, had no conscience, no hands, and no brain, and therefore could not practice medicine. With the assistance of my attorney friend, we drew up articles of incorporation and soon had formed Somerset Clinic, Incorporated. This was the only such corporation at that time in the entire United States.

With incorporation behind us and with architectural plans ready, construction began. It became my job to oversee construction, prepare payrolls, and generally look after the business end of this project. When time would permit I would travel to established clinics, including Mayo, Oschner in New Orleans, and a number of smaller clinics, to learn how they did business.

133

Soon we were nearing completion of an excellent facility and approaching the time to move in and begin "practicing medicine".

～　～　～　～

When Nina and I went to Kentucky, we lived in an apartment in the home of Mr. and Mrs. Revel Gooch, an exceptionally nice couple. With the birth of our first child, we needed more space. Luckily we found a newly constructed two-bedroom garage apartment which was ideal for us. The only problem was that we had no furniture and we were in the midst of paying for our first new car, a 1949 Hudson.

Jack Goldenberg of Goldenberg's Furniture Store was a friend. He outfitted our apartment without any down payment. As I recall, we purchased everything we needed for about $500.00. At that time I was earning what then was a very good wage, between $300 and $400 a month. Nina was working at the hospital, so we were doing very well financially.

Elizabeth Ann Thomas, our first child, was born December 20, 1949. Nina's only request after delivery was for a quail dinner. I didn't have a "bird dog" for hunting quail, so I simply went out of town to a likely looking place and climbed over the fence. Just as I touched the ground inside the fence a covey of quail flew up. I killed three. Knowing I had enough for her, I returned home to prepare them. I wasn't gone from the apartment more than an hour, which I think is probably the best luck I have ever had on any hunting venture. I intended to "do it up right," so, after cooking the quail I put them in a sterling silver dish and put that inside the oven to keep warm while I prepared the balance of the dinner. This, I learned, was a mistake. The cover of the dish and the bottom melted to the point I had difficulty getting them apart. Needless to say, I ruined a perfectly good dish. Notwithstanding, I took the quail to Nina in sterling.

Nina was determined to be home for Christmas during a time when most mothers who had just delivered stayed in the hospital for at least a week. Soon we were in one of the most serious crises of our lives. It was back to the hospital for Nina in the hope of controlling a very serious case of septicemia. Instead of improving, she grew steadily worse. We knew that her mother had died of the same problem following Nina's birth. Three or four days later Dr. Robert M. Bateman, her obstetrician, and a member of the Somerset Clinic, emerged from her room and stood talking to me in the hallway. Not known for his diplomacy, he bluntly told me she probably would not live more than four or five hours and "that I might as well get things ready for it." God had to have been listening because Dr. Mcleod Patterson, an internist in the Clinic, walked past and heard what was said. I shall be eternally grateful he was there. He literally pushed Dr. Bateman aside. They did not get along really well professionally, anyway.

Dr. Patterson emerged from Nina's room four hours later. I know he had not left the room, although many others had come and gone, because I stayed in the hallway the entire time. When he emerged, the first thing he said was, "I think she'll make it. We won't know until morning." He said he had arranged for a new antibiotic, acromycin, not yet used in the Somerset City hospital, to be flown in by private airplane from Louisville, Kentucky. She had already taken the first dose. Dr. Patterson advanced the opinion that if she survived she probably would be unable to have any more children. At that moment this was not our primary concern. She did, of course, recover and had two more children, Susan and Larry.

135

The challenges presented by the clinic were ongoing. I was introduced to double-entry bookkeeping, personnel matters, the purchase of medical equipment and supplies, federal income tax matters and a multitude of other responsibilities.

As a member of the National Association of Clinic Managers, I had the privilege of traveling a couple of times each year at the clinic's expense. One such meeting was in Los Angeles, California, in November of 1953. Dr. Moore of the Jackson, Tennessee Clinic, Cecil Colvin of the Green Clinic in Ruston, Louisiana, and I had decided to drive out together. When I got to Jackson, Tennessee, to pick up Dr. Moore, I had some difficulty convincing him to go in my car rather than his big Buick sedan. I had just purchased my second new Hudson, a 1954 Hornet, with twin H-power. This meant the six-cylinder in-line engine was fitted with two carburetors. They each fed three cylinders. Hudson Motor Cars, at that time, were winning almost every stock car race they ran in, so I knew it was a fast car. It wasn't until later I learned just how fast it could go. I never found out what its maximum speed really was.

We hadn't been on the road long until Dr. Moore and Cecil relaxed and agreed that we were in the right car. It was not only a fast-running car, but it was exceptionally comfortable and was considered the safest car on the road, partly because of its very low center of gravity.

We were staying in the Statler Hilton Hotel in Los Angeles. It was new, having just opened. While checking in I was advised that they were holding a message for me. I was told to call my Uncle Henson Thomas, who lived in the area. I had no idea he knew I was there.

You would have had to know my late Uncle Henson to appreciate the following. He was known for being "closed-mouth". He never talked about his personal life.

He was also well-known as a practical joker. Before going to California he owned two drug stores and a beautiful home in Nashville. He sold it all and moved to Los Angeles when his daughter Yvonne obtained a contract with one of the major movie studios. Each summer thereafter, he, his wife Madeline and Yvonne would come to Tennessee in an old black Chevrolet sedan that looked like it had never been cleaned even once. Everyone presumed that Uncle Henson had either lost or spent all his money.

Uncle Henson, the practical joker

I called Uncle Henson from the hotel and he insisted that I stay with them while I was there. I explained my need to be in attendance at the convention. Because of the uniqueness of our clinic's operation I was expected to discuss our clinic at a number of the committee meetings. He then insisted I must come that evening for dinner and that he would pick me up in a few minutes. At exactly the appointed time he drove up to the entrance of this elegant Hotel in his old Chevrolet. He stepped out to meet me in his Tennessee bib overalls. I hoped to get out of there before anyone I knew came along.

Soon we were driving through an elegant residential area, making me wonder what kind of home he lived in. We drove slowly down this winding driveway then atop the hill where I could see the Pacific Ocean. We were in the Pacific Palisades. We pulled into a vacant spot in a four-car garage. Parked there also were a new Packard, a small sports car, and a white closed-in truck that looked refrigerated. His home was one of the most beautiful I had ever seen. I looked at him and without a word being said, we both started laughing. I asked as I sat there why he had just driven the Chevrolet to Tennessee when he could have driven the new Packard. Quite seriously he said, "I don't want them to know what I'm doing." I never told this until after he died. Until much later, I was the only member of my family to visit him.

The truck, he said, was his business. He showed me a steel ring, probably 8 or 10 inches in diameter, and full of keys to the homes of movie stars. He was a milkman and would put the milk directly in their refrigerator. He often commented that I would be utterly surprised how many people he saw coming out the back door of some homes at 5:00 AM, Betty Grable's in particular.

During the week he arranged a private tour of the 20th Century Fox Studios. I was introduced to Susan Hayward. Later in the week, he called and wanted to know if I would be willing to escort a young starlet to her "coming out party." I said, "no, I have a wife back home." He explained that it would all be above board, simply put — it was a business deal. I would show up properly dressed, she would provide the money for the evening, and we would be off. I finally convinced myself to call Nina and ask her what she thought about the idea. I was a bit surprised when she said, "Go for it on one condition. Stay out of her bed."

I scouted about and got a tuxedo and all the accouterments and showed up at the appointed place at the appointed time. Waiting there was truly a "goddess". She was, I believe, the most beautiful woman I had ever seen, including my lovely wife. I truly do not recall her name, so forgive me for the "her's" and "she's". She handed me a roll of money and when the limousine arrived we drove away like royalty.

The party was at one of the movie studios. It seemed as though hundreds of people must have been there. I was glad we had decided that I was to be "Larry Bates" that evening with no reference whatsoever as to where I was from. I tried not to let it show that I was overwhelmed and I think I succeeded. I relaxed only when we got on the dance floor and started doing a Tango. She was an excellent dancer. I had just finished a course in ballroom dancing at Arthur Murray's in Lexington, Kentucky. Soon we found ourselves, quite literally, putting on a one-couple show. When the party was over we returned in the same limousine. I gave her the unused cash and returned to reality. Uncle Henson called the next day to let me know that she was very pleased, but was having trouble trying to explain who her "mystery" companion had been.

On the way back to Kentucky we stopped for gasoline late one afternoon just as we approached the southern portion of the Rocky Mountains. We intended to spend the night nearby. At the station we learned that a severe snow storm was approaching and if we wanted to get over the mountain any time within the next three or four days we had better do it before midnight. We decided to make a run for it.

The sky was clear, and the full moon so bright you could read a newspaper by it, to use an old Tennessee expression. With a full tank of gasoline and my two companions asleep, I decided to "let it roll." The highway, once over the mountain range, was straight and virtually flat. Four hours later I stopped for more gasoline. It took a bit of effort to convince my colleagues where we were and that we had covered 410 miles while they slept.

I arrived home to face another major decision, one I had not expected. I knew the doctors in the clinic had been arguing among themselves about the division of the money, but I did not know how serious the problem had become. Dr. Patterson, my close friend, sought me out and told me the clinic was about to dissolve and that when it did, I would have to leave. He suggested I resign to avoid any stigma that a dismissal might bring.

⸎ ⸎ ⸎ ⸎

After we moved to Kentucky, the Wolf Creek Dam was built, creating a lake that backed water up well east of Somerset. Bass fishing was exceptional and I loved to catch them. Dr. Morgan, a member of our clinic, knew I had been using a flat-bottom boat to fish from and cautioned me about how dangerous the lake was, especially when using such a boat. He called me to his office and pointed to a beautiful Whirlwind boat, with an Evinrude motor attached. Both were setting on a trailer. "Take that," he said, "and when you get an extra $300.00, pay me for it." I fished three times a week, Wednesday, Saturday, and Sunday afternoon, for two or three years. I have fished when it was so cold the line would freeze on the reel between casts.

Unless you have caught a two- or three-pound small mouth bass when it is cold, you have no idea the thrill it offers. The fish like the cold water and it makes them very aggressive when hooked. When they take the bait a fisherman would think he had a 20-pound "ball of fire" on the end of the line. With the right bait I had only to move quietly close to the shore and attempt to cast right at the water's edge. In fighting they would make the water boil.

Only once did I come close to getting in trouble on the water. This lake was bounded by steep hills and in many places the water was 165 feet deep. One could hardly hope to touch bottom. One afternoon I had gone some distance from the dock and was fishing on the far side of the lake watching an angry-looking cloud approaching. I wanted to stay until the very last minute and ended up staying too long. Suddenly the wind became fierce, whipping up waves and whitecaps two to three feet high.

When I was about halfway across the lake it started to rain very hard. Hoping to prevent the boat from filling with water from the rain and the waves splashing into it, I managed to pull the heavy canvas cover over the boat. By getting in the rear of the boat and steering by hand I could put the cover over almost the entire boat. As I struggled to remain "into the wind", I realized the boat was half-full of water and about to sink. A piece of the cover had acted much like a funnel and was about to fill the boat. With waves about to turn me over, I continued to steer into them with one hand while bailing water with the other hand. I'm still here to tell you about it, but truthfully I thought that was to be my last day. I cannot swim and even though I had on a life preserver with an extra one tied to me, I probably would have drowned had I capsized. I never let that happen again.

I had to sell this treasured possession when I entered the Federal Bureau of Investigation. When I went to pay Dr. Morgan, he said, "You owe me nothing."

Wedding Day
March 27, 1948

Wedding Departure

 The Family Begins

With our first child,
Elizabeth Ann

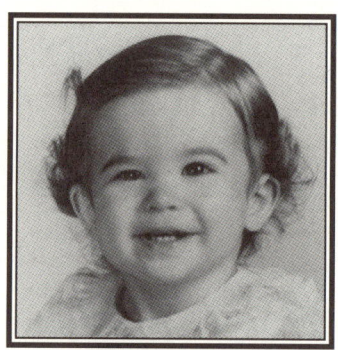

Elizabeth Ann

Our second child,
Susan Carol

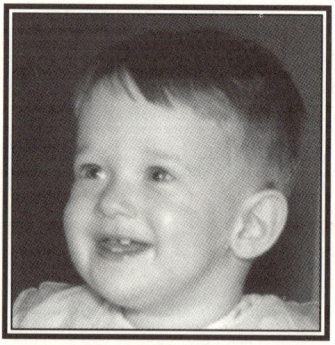

Our third child,
Lawrence Gray

142

Elizabeth Ann's
First steps

Elizabeth Ann
and Daddy

Elizabeth Ann
in Daddy's hat

Elizabeth Ann
and Susan

Susan and "Little
Larry"

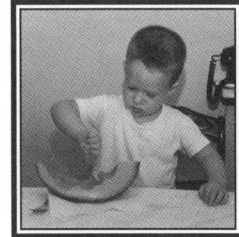

"Little Larry"

Christmas 1956

Elizabeth, Susan,
and Larry

With Nina and
"Little Larry"

Elizabeth Ann

Susan

Larry

Nina and I at "Topknot"
cabin in Gatlinburg

Nina and I - 1988

Nina and I with the children
Christmas 1991

The children and I
1996

My graduating class at the FBI Academy

Me? Drive?
In New York City?

Ready for assignments

Larry Thomas Retires After 26 Years in FBI

Larry F. Thomas, Special Agent for the FBI in Maury and nine other middle Tennessee counties for the past 12 years, retired today after serving a total of 26 years with the Bureau.

Born and reared in South County, Agent Thomas is the son of Mr. and Mrs. J. Melvin Thomas of Route Creek, Tenn. He served during World War II in the U.S. Army and was wounded in combat after the Battle of Remagen Bridge in Germany.

He received his LLB degree from the Cumberland School of Law in Lebanon.

From 1946 to 1954, he was manager of the Somerset Medical Clinic at Somerset, Ky.

From January 1954 to present, he has been a Special Agent for the FBI. As Senior Resident Agent, he has handled all matters of jurisdiction in the area comprising southern Middle Tennessee.

Thomas' first assignment with the FBI was at Indianapolis, Ind. His next assignment was New York City from Feb. 1956 to June 1967.

It was in New York where Thomas worked National Security for the FBI, particularly in the field of espionage. He worked on the case of the Russian Master Spy Rudolph Ivanovich Abel from beginning to end.

While Thomas will not comment on the details of the case, news accounts of the day revealed that Abel was a top spy of the Soviet KGB who entered the United States illegally. It appears there are legal spies and illegal spies, and Abel was one who had entered our country illegally. In the spring of 1957, he was cornered in a New York Hotel room by Agent Thomas and other agents who arrested him as a deportable alien. After agents searched Abel's room and found cipher pads, 18 micro films, and a phony birth certificate, Abel was then charged with espionage. He was later convicted, fined $3,000 and sentenced to 30 years in prison.

When now U.S. pilot, Francis Gary Powers, was shot down while flying over Russia on May 1, 1960, the groundwork was laid to exchange our spy for their spy. On Feb. 10, 1962, on a bridge between East Germany and West Berlin, Abel was swapped for Powers who had also been sentenced for spy activity.

Thomas recalls his work with other agents in the Weinberg kidnapping case where a cab driver kidnapped and killed the child. Agents matched writing on the ransom note with over two million driver's licenses in New York and finally found a match with the killer.

Then there are funny memories such as when Agent Thomas presented his credentials with his photo to a person and said, "FBI, I am looking for a criminal named John Doe." The individual looked carefully at the credentials with photo, and then stated emphatically, "Nope, I have never seen this person before."

LARRY F. THOMAS

Assigned to Columbia and the ten surrounding counties since June 1967, Thomas has worked on all matters under FBI jurisdiction in this area. He has been instrumental in solving many bank robberies and crimes involving auto thefts and stolen property which crossed state lines.

Thomas and his wife Nina are the parents of three children.

A daughter, Mrs. E.J. (Elizabeth Ann) Kisly, is a teacher at Milan, Ill., where her husband is employed as sales manager with Montgomery Elevator Co.

Another daughter, Mrs. Dawson (Susan Carol) Gray, is a third-year student at UT Memphis Medical School. Her husband is an attorney here in Columbia.

A son, Lawrence G. Thomas, is in the school of engineering at the University of Tennessee.

Thomas and his wife will remain in Columbia after retirement.

145

FEDERAL BUREAU OF INVESTIGATION

The following information and events occurred during my twenty-six years as a Special Agent of the Federal Bureau of Investigation. This represents only a small example of the matters assigned to me personally, or cases assigned to other agents on which I worked. It is fair to say there were several cases in the "security field" which I have elected to exclude, either because they were extremely sensitive in nature or involved matters I feel should not be divulged even at this time.

The information in this book under the section heading "FEDERAL BUREAU OF INVESTIFGATION" was approved for publication by the Federal Bureau of Investigation by letter dated March 9, 2000.

With Christmas, 1953 approaching, it wasn't the time we would have chosen to move. From time to time I had received offers of employment from other clinics, but none were forthcoming at that time.

Nina knew how much I had always wanted to become an FBI agent. In 1947, I had applied while still in college. Some investigation was conducted because friends in Hickman told me an agent had been around asking questions about me. Then I received a letter from Mr. Hoover pointing out that through an oversight it had now been determined that, at twenty-two years of age I was not old enough to qualify. It was suggested that when I reached twenty-four years of age I could reapply. Nina and I agreed that I should now go to the FBI office in Louisville and reapply. By now I was approaching my 29th birthday. I knew they would not accept anyone over 30 years of age, because the law then required an agent to have 20 years of service by age 50 in order to retire.

At the FBI office in Louisville, I was met with open arms. I suppose my ego became very inflated hearing how well qualified I was and how my experience would almost guarantee my rapid advancement through the FBI ranks. Little did I know then that President Dwight

Eisenhower had ordered the FBI to expand their coverage of the Soviets in the United States. The FBI said they needed 500 new agents to do it. Every office was scrambling for qualified applicants. I was about to be one of them.

When I told them about the earlier investigation they immediately called headquarters in Washington, DC to verify it and ascertain the results. While I waited it was suggested I take the entrance exam. It was short and easy, being mostly legal questions with which I was familiar. I was told to go to lunch and return to find out what headquarters had said.

When I walked in the door after lunch I thought they were going to hug me. They said I had been accepted pending further investigation and wanted me to report to Washington, DC the following week. Even though I needed employment, this was a bit too fast. I insisted on a month to notify the clinic. Besides, I wanted to get through Christmas.

I was offered an appointment and told to report to the FBI headquarters in Washington, DC on January 25, 1954. FBI training was a minimum of twelve weeks, most of which was at the academy located on the Quantico Marine Corps base in Quantico, Virginia. Wives could not accompany us there. So we decided that Nina would remain in Kentucky during my training period.

I left Somerset driving our car. There was no interstate highway system at that time. After a very hard day's drive I arrived in New Market, Virginia. I decided to spend the night there and go over the mountain the following day. It was cold with a light rain falling. The real surprise came in the morning. Everything was covered with a thick layer of ice. So much was on the car that the tires looked half-flat. I couldn't get inside the car because the doors were frozen shut. Using a pocket knife, I chipped away the ice around the door and finally got it open.

Crossing the Appalachian Mountains was another feat. As I approached the top I was met with very deep snow. Going up was much easier than going down the other side. Cars and trucks were stalled every few yards. Some almost completely blocked the roadway. One truck in particular left just enough room to get past by getting dangerously close to the drop-off side. I had no choice but to try it. It was impossible to stop. I was gaining speed, all the time doing everything I could to slow down. Fortunately, some of the curves allowed me to swing into the heavy snow against the side of the mountain. I said a prayer of thanks when I got to level ground again.

I pulled into the first gasoline service station I saw to get fuel. I couldn't get out of the car. The door had frozen shut again. The attendant couldn't get gasoline in the car. I pulled inside the service bay and waited until it thawed so I could get out. Here I learned that anyone coming into Washington DC without chains on his car would be given a ticket if they got stuck. So I bought my first pair of tire chains.

I arrived in Washington early enough to get a furnished room near FBI headquarters. After reporting in, I learned that we would be moving to Quantico the following day and that no personally owned cars could be taken down there. This created a major problem. I didn't have enough money to store it. I remembered that the Chief of Police in Somerset had a sister living in Washington. I arranged to park the car there temporarily.

From the very first day it was apparent that all agents were to fit the same mold. Dark blue suits, white shirts, subdued ties, and a hat was acceptable attire, but no argyle socks, which were the rage of the day. Within the first hour, Assistant Director, Hugh Clegg, who was giving us the official welcome, singled out a young man in the back of the room and told him to get rid of his argyle socks at the first break period. While Mr. Clegg was still speaking we all became aware of a commotion at the rear of the room. The man with the argyle socks was digging through a mound of luggage looking for his. He was asked to sit, but instead stood straight and said, "I'm leaving. I would never work for such a chicken s___ organization." He walked out. No amount of cajoling could stop him. I think we all admired him at the time. The next twelve weeks were something less than a picnic.

Except for the fact that Dr. Robert McLeod, one of the doctors at the clinic, had said I would never make it through, I would have gone home and looked elsewhere for work. Had I left, I would have regretted it the rest of my life.

Every day included a lecture on morals, the places where we might go, and places we were not to go. Everything seemed to be designed to put new agents in fear of the system. Yet when we finished the course we were given credentials, a badge, and a gun, and sent out to represent the United States Justice Department. I had spent the last five years trying to build initiative and self-confidence and they seemed determined to reverse the process.

Immediately after I arrived at the academy on the Quantico Marine Corps base I set about trying to figure out how to get my car down there. It was an inconvenience where it was. I learned that the town of Quantico was not located on the Marine Corps base. The Chief of Police, when learning of my dilemma, offered to let me park my car in front of his house and leave it as long as I wanted, since he had an abundance of space. The first weekend I was free I took a bus to Washington and brought my car back to the Chief's house and parked it. Thus began about 10 weeks of constant harassment by bureau officials.

Classroom lectures began at 8:00 AM. At 8:05 on Monday I was called out of class and reminded of the admonition against bringing personally owned cars to Quantico. The fact that it was not on the base, but on private property by permission, meant nothing. I was told to remove it immediately. Having no place to take it, I simply refused to move it.

The following day a Bureau official, "Doc" Watson, came to the academy and called me out of class. Without the slightest explanation he began giving me an oral quiz, designed purely to harass and demean. I clearly recall that he asked me to spell "and so forth." I spelled it A-N-D S-O F-O-R-T-H. His displeasure was apparent. "What I mean," he said, "is etc." My reply was that "etc." is an abbreviation. If he wanted me to spell "et cetera", he should simply ask me to do that. We all came to know "doc" as not the most intellectual official there. He left without any further demands or threats. Then they brought in G. C. Gearty, three or four levels below Mr. Hoover. The vehicle stayed where I had parked it.

Midway through our training we were required to move back to Washington for completion of the course. We were instructed to go up in advance and arrange for a place to live if we had not already done so. Our move

150

was scheduled for mid-week with the balance of the week and Monday of the following week off, since it was a holiday. We were not made aware of this until the day before we were to leave. Seeing this as a perfect opportunity to go to Kentucky and see Nina, I set about getting ready. Then I was told I had to ride the bureau bus to Washington. No exception had ever been made. One was made that day. It was finally agreed I could drive my car if I stayed very close to the bus. When I got to the intersection leading toward Kentucky, I turned West.

The rule was that if we were going to be away from your residence over a weekend we had to have approval in before Thursday. I called Mr. Gearty to advise him where I was going. His immediate reply was, "You can't go; you did not get approval according to the rules". After a very long harangue I finally told him I had not called for his approval; I simply had called to tell him where I was going. Before I could hang up he informed me that if I was not back by 10:00 PM Monday night I would be fired. With Jim Holbrook, a member of my class whose home was Ashland, Kentucky, I took off. Nina was to meet me in Ashland.

We were to drive all night, but knowing our wives would be there when we arrived made it all worthwhile. Around 2:00 AM we were passing through a small town in Virginia. Not a person was in sight. Suddenly, from nowhere a police car appeared, with lights flashing.

I knew that if Mr. Gearty found out we had been arrested or even given a speeding ticket, he would probably fire both of us. I pulled to the curb and watched this enormous policeman writing down my license plate number. We had not yet been issued credentials, but we did have our badges. I felt I needed this man's attention right then before he made out the ticket. I began tapping my badge on the side of the door. The officer bent over and

151

began reading "F-e-d-e-r-a-l B-u-r-e-a-u...". Then he stopped, extended his hand with a smile, inquired about our health, and wanted to know where we were going in such a hurry. I stretched the truth somewhat and told him we had a hot assignment in Kentucky and we were already behind schedule. By now cars had stopped on the narrow road, blocking it in both directions. The officer set about clearing away the traffic and escorted us to the edge of town with a wave and blinking lights, sending us on our way. No two FBI agents ever felt more relieved. We knew then it was going to be different once we got our credentials and got out into the real world.

I shall jump ahead a couple of months to say that following completion of our training Jim and I, on our way to Kentucky, passed through this same town, but this time, I slowed to below the speed limit. At just about the same spot the blinking lights appeared again. I wondered why because I knew I had not exceeded the speed limit. This same policeman approached my car, extended his hand and said he simply wanted to know how things came out in Kentucky. I assured him all was well and the slight delay when he had stopped us had caused no problem whatsoever.

Following our initial trip to Kentucky, and with our brief second honeymoons over, Jim and I started back to Washington. We failed to take into account that a late winter snow storm might come along. As we approached the Appalachian Mountains just where I encountered the snow in January, we found ourselves barely able to make it through deep snow. We remembered Mr. Gearty's admonition and struggled on. As the critical hour of 10:00 PM, the time "we must" be back in Washington approached, it became apparent that we would never even come close to getting back by then. Almost as if God had put it there, in the middle of nowhere, stood a public coin-operated telephone, lighted as if calling attention to our need.

Knowing I did not want a long-distance operator's voice messing up my idea, I identified myself, said that I wanted to make a very short call to the FBI and would like to pay before the call was completed. The operator saved the day by completing the call without saying a word. So at exactly 9:55 PM, I spoke to the FBI clerk handling availability records and asked that she sign us in. I recognized her voice and even knew her name.

Jim and I arrived in Washington just in time to take a shower, put on fresh clothes, and go to work. We had no telephone in our apartment. Sensing I might need a bit more proof, I stopped at the neighborhood pharmacy and jotted down the number of an outside telephone. Jim and I agreed, if questioned, he would say that I had handled the availability checks for both of us. It was true that I had.

I was in class about an hour, beginning to feel that all was well, when I was called out and asked to report to Mr. Gearty's office immediately. His office was on the fifth floor of the FBI building just down the hall from Mr. Hoover's office. Mr. Gearty's secretary directed me to a seat saying he was busy at the moment. He was still busy two hours later. I could tell from what I heard inside that I was being allowed to "stew" for a while. I did become irritated and told the secretary I would come back to see him when he wasn't so busy. I was ushered into his office immediately.

Mr. Gearty's normally sallow complexion was even more gray this day. His displeasure was apparent. I sat through his tirade without one word. He pointed out I had violated his instructions by not signing in before 10:00 PM, and that he had no choice but to dismiss Jim and me from the FBI. I had no choice but to play the bluff, feeling he had no way of knowing what time we had gotten back to the city. Knowing I had, in fact, signed in at 9:55 PM, I announced, as I was about to depart from the room, that he had made a grievous mistake and that I would walk down the hall and present my case to Mr. Hoover in person. His facial expression clearly indicated he did not want me to do that. He asked me to take a seat while he tried to work it out. It was not until then I told him I had signed in at 9:55 PM, and could prove it. He hadn't even bothered to ask. Nothing was ever said about what time I had actually returned to the city.

After another hour he returned with a much improved disposition. He said I should forget the whole thing and return to class. Maybe I pushed it a bit too far, but I chose to ask for an explanation and an apology as to why I had been kept waiting all morning and it was now lunch time. He did offer a half-hearted apology saying I had been signed in on the wrong register.

On the way back to class I had to pass my class counselor's office. I heard him talking with the counselor of another group, relating my encounter with Mr. Gearty, and the fact that Gearty had said I threatened to go to "The Old Man", meaning Mr. Hoover. Mr. Gearty, felt I would have done it. You can be assured that I would have done it. From that day until I finished training I had no further problems with the training staff.

I trust I have not belabored the forgoing to the point of boredom, but even the "very good" generally has a bit of "not so good" mixed in. So it was with FBI training. This is not a condemnation of the Bureau, but rather a criticism of the system that existed at the time. My contacts with Mr. J. Edgar Hoover, Director of the FBI, limited though they were, convinced me he was a totally fair, honest, and compassionate person. He expected a great deal of his agents, but then that was what built an esprit de corps second to none. Mr. Hoover invariably exhibited an understanding, fair approach to personnel matters actually reaching his desk.

154

The problem was with those working under Mr. Hoover. Knowing what was expected of them, they simply set forth rules designed to instill fear sufficient to prevent any possible transgression that might bring them into disfavor with Hoover. An accumulation and compounding of the rules as they drifted down often made them ridiculous by the time they got to the Special Agent in training school or on the street doing the actual work. It was often pointed out that the Bureau succeeded in spite of itself. I can only attribute this to the fact that there were enough competent men there willing to take the chance needed to get the job done.

It was interesting to note that in training school the overall attitude of the class was clearly divided among those who had come up through the FBI system, such as those in clerical positions, and those like myself coming directly in from outside pursuits. The former clerks had already been indoctrinated and had no trouble fitting this new mold. Maybe it all did, in the end, have a beneficial effect on my remaining twenty-six years.

∽   ∽   ∽   ∽

Being a Law School graduate, the study of Federal Criminal procedure was easy. Training in the use of firearms and arrest procedures was something new and interesting. Some of it was new, anyway. After having fired hundreds, even thousands of rounds of ammunition through Dad's shotgun, I knew that portion pretty well. The first time I fired on the skeet course I broke 23 of 25 targets missing the two at the "center" position, but I soon learned how to do it from there.

I came very close to being immortalized by being the first trainee to make a perfect score of 100 on the practical pistol course. I was just finishing a "record run", lacking only twelve rounds to finish. The firearms instructor eased up behind me and said that up to that

155

moment I had a perfect score but I only had twelve seconds left to finish. I knew I probably could not fire twelve shots in twelve seconds since I had to reload, so I hurried a bit. One of the last twelve shots narrowly missed, giving me a 99.8% score. As it turned out, I had more than twelve seconds. Even so, I was proficient enough for them to ask me to become a firearms instructor. Seeing how adversely it had affected the hearing of the permanent instructors, I declined. Besides, this was not what I wanted from the Bureau.

It was essential that every Special Agent know how to drive an automobile. One classmate, Arthur Koppel, who was a young Jewish man from Brooklyn, did not know how to drive an automobile. I was assigned the responsibility of teaching him. I don't know how many large metal garbage cans he destroyed before I gave up trying to teach him how to park a car. I refused to certify that he could drive. As it turned out, Art and I were both assigned to Indianapolis, Indiana as our first office. Art wrecked a Bureau car the first day he was there. I was especially glad I had not certified him.

❧   ❧   ❧   ❧

We had another former clerk from Brooklyn who knew how to drive but had never held any type of firearms in his hand before we began the training. The first time he fired a shotgun he was so startled and frightened that he "lost his cool". The recoil caused him to stagger backwards, since he was already leaning back in anticipation of the recoil from the gun. About to fall, he turned around with a loaded shotgun waving in all directions. We literally hit the ground in a prone position. As you can imagine, he had to have a bit of private instruction. I knew then I hoped I would never be called upon to go out with him on an arrest situation.

❧   ❧   ❧   ❧

One more event and then we will go forward to something else. A new pistol course, which electronically recorded how long it took to draw the weapon and fire after a light had come on, had been installed. The instructions were clear and very proper: do not pull the trigger until the gun is out of the holster and pointed at least in the direction of the target.

The agent in front of me, in his haste to beat the clock, committed the inexcusable mistake and shot himself through the right buttock with the bullet going in high on the hip and coming out just where the buttock meets the leg. Fortunately for him, we were using what we called "ball" ammunition. That means the bullets were round on the end rather than flat like a wad-cutter bullet would be. Had he loaded with wad-cutters the exit hole would have been horrendous. He seemed almost unaware he had been shot, and later told me his first thought was about what they would do to him administratively rather than the severity of his wound.

We took him to the Marine Corps Hospital in Quantico in a Bureau car, having been cautioned not to let him bleed on the upholstery. The doctor ran a swab all the way through the wound to clean out any remaining gunpowder, bandaged him up, and we took him back to the range. Believe it or not, he continued on the firing range, doing whatever he could do standing up. He stood most of the time for the next three or four days.

❧ ❧ ❧ ❧

My first assignment was Indianapolis, Indiana, with a month between the completion of training in July, 1954, and the date I was to be there. The policy then was for a new agent to be in his first office no more than a year and then he could expect to be assigned to one of the larger offices: Chicago, Los Angeles, or New York City. Nina and I agreed I should go on to Indianapolis alone, look for a place to live, and simply see how everything developed.

The Agent in Charge of the Indianapolis office suggested that I simply get a furnished room because I would soon be assigned to road trips. This meant I would go out on Monday to a resident agency needing help and work there as long as needed or until Friday, and then return to Indianapolis. This was financially beneficial for me, since I would be traveling on a per diem basis. I was assigned to work several weeks in Evansville, Indiana. This was ideal for me since I could easily go to Somerset to see Nina and Elizabeth on the weekends. So we just let this continue without trying to move Nina to Indianapolis. Before long I was assigned to the Lafayette, Indiana, Resident Agency on as permanent a basis as one could be at that time.

There were two other agents assigned to Lafayette. The senior Resident Agent was John Smock, and the other was Fred Wilt. Fred was a world-class track star, having participated in the International Olympics once already. He was in training much of the time while I was there. Often I would go to the Purdue University field house and time his laps as he ran. That was as close to the Olympics as I ever got.

The first Monday morning I was in the Resident Agency, John asked me to go with him to "check the houses." "What houses?" I asked. "The whorehouses," he replied. Prostitution was legal in the city of Lafayette, and was tightly controlled by the police. All seven houses were closed at midnight every Friday and could not open again until Monday, and then only after every working girl had received a physical exam and a blood test. Our job was to interview every new girl in an effort to identify where she was from and who her pimp was. Due to our proximity to Chicago, most girls were from there. They rarely identified their pimps. This was a real revelation to a country boy. John knew every madam and they knew that if they did not cooperate with us they would be closed down, so they always had the new girls waiting for us. The very first girl we interviewed sat in front of us wearing nothing but a "trick suit." A trick suit is made much like the top half of pajamas without buttons. She wouldn't have closed it even if it had fasteners, since she had made no attempt to keep what she had on closed. That wouldn't have made much difference anyway, since it was so sheer anyone present could see right through it.

The girls were intimidated by us, but the madams were entirely different. John warned me in advance. The madams had at one time all been working girls but had saved enough money and had sufficient clientele to open their own places. Most were middle-aged or younger and usually attractive. Since I was the new man, almost every one of them made it abundantly clear they were no longer in the business themselves but were available to me if I called.

⚬ ⚬ ⚬ ⚬

Shortly after I arrived in Lafayette, information was received that a Chicago mobster, traveling through Lafayette, had wrecked his truck loaded with stolen merchandise. The truck had been towed to a local junkyard while the driver went for another truck onto which he could load his cargo. We were to set up coverage on the truck and await his return.

It was already Fall and the weather was very cold. When the information was first received no one had known what we would be doing, so I had not dressed for a cold night. Soon I found myself sitting in an Indiana Highway Patrol car parked inside a shack where the wrecked truck was stored. My colleague in the FBI and senior man were inside the junk yard guard's shack.

Their shack was heated, but ours was not (one of the benefits of seniority). We had arranged the outside lock on the shack's door to make the building appear secure, when actually we could push the door open from the inside. In just a few minutes my car was very cold. The solution seemed easy — just start the engine. The shack was well ventilated with cracks between each plank. The problem was that our exhaust went out underneath the door, clearly indicating someone was inside. So the trooper and I resigned ourselves to a cold night, and a very cold one it was. It wasn't until later that I learned the Trooper was as new to this business as I was.

The reports we had indicated that the driver of the truck was known to be armed and dangerous. We expected he would, in all probability, bring someone to help in reloading his cargo. Periodically throughout the night, one or both of us would doze off only to be rudely awakened when ice would break off the roof. One time the Trooper awoke with a start and I found myself looking into the barrel of his gun. It was then I volunteered to handle any situation that developed and suggested he could holster his pistol. With a shotgun at hand, we waited.

Just as it began to be daylight a vehicle entered the yard. The yard covered several acres and we watched the headlights winding along the road, coming ever closer to us. I had positioned myself at the doorway and waited. The truck pulled up within three or four feet of the door. Just as the driver, who was the only occupant, stepped out I pushed the garage door open with authority and pointed the shotgun at him. He fell to the ground, having fainted.

As it turned out, this man had wrecked his car the previous day and knew it had been put in the shed where our patrol car now sat. He simply had come out to check the damage. He admitted that when he entered the junkyard he was drunk or nearly so. When we revived him, he was clearly sober. The Chicago police had arrested the driver of the truck during the night, so no one ever came for the truck.

⌒ ⌒ ⌒ ⌒

A telephone call was received at the Resident Agency in Lafayette advising me that one of the FBI's "Ten Most Wanted" fugitives was working as a desk clerk at one of the local hotels. The fugitive had previously been known to pursue such employment. I took a photograph to show the caller. There was no doubt, she said, "That's him." Our poster listed the fact that the last joint of the little finger of his right hand was missing. Identification seemed easy.

John Smock and I went to check it out. We sat apart from one another in the hotel lobby, looking at the suspect and then at the photographs we had. It certainly looked like the fugitive with every feature matching, except that he would never put his right hand on the counter. Finally John nodded, which was my signal to move in. I walked up to the desk, drew my revolver, and ordered him to put his hands on the counter. Believe it or not, the last joint of the little finger of his right hand was missing. John and I knew we were heroes, having captured a dangerous Top Ten fugitive all by ourselves. As it turned out, he was not the fugitive nor was this the first time he had been mistaken for the fugitive. To use a common expression, he was a "dead ringer."

⌒ ⌒ ⌒ ⌒

A dministrative duties, dictation, file reviews, and the like, were handled in Indianapolis, so I went there often. On one particular occasion I had driven my own car, the Hudson. It was getting rather late at night when I started back to Lafayette, 60 miles away. Indianapolis and Lafayette were connected with a new four-lane divided highway which was straight as an arrow. Just as I entered onto this highway a 1949 Mercury passed me. I knew it was "souped up" since it had twin tailpipes. Right behind it was a State Trooper with lights flashing, trying to stop it.

The trooper was driving a new Chevrolet with an eight-cylinder engine similar to the new Oldsmobile Rocket 88. Although it was a fast car, it was obviously unable to overtake the Mercury. At first I let them get out of sight. Then I decided that maybe I could help. When I caught up to the Trooper the Mercury was nowhere in sight. I passed the trooper with my speedometer, which showed up to 120 MPH, starting around the second time. I caught the Mercury just before it reached Lafayette. As we approached the first traffic light at the edge of town, the light was red and heavy traffic was crossing. The Mercury, trying to stop, slid into a telephone pole. With my car blocking any retreat, I held the subjects until the trooper arrived.

His first comment was, "Do you have any idea how fast you were going?" When I had passed the Trooper he said his speed clock (this was before the days of radar) had gone past 120 MPH and started around again. I had passed him, he said, with nothing more than a slight swishing sound. He estimated my speed at somewhere between 135 and 150 MPH. The subjects, it turned out, were wanted for burglary.

❧   ❧   ❧   ❧

By now Nina was pregnant with our second child, Susan. From her observation and experience at the Somerset City Hospital, she felt that Dr. E. V. Weddle was the best obstetrician she ever knew. Knowing that she almost died when Elizabeth Ann was born, she wanted to stay very close to Dr. Weddle until delivery.

It was decided that I would get an apartment in Lafayette and move our furniture there. Nina had been invited to live with Helen and Clarence McNeilly, our very dear friends.

I must say here that no two people, except for our immediate families, were ever more loving or more helpful to us than the McNeilly's. Nina lived there until Susan was born and I could come to get them. They would accept no payment for food or rent. Nina stayed with them about eight months for free. Helen died January 6, 1994. "Mac" still lives in Maryville, Tennessee.

I had barely gotten the apartment in Lafayette set up when a transfer to New York City arrived. I called Nina to tell her. We cried together over the telephone. This meant leaving her to have the baby alone and I probably would not see her again until after Susan was born. I considered resigning, but then I had no other prospects for employment. With Nina having to stop work soon there was no choice but to go to New York. I was given four weeks to get to New York. I arranged to take some leave to spend with Nina. This was the most difficult separation we had ever experienced. I think I cried halfway to New York City.

I left Somerset, Kentucky, in the Hudson automobile in mid-January, 1955. By the time I got to the Pennsylvania Turnpike near Wheeling, West Virginia, I was again in the midst of a snow storm. The highway was already down to one lane and that lane was covered with snow, which was still coming down. Fifty miles per hour was maximum safe speed. A man in the Cadillac behind me began blowing his horn wanting to pass, but there was no place for him to get around me. Finally, we came to a Howard Johnson's rest area on the turnpike. I pulled in, only to have the driver of the Cadillac berate me for driving so slowly. I suggested he get in front of me when I left.

As it turned out I left first. He was soon behind me again trying to pass. We came to a spot going down grade that afforded him an opportunity to try. I slowed to give him more room. Just as he got in front of me he started to spin, making three long, slow, complete revolutions, the last one taking him through the guard rail and into the median. The last time I saw him he was pointing in a westerly direction while I headed east.

I arrived in New York City on January 25, 1955, late on a Sunday afternoon with no idea where I would stay or how to get around if I had a place. The office always offered assistance and suggested a small hotel on 14th street that would give me an excellent rate. The streets were deserted, dispelling all the stories I had heard about the horrible traffic jams in NYC. The next day brought on a couple of unexpected crises. During the night burglars had emptied my car. All I had left was what was in the hotel room with me. Then when I got to the office I could find no place to park my car. Millions of people were everywhere.

After reporting in, I went in search of a furnished room and found an acceptable one in Brooklyn, just over the river from the office. This would suffice while I searched for an apartment, which had to be right away since the moving van was already on its way with what furniture we had. One morning on the subway during rush hour motivated me to search quickly. I felt fortunate to find an apartment which I could afford in Ridgefield, New Jersey. Rent was $80.00 per month and I had to make a deposit and pay a month's rent in advance. I didn't have enough money to do it. For the only time in my life I called my father for money. Dad sent me the $300.00 I needed to get in. I mailed him a promissory note as evidence of the debt. Later when I was able to repay he said no, that he had given my brother and sister $300.00 each, and that it was all even.

164

As soon as I was established in the apartment life became a bit more bearable. A classmate of mine, Francis X. O'Brien, lived with me for a while until he found an apartment for his family. This helped with the adjustment. Even though only two or three weeks had passed I began to feel comfortable with the commuting and working conditions. I lived near enough to see the towers of the George Washington Bridge. During the off-hours, I could get to the office in fifteen to twenty minutes. During rush hour it took an hour or more, depending on how many stalled cars were up ahead.

When it came time for my assignment in New York, God blessed me again. I was assigned to the Soviet Intelligence Squad. I did not know it then, but this was far better than working criminal cases, applicant squads, or any other place I could have gone. It was considered a choice assignment and generally reserved for those who had more seniority than I. Except for a couple of brief temporary assignments to work a special case, the Weinberger Kidnapping being one of them, I remained on the same squad. In fact, I had the same desk until my transfer to Tennessee, twelve years later.

My introduction to Soviet Intelligence work consisted of being assigned to a three-man surveillance squad. Since I was the new man, the team leader handed me the car keys and said that I was now the driver. I objected but was told there is no better way to learn New York City than to get in the car behind our Soviet subject and follow him wherever he went. I was directed to an address somewhere on the upper West side of Manhattan and told to park in a given spot on the left side of a one-way street. I was given a photograph of our subject for the day, Vladimir Molchanov. Vladimir was a handsome man with beautiful black, wavy hair. I asked where he lived. My team captain pointed to the doorway nearest me, not ten feet away. I asked if we were not just a little too close to his doorway, since he could not possibly get out without seeing us. Some days you get in close, I was told, so that when you want to be discreet and drop back they wonder where you are. I didn't subscribe to the idea then nor now, but it proved interesting. Vladimir came out and looked me straight in the face. He walked a few steps in front of our car, then reversed himself and came back. He bent down by my window and said, "Good morning," and then left for the Soviet mission. I came to know Vladimir well enough that I could pick him out of a multitude of people by seeing just the back of his head.

Subsequently he was transferred to the Soviet Embassy in Washington, DC. Years later, as I sat in the railway station in Washington waiting to board a train for New York City, I saw Vladimir at the far end of this very long terminal. Soon I realized he was walking straight toward me. I wondered why, because we had never spoken in all the years. Wondering if he had me confused with someone else, I said nothing until he offered his hand in greeting. It was only then he realized that I was not a KGB agent, someone he had not seen for years. At my invitation he sat down and we talked for several minutes. It was a truly enjoyable encounter. I never saw him again.

❦ ❦ ❦ ❦

Late one evening I was asked to follow a certain KGB agent home, since he had apparently been taking some diversionary routes and getting home later than he should have. It was already late, almost midnight. He started walking and entered Central Park at about 67th street. He lived on West End, almost exactly opposite the 67th Street entrance. There was not a direct trail between the two points, but if one were familiar with the park there was a way to go that would be virtually direct. He did not take that route. Instead of going west he went northwest. I knew this would take him through

166

"The Brambles." The Brambles is a fairly large area in the park bounded on one side by Central Park West. It was known throughout the world as a homosexual hang-out. It really was not a place one ought to be late on a spring night. As we got further into the park the bushes were thicker and the street lights were much too far apart. One could hardly see the walkway. As I walked along, I could hear people talking and moving about. I was walking with my gun in my hand. The Soviet realized he was in the wrong place but he had no idea how to get out. He stopped just ahead of me. I approached him and asked if he was lost. He was lost and his fear was evident. I simply told him who I was and suggested he walk out of there with me. He was obviously relieved and thankful.

At this same time, I had asked for and received the cooperation of an internationally known physicist who was to help us in an ongoing double-agent operation. He lived on the west side of Manhattan in the same general area as the brambles. He was not homosexual. Apparently he made the same mistake as the Soviet I was following and was found murdered in the brambles just a few weeks after I had gone through there. The New York City Police Department identified the murderer as a Dutch sailor, whose ship was still in port.

❧ ❧ ❧ ❧

Ivan was a KGB agent assigned to the Soviet Embassy in Washington, DC He held an important position in the KGB, rather like an inspector. When he came to New York it was a matter of concern for us. I knew him better than anyone else, so when he came, I was assigned to keep tabs on him. He often traveled by train. While waiting for him in New York City one day, I had the good fortune to meet the well-known writer William Faulkner. We sat on a bench in the waiting area and visited for an hour or more. On this particular trip, Ivan went directly to Soviet's United Nations mission but soon emerged driving a car. He drove to the vicinity of Radio City Music Hall and parked. After the show was over, he went across the street to the York Bar for his usual drink, or drinks. By the time he came out, now after midnight, there were only three people on the street, all FBI agents.

First he walked in one direction, then reversed himself and came back towards us. This poses real problems when a person is trying not to be seen and there is no one else on the street. After he did this several times, I concluded he had forgotten where he parked his car. So I simply stood my ground and let him walk toward me. He stopped and asked, "Do you know where I parked my car?" I offered to take him to it. He was so drunk I knew he would never find it even if I told him where it was. We walked along together, with my two colleagues trailing behind. When we got to his car he couldn't get the key in the door lock. He acknowledged he was drunk, and asked if I would drive his car to Soviet Mission for him. This I declined to do, knowing I had no intention of going into their guarded parking garage. I offered to let him drive along behind me and that I would point him in the right direction. So here we were, driving up Sixth Avenue at about 5 MPH, me in front and Ivan a car length behind. When we reached the Mission I pointed to the entrance to his garage and waited to see if he could get through the doorway. When about halfway through he stopped, blocking the street, came to my car and effusively thanked me for the assistance. I often wondered how he ever explained this to his people.

We subsequently talked, when he was sober, about his assignment in this country and how much he enjoyed living here. I have always believed that if I had been able to spend more time with him, and rules had been different, I could have brought about his defection.

With some urgency my radio sounded seeking any unit that was near Idlewild Airport (John F. Kennedy, now). As it happened I was the one. I was instructed to proceed to the airport as fast as possible and meet an airplane coming in from Europe with two very high-level Soviet intelligence agents on board. Given the arrival time, I knew I had only minutes to get there. As I proceeded along the Queensboro Expressway, a major thoroughfare, weaving in and out of traffic with emergency lights flashing and siren on, I was overtaken by a New York City Police car occupied by three officers. The passenger riding in the right front seat was a Captain. As he pulled alongside, he ordered me to pull to the curb. Even though I was driving, I displayed my FBI credentials with him no more than two feet away. With a few expletives and a negative shake of the head, he ordered me to pull up on the grass alongside the roadway. I refused to do it, knowing I was perfectly legal in what I was doing and if I had stopped I would miss the arrival of the plane. His driver managed to maneuver in front of me and attempted to force me to stop. I simply steered clear of him and continued on wondering if the Captain might not be so angry by now that he would shoot at us. He was livid.

At the airport, I sent my two colleagues inside while I remained with the car to await the Captain. To say that he created a scene was an understatement. He threatened to arrest me, along with a number of other actions he said he would like to pursue. With his identifying number present on his shirt I took it down along with his name and suggested he go ahead and do whatever it was he was going to do. In the end he did nothing.

The New York City Police Commissioner at the time was a former FBI agent. I immediately reported the grossly inappropriate conduct of this officer to the Commissioner's office. I was told the Captain had been turned down for attendance at the FBI National Academy and ever since had hated all FBI agents. The Captain was fired that evening. This was the only such incident I experienced in my 26 years with the FBI. Without exception other officers were cooperative, some more than others, but none attempted in any way to obstruct my efforts.

❧ ❧ ❧ ❧

I had worked very late one night and had to take the bus home. When walking from Times Square to the bus terminal the most direct route took me past the old Metropolitan Opera House. It was about 2:00 AM on a cold night and several itinerants were huddled around a fire built on the sidewalk alongside the building. The streets were deserted. As I approached this group one got up and stood waiting in front of me. I stepped between parked cars onto the street. So did the man waiting. At this point I realized that another one had gotten in behind me. I stood in the middle of the street holding my gun inside my topcoat pocket. As they came near I drew my pistol and said, "You men are about to make the biggest mistake of your lives." Just as if it were a daily occurrence the one in front said, "Yeah, I believe you're right." They both returned to the fire and I continued on to the bus terminal. Just another day in "The Big Apple".

❧ ❧ ❧ ❧

Many of the top scientific minds in this country were to gather outside Chicago to discuss some of the most secret undertakings underway in this nation at that time. All had "Top Secret" security clearance. Being at the height of the "Cold War" there was a concern that a Soviet KGB Agent might try to infiltrate the proceed-

170

ings. Along with another agent who was familiar with most of the known KGB agents in New York City, I was sent to this meeting to identify any unwelcome guests. Only one or two of the top organizers were to know that we were there. When we arrived we were given fake identification lapel documents. I was Larry Bates, Lockheed Corporation - Celestial Travel." This was selected, I was told, because at the time there was no such project and that we could say anything we wanted to if asked about it and no one else would know whether we were correct or not.

Near the end of the three-day meeting my colleague and I were on the elevator en route to our rooms when two other attendees boarded. I noticed immediately they were from Lockheed and tried to position myself so they would not see my identification. It seemed they were bent on making conversation and rather insisted on moving in position to see who I was. Seeing "Lockheed", they expressed concern they had never seen us at Lockheed and had never heard of the Celestial Travel Research Program. Obviously, it was time for a "snow job". I offered the opinion that it should not be of any concern to them since ours was a very small group working on the most secret of projects. Even this did not satisfy them and the questions persisted. Finally, realizing I was about to the end of my snow job, I told them we were working on a project for travel to the moon. I thought this was about as far out as one could go. Fortunately, we reached our floor about this time and made a hasty exit. I wondered many times subsequently, when the Apollo moon project was announced, what the two men really thought. Maybe they said to themselves, "I met the two men working on this project when I was in Chicago."

❧ ❧ ❧ ❧

Susan Carol Thomas was born May 10, 1955. We would very soon be a reunited family. As difficult as it was for me to arrange a two-week leave of absence, I was determined to be in Kentucky the first day they were able to travel.

Having already experienced the new environment, I was truly concerned about Nina and the culture shock awaiting her. I did all I could, which I am afraid was not a great deal, to make our small apartment an inviting place for her. Awaiting her arrival was a new electronic device, our first television set. Nina adjusted quickly, making friends with a couple of very special tenants. They could commiserate about their plight. Soon all of us were acting like natives. On second thought, we were determined never to act like most natives.

Our apartment complex in Ridgefield was inhabited almost entirely by Jewish and Italian families that had moved from New York City. Most of them had never been further away from home than they were at that moment. Weekends brought a host of their New York relatives who would stand outside, looking at trees and grass, being thrilled "to be out in the meadows." The nearest real meadow was still miles away.

The vast majority of our neighbors were very nice people. There were a few, however, who spoiled it for everyone. Laverne "Rick" Rickles, a fellow colleague, and his family lived in the apartment complex. He and I had worked very late one night, arriving at our apartment at about 2:00 AM. Parking at that hour was usually at a premium. However, on this occasion there was one space awaiting us very near our front door. Rick pulled slowly past this spot, talking while preparing to back in along the curb. Just when he was about halfway in a small Studebaker nosed in behind us getting about halfway in place so that now neither he nor Rick could actually park there.

Within an instant both of us were out of our car. We immediately recognized the driver of the other car as an apartment resident known as a bit of a trouble maker. Rick, all six-feet-four-inches of him and still sporting the physique of the standout college football player he had been, approached the driver. With calmness unbecoming the situation Rick inquired what the driver thought he was doing. "Can't you see, you FBI son of a bitch?" Without a word Rick reached inside, taking hold of the driver's right shoulder with his left hand, and started pulling the man through the car door window. The mistake the driver made was not having rolled the car's window all the way down. Rick continued to pull, finally getting the man's rib cage over the window. By this time the driver was begging for a truce and volunteered to move his car. Rick, realizing the man could not drive his car with half of him sticking out the door, promptly started stuffing him back in. Having his ribs go back over the partially raised window was even more painful now than when he was dragged out. With our car in place we went to bed and watched the next day as the man moved out.

❧   ❧   ❧   ❧

Our third (and last) child, Lawrence Gray Thomas, was born January 5, 1961. This addition, coupled with the normal accumulation of things, made the apartment seem even smaller. Our constant desire to find a house of our own was now even more compelling, yet we simply did not have enough money to do it.

In the summer of 1961, still driving the Hudson, we left New Jersey en route to Shreveport, LA, and then back to my family in Tennessee before returning to New Jersey. Even though it was July, we left wearing sweaters. Two days later, we were driving through Eldorado, Arkansas, concerned about the heat and the fact the children were complaining about nausea. The temperature was 104°.

We swore then that if it was at all possible we would purchase an air-conditioned car before making the trip again. Besides, the Hudson now had about 125,000 miles on it. We did subsequently purchase a new 1963 Pontiac with air conditioning. At that time very few cars, except the newer Cadillacs, had air conditioning. We were even asked on occasions when we pulled into a service station in the summertime how we could stand the heat in there with the windows rolled up. I remember once asking the attendant to touch the cool steering wheel. It was the first car he had ever seen with air conditioning on it.

Our first air-conditioned car:
a sky-blue 1963 Pontiac LeMans

We had a friend, Forrest Nettles, who was the Chief Pilot for Texas Eastern Gas Transmission Lines headquartered in Shreveport. He was able several times to arrange to take Nina and the children to Shreveport at no cost. In 1963, Nina had gone to Shreveport with the children to spend a month with Sis Foster, her adopted mother. When it came time for me to go get them I couldn't get there fast enough. The last day I had driven hard for over 12 hours and was looking forward to getting out of the car and resting. Just as I pulled into the driveway in Shreveport, Nina, wet with perspiration, came running to the car got in where it was cool and said, "Please take me for a ride before I suffocate." We laughed then and many times thereafter about whether she was more glad to see me or the cool car.

Nina's father died in 1963, leaving her a cash inheritance of about $2,000.00. I had been blessed with having invested a small sum of money in a stock that had tripled in value. We sold the stock and now felt ready to look for a house.

A local real estate agent agreed to give us the first chance at the next house going on the market in Ridgefield, New Jersey that she thought we could afford. Ridgefield was considered a choice place to live. Commuting was excellent, the school system was superb, and property taxes were very low because the city received more money than it could use from a public utility it had accepted when no other municipality would take it.

Fortunately, I was home the day the real estate agent called with some urgency, saying she had a house we might be interested in. It was ideally located only about two blocks from our apartment. We looked at 518 Morse Avenue with unbelievable hope in our hearts. It was an old house, more than fifty years old in 1963, but very sturdy and most of the inside had recently been reno-vated. We were the first prospective buyer to look at it, but soon the house was full of them. The agent whis-pered to us say-ing that if we wanted the house we had to make up our minds within thirty minutes. She pointed to the man behind me and said she knew he wanted it and had the $30,000.00 pur-

518 Morse Ave, Ridgefield, New Jersey

chase price in his pocket. The house had been priced for a fast sell so there was no negotiating the price. It was located on four levels, including a full basement. On the street level were the living room, dining room, kitchen, and a large entrance hall with a beautiful winding stair-case going to the top floors. There was no time to do more than a quick walk-through looking briefly at the plumbing and heating system. We were assured that

175

everything was in good working order. We bought the house within the thirty minute deadline, knowing it would keep us busy making repairs as long as we lived there. Now we had more than enough bedrooms for everyone to have their own. One could even look out the top floor window and see the Empire State Building.

We moved into this house, getting set up just about bedtime. We were just getting ready for bed when we heard water dripping. A close inspection revealed a sizable leak in a long pipe with a few small leaks at other places. A plumber took a look, shook his head, and told us we had a problem. The large pipe was made out of brass. Other portions were galvanized pipe while still others were copper tubing. This mixing of metals, he said, had caused electrolysis and that everything, except for the new copper tubing, needed to be replaced. As soon as I learned the approximate cost of his repairs I purchased two large pipe wrenches, a propane torch and some solder, and started learning how to plumb a house. Before I left I had replaced all of the plumbing as well as the outdated electrical wiring. While working on the wiring I learned that the house at one time had been lighted with gas lights and had subsequently been wired with cloth-covered wire, some of which was now exposed. All of the switches were ceramic. The plumbing and electrical wiring was made much easier by virtue of the fact that at one time the house was equipped with a dumbwaiter running up the center of the house, from the basement to the top floor. This shaft gave easy access between floors. Aside from the usual cuts and scratches, I had no real problems except for the time I was introduced to what a full 110 volt electric charge feels like. The power company had failed to make an adequate ground outside the house, so when I touched the circuit breaker box I became the ground. Try to avoid that whenever possible.

❧   ❧   ❧   ❧

According to local ordinance only a gas company employee could turn on a gas furnace. In the interest of economy we waited until we needed heat before having it turned on. The furnace itself was intimidating. It was huge with a steel wall several inches thick. It had once been coal-fired, but had since been converted to natural gas, with a circulating hot water system. Just when it was about ready to start heating the service man took one look at the pressure gauge on top of the furnace. It read 120 lbs. of pressure with the maximum safe pressure being 12 lbs. He turned off the gas and insisted that we evacuate the house until it cooled off. He suggested that the pressure tank might be filled with air and that we call a heating system repairman. Here came our friendly plumber again. He found a little air in the system but not nearly enough to cause the pressure to rise to that degree.

So the next day the gas company employee came back and turned on the system with exactly the same result as before. He turned off the gas and left. It was beginning to get really cold by now. Back came the service man this time with no idea of what to do. He gave me the name of a nationally-known heating and cooling expert in New York City and suggested I present the problem to him. The next day found me pleading with this man's secretary to let me see him, even though "I was not a tradesperson and they were strictly wholesale." After listening to my presentation and asking a few questions about the face of the pressure gauge he excused himself and promptly returned with a new gauge. I asked the cost and was profoundly surprised when he said to take it home, put it on the furnace, and fire it up. If it didn't work I was to promptly return it and owe nothing.

It took almost an hour to drain all the water out of the system. It was impossible to replace the gauge without draining the water because of the high water pressure. I learned this because I tried it once, but succeeded only in getting wet from head to foot and flooding the basement before I could get the water turned off.

With the new gauge finally installed I called the gas company to try again. We all sat watching the temperature and pressure rise. The gas company employee seemed the most apprehensive. I had declined to tell him what I had done. The pressure promptly rose to 12 pounds and held solid. He presumed the gauge was stuck and started to hit it, thinking the system must surely be about to explode. Within less than an hour this big house was uniformly warm in every corner.

I went back the next day to pay for the new gauge and then learned that there was nothing whatsoever wrong with the system. Just from my description the heating expert said that when the system had been converted, it was equipped with an open venting tank in the attic. When it was updated to a closed system the pressure gauge should have been changed to what I had just put in place. Throughout our stay in this house we gloried in the quiet, efficient, uniform heat, even in the most extreme cold weather. Never was a gas bill more than $30.00.

The house took most of my free time not because it was about to fall down, far from it, but because we wanted it as perfect as we could make it. Nina spent her time inside finally resolving to refinish the staircase. I tried to discourage her, pointing to the fact that it ran all the way to the top of the house. With gallons of paint remover and some piano wire, she began. She toiled with it for weeks, removing seven coats of paint, by actual count. I certainly was pleased to see the beautiful chestnut wood in the railing and supports and oak in the floor and staircase risers. Her efforts were rewarded when the last coat of satin-finish varnish went on. It truly was beautiful. Knowing each summer while on vacation that we had this place waiting for us made returning to metropolitan New York much more enjoyable. She cried when we sold the house because she had to leave this staircase behind.

～ ～ ～ ～

After a period of time on the surveillance squad I was assigned to case work. Our subjects were known or suspected KGB agents. The objective of our investigation was simply to ascertain their contacts and assess them for any risk to our national security. Realizing that KGB agents generally went through four years of training in contrast to our twelve weeks, we were not up against amateurs. A well-known KGB agent once described FBI agents as "children walking around in soft-soled shoes." I certainly question his characterization.

～ ～ ～ ～

Reino Hayhanen, a Finnish national, but also a KGB agent, had been dispatched to the United States almost four years earlier as an "illegal agent." This means he was here illegally under an assumed name and identity. Hayhanen had been given money to set up a photographic shop in New York City as a front for his activities. Instead he used the money to finance his drinking habit and to support an American wife he had married in violation of KGB rules. Then he was ordered by the KGB to return to the Soviet Union for a sort of in-service training. He knew that if his superiors ever found out what he had really done, and they probably would if he took a routine polygraph test, he would be executed.

He got as far as Paris, France, but lacked the nerve to continue on to Moscow. Instead, he walked into the American Embassy, identified himself, and offered to defect. After a very quick debriefing he was returned to the United States. The most important information he was able to furnish was that his boss in the United States was another illegal KGB agent, known to him only as "Colonel Abel." Hayhanen knew almost nothing about Abel, not even his full name. He did not know where Abel lived or anything about his network. Hayhanen did remember that once while he was driving about with Colonel Abel, Abel pointed to a large building in Brooklyn and expressed some interest in it, indicating that possibly Abel had a "shop" there. We drove about Brooklyn with Hayhanen in our car for three days, hoping he would recognize the building. Finally, he pointed out a building that he thought was the right one. A discreet inquiry revealed the owner to be a member of the Communist party, ruling out any direct contact with him.

This building appeared to be more of a warehouse than anything else. As I recall, it was about 15 floors in height. We established 24-hour coverage on all sides of the building. After a few weeks it was noticed that the lights in one section remained on well into the night while the rest of the building was totally dark. By gradually moving in closer we were able to get a photograph of the man whom we thought was using this room. Hayhanen readily identified the man in the photograph as Colonel Abel, who later came to be known as Colonel Rudolph Ivanovich Abel.

In the course of an exhaustive investigation, it was determined that Colonel Abel was an illegal alien, making him subject to arrest. Elaborate plans were set up so that we could arrest him in his "shop", which would give us access to whatever might be inside. We were surprised at the volume of the material. The truck we had available was too small to hold it all. The US Department of Justice had laid down very specific and somewhat confining rules as to how long we could remain in his shop, forcing us to be selective as to what we took.

Once back in our office the contraband was sorted and a minute investigation began. The agent working near me was intrigued by what appeared to be a solid block of ebony. Knowing that he was skilled as a machinist and carpenter, the agent concluded that Abel used it as a sanding block. In frustration, the agent threw the block on the floor. It had defied a careful examination and appeared solid, but it was, in fact, hollow and had burst open upon hitting the floor. Inside were cipher pads used by Abel in preparing his clandestine communications with KGB headquarters in Moscow. Being a good agent, and Abel was, he had separated the key to his code from all other items. We never did find his key nor would he reveal it. Subsequently, after Abel was exchanged for Francis Gary Powers, Abel's personal possessions including his guitar, were returned to him. It was then we learned through another informant that the key to his code was taped inside Abel's guitar, which was left hanging on the wall when we had searched his shop. One would hardly expect a guitar to be of intelligence value and since our time and space was limited, it was not taken. The most complete investigation we could conduct revealed little about Abel's network or his activities. Notwithstanding, he was tried and convicted of espionage. Throughout, Abel remained totally composed.

During the months prior to the trial we literally lived with Hayhanen. I have spent many days and nights at his home near Poughkeepsie. As the trial date approached, we were instructed to be sure he did not have access to any alcohol. It was imperative that he appear in court sober. By the time we got to the federal courthouse with him he was shaking all over and was in no condition to get on the witness stand. We quickly obtained a bottle of vodka, his favorite drink. In no time he was calm and went on the witness stand and made a great witness.

Throughout the case Abel was treated as the adversary he was, yet each of us respected him for the professional he was. We wondered if we would be as equal to the task as he, if the situation were reversed.

～ ～ ～ ～

Soon we entered a period of 4 or 5 years of unheard-of success in the intelligence field. Defections scattered about the world yielded invaluable information, often helping to identify most KGB agents and their sources of information or targets in the US. We were especially fortunate to get a new Special Agent in Charge (SAC) in our section who offered us a relatively free hand.

About the same time, we were blessed with the defection of an agent whose code name was Fedora. Fedora was in charge of the entire KGB operation at the Soviet mission to the UN. In that position he was familiar with what each of approximately 100 KGB agents was doing. This was a "gold mine" practically laid in our laps. Although I did not participate in the direct debriefing of Fedora, I did work closely with various aspects of the case.

I was called to the office of my upper-level superior and shown an advertisement from the New York Times. It was offering for sale a Concord tape recorder secreted inside an attaché case. At that time, Concord was a leader in the tape-recording field. I was asked to go look at it discreetly and assess its potential for our purposes. After being allowed to examine it at length I had no doubt that we could benefit from it, but it cost $1,100.00. A unit today of comparable, maybe even superior quality, would only cost a small fraction of that amount. This unit was well-designed, with a microphone hidden under the handle of the case. It could pick up conversations from 8 to 10 feet away with exceptional clarity. An accessory cord of approximately 15 feet offered other possibilities. I doubted the Bureau would pay the price. When I reported my findings and opinions, I was immediately handed $1,100.00 in cash and told to go get one. When I returned with it and offered it to my superior he said, "This is yours. Take it home and when you are satisfied you know all about it let me know." Before I left New York City, I had worn out this unit, having used it successfully in two or more defections brought about through our own efforts.

From the inception, some Bureau Officials doubted Fedora's truthfulness. There were those who questioned reports they were getting, contending the information was too good to believe. It was even suggested that we were enhancing what he told us. My superior in New York asked if I could get a recording of one of the interviews. I knew Fedora had said that if we ever recorded him, he was through. I knew I must be very careful and not be detected. After looking at the interview site, a room in a better midtown hotel, I concluded I could hide the recorder inside the bed's box springs and run the remote microphone under the bedspread to within two feet of where Fedora always sat.

The recording was so clear I could hear the vodka being poured into Fedora's glass fifteen feet away. Again the report of the interview was questioned. We compared the report with my recording and found it almost verbatim. Desiring to prove our point, I was asked to take the recording and the recorder to headquarters in Washington, DC so the skeptics could hear it. Because the recorder used a special speed, the tape could only be played back on that particular recorder.

The late William Sullivan was an assistant director of the FBI at that time. I was assured he understood the risk we had taken, the value of what we had, and the fact that he would protect me from any overzealous Bureau supervisor. Further, he personally assured me I would be protected. I had gotten no further into the recording than two or three minutes when one of the two supervisors he had called in asked who had made the recording. I waited, hoping Mr. Sullivan would handle it, but when he didn't I acknowledged that I had. The next question was, "Are you an approved sound man?" meaning was I certified to make surreptitious recordings. I still remember Mr. Sullivan's admonition, "You ask too many questions. Don't ever mention it again." I tell this only to show how narrow the thinking of some supervisors were and to show, in a small way, that we succeeded in spite of the system.

❧   ❧   ❧   ❧

Another case was especially satisfying for me: A member of another squad was talking with a Polish intelligence agent who was thought to be a candidate for defection. The Polish agent insisted that our agent take no notes during their conversation and was especially adamant about not being recorded. It was thought that if we were able to get a good recording that would incriminate him, he would defect.

He flatly refused to enter a Bureau car. He wanted us to use rented cars. He preferred that we use the Ford Mustang. He invariably looked for a potential recorder. My recorder was hidden under the mat in the trunk, with the microphone tucked neatly under the floor mat and positioned along the console nearest him. It produced superb recordings even when he turned on the radio in an effort to make our recording unintelligible. This man became a valued informant, due in large part to my recording efforts.

❧   ❧   ❧   ❧

Mikhail Sverin was recognized as a veteran KGB agent. He was a tall, handsome man who had been in the US long enough to become "Americanized". He knew New York City as well as or better than I. After many months of observation it became apparent that he was doing something different on the third Friday of each month. On these nights he never arrived home until very late. Otherwise he appeared to be a family man.

I had hoped to arrange extensive coverage on a given Friday night. At the last minute my manpower was diverted to something else. I asked FBI Agent Bill Stitler if he would help me. Bill and I worked together often. Bill was very good at surveillance. At 5:00 PM Sverin left his office just as he did every day. He joined the throng going home, but instead he went the opposite direction. First he took the Third Avenue Subway, darting on and off the car at the last moment. He rode one stop, got off, and walked to Fifth Avenue and Central Park South. There he rented a "handsome cab" (a horse-drawn buggy) and started a tour of Central Park. Less than a quarter of the way around the park he got off, walked back to Fifth Avenue and caught a downtown bus. At 42nd Street he left the bus and entered Grand Central Station. By now it was abundantly clear that he was on an important mission. It was obvious he was trying to detect our surveillance. On occasions he would walk very fast, even running to a corner, go around it and wait to see if we followed in kind.

He continued, convincing us that we had been successful up to that point. Finally, he boarded a train to Long Island and rode it to the very end. When we got off it was raining heavily. Sverin took a cab and rode further out on Long Island, leaving the cab on a darkened street in Levittown, Long Island. Here he began walking in a driving rain. Not another person was in sight. We had to remain several blocks behind him in order to prevent detection.

Bill and I met under a street light. He was without any rainwear of any kind. I looked down and water was bubbling out of the tops of his shoes. We knew we had a "live one". We continued on, wet or not. Up to this point we had done our job well. Sverin eventually entered a small isolated restaurant with only one car parked in the lot. We took the license number knowing that we could not go inside, since we could see only two customers in there – Sverin, and the man he came to meet. I entered the open back door of the restaurant leading directly into the kitchen. Fortunately, the manager was there and was very cooperative. He didn't know either man but knew they met there about once a month. Not desiring to have our presence become known to Sverin, we left knowing I could ultimately identify the man he met. He was a business man and long-time Communist Party member who was not in a position to do any great damage to the US. In due course I interviewed him, neutralizing his effectiveness to the Soviets.

One feels proud of such an achievement, even once in a lifetime. It is rare that a trained intelligence officer is able to go through so many diversionary tactics without being detected. Mr. Hoover expressed his pleasure by giving me a cash award of $500.00, the maximum given at that time.

~ ~ ~ ~

Agents would always try to be prepared for the unexpected. Payday was approaching and I had with me only enough money for lunch, subway and the telephone. I unexpectedly found myself following a KGB agent who ultimately led me to Boston, Massachusetts, having ridden the subway, taxis in New York and later in Boston, and an airplane sandwiched in between. I had not paid anyone. I barely had enough money left to telephone the Boston office and ask for help.

The pilot of the airplane was actually pleased to have me aboard when he learned that he had a full-fledged KGB agent as a passenger. Those were the days when "KGB" was truly a bad word. I was invited to ride in the cockpit and was told I did not have to pay if I chose not to.

I went into the Boston office, picked up a book of GTR's (Government Travel Vouchers), and backtracked the route to New York, paying everyone as I went. Once I was back, I put a generous amount of "mad money" in the back of my billfold. I continue this practice to this day.

❧ ❧ ❧ ❧

I made another trip aboard an airplane, riding in the cockpit. This time it was not by choice, and with not nearly the same hospitality. I was the first FBI agent to board an airplane at LaGuardia airport in New York City after the US Congress passed the law making it a crime to carry a concealed weapon aboard an airplane. The act specifically exempted FBI agents. I boarded, well-informed about the exemption and the procedures we were to follow. I was simply to identify myself to the stewardess when I boarded and tell her I was armed. Prior to this new legislation, agents had already been doing just that, so it should have come as no surprise to her. The plane taxied to the end of the runway and was getting ready to take off when I was summoned to the cockpit by the captain. He informed me that I would have to get off the aircraft and that a car was coming to get me. I explained my position and that I was in full compliance with the provision of the law he was citing and that I was not going to get off.

I was carrying some highly secret materials to be used in a clandestine operation and people in Washington were awaiting my arrival. It was obvious the pilot had heard about the new law and its prohibitions, but he was either unaware of the exceptions or chose to be difficult because he was in a position to do so. On rare occasions a pilot would remind the passengers that he was the absolute boss of his plane. I was told then that I would have to surrender my gun to him. This I declined to do. Then he wanted it unloaded with him holding the cartridges. We finally compromised when I agreed to sit next to him in the "jump seat".

❧ ❧ ❧ ❧

One afternoon I was riding the Lexington Avenue Subway north toward the Bronx. Just as we were about to reach the 125th street stop I realized that something serious was going on among a group of high school boys and girls. I could hear a girl screaming "No! No!" She was surrounded by 25 or 30 others. Tempers were getting nasty and a fight was brewing. A young girl on the floor of the subway was being raped while those around watched. Tempers flared, then someone broke a window and started to wrap shards of glass with cloth as a weapon. I stood atop a seat just behind the crowd, drew my gun and ordered a stop to what was taking place. At first a few pushed toward me with their home-made weapons. They soon decided their weapon was no match for mine. When I realized that the first car had reached the station I pulled the emergency cord, stopping the train and in effect trapping the occupants of the car in the tunnel.

It was a criminal offense to pull the emergency cord without good reason. The subway security police responded immediately. I identified the victim and the perpetrator, and left the train just as if these things happened everyday. And they probably did.

I had boarded the same subway line in lower Manhattan during afternoon rush hour en route to our office at 69ᵗʰ Street and Third Avenue. I had missed the express train, so we were stopping at every station. As we traveled north two men of apparent Puerto Rican descent started playing a little "game". They had positioned themselves close to the double doors of the car, and when the train stopped they would not let anyone board or leave the train through that door. Normally this would cause little problem, but with the platforms full of people trying to board the situation became progressively worse. I had been sitting behind this pair hoping they would tire without my having to get involved. As they continued I became more incensed with their conduct. When we pulled into Grand Central Station a horde of people were pushing trying to get on, yet they stood their ground with their arms locked together.

I hit them both in the small of their backs with my fist knocking them outside the car onto the loading platform. They stumbled and fell one on top of the other. I heard the "click" of a switchblade knife. I drew my pistol and pointed it squarely in the face of the one with the knife. The one underneath, unable to see my gun said, "get him". His partner replied, "Get him yourself, you son of a bitch!" The last I saw of them they were running up the stairway leaving the station amid a cheer and thanks from the crowd.

❧ ❧ ❧ ❧

Through a very sensitive source, information was received that the wife of an illegal KGB agent was coming to the US to join him. We had a photograph and description of her, and a general idea of when she was to arrive. We sat at Idlewild International Airport for days before she finally arrived. I will call her Martha, though that was not her real name. Martha's husband George, had been in the United States for several years.

Martha proceeded to midtown Manhattan and checked into a hotel. Our instruction from Mr. Hoover himself was "NOT TO LOSE HER". All went well for a couple of days until Martha failed to be seen leaving her room. She no longer resided at this hotel, apparently having slipped out the service entrance in the middle of the night. No one dared tell Mr. Hoover that we did not know where she was. Every man in the office of approximately 1,200 agents was involved in an effort to locate her.

Fortunately, one of our men, while reviewing the guest registration cards at a small hotel located on the west side of Manhattan, noticed certain characteristics in the hand writing of a recent guest which compared to that of Martha. It was known that Martha was sent to meet her husband at a particular location in Yonkers, New York on a Sunday afternoon.

Our supervisor was a bachelor who was married to the Bureau. He loved to have conferences. One hundred men, including me, were called to the office at 1:00 PM, just hours before the anticipated meeting between Martha and her husband, George. The conference droned on and on to the point we were about to run out of time. Finally I mustered enough courage to suggest that we needed to get in place. The supervisor, obviously displeased with the interruption, suggested that if I felt that way that I should take two men with me and go on to the meeting site in Yonkers.

The three of us pulled up to the anticipated meeting site only to find there was no parking place available. It had been presumed that we would have no trouble parking, since it was Sunday. Our plans were to put a closed van

190

of ours in a spot directly in front of the meeting site. This was the first of a number of miscalculations that day. Being unable to find a spot for myself, I pulled into the front end of a bus stop. Just as I did I looked into the rear-view mirror as passengers were getting off a bus. There in the midst of them stood Martha.

When I radioed the office I was told I had to be incorrect, that Martha had not left her hotel. I was reminded this was well in advance of the anticipated meeting time. I was certain of my identification. I probably knew her better than anyone else at this point. Instead of going in the direction of the meeting site, Martha started walking in the opposite direction. I parked the car in the bus stop and locked it. The three of us followed her. Martha never went near the anticipated meeting site. She walked several blocks and entered a neighborhood theater. The theater was virtually deserted, making us all the more obvious. I stationed the other two men near the front door in case she slipped past while I was looking for her. I found the stairs that led to the projection booth. This took me to the very top row of seats, behind everyone. There were only four or five people in the balcony and Martha was one of them. I watched as she changed seats several times, always moving toward the center. At the same time, a man began changing seats, moving ever closer to Martha. Finally, they sat together and hugged each other. I knew she had just met George.

I rushed downstairs and had one of my colleagues to set up outside. I asked the other one go get the car. I telephoned the office to get them in motion only to learn the conference was still in progress. I needed help. Just then, George and Martha walked out. Instead of going in the direction of the populated area, they started walking south along the northern-most part of Broadway. This is the same Broadway that goes all the way to the southern tip of Manhattan. At that time it was a wooded area for a couple of miles or more. By now it was dark.

With no way to follow closely without being detected I dropped back until I could barely see them, planning to run and catch up when they got to a populated area. We had not gone far when a City bus passed me. George and Martha managed to get it to stop for them, even though they were not at a regular bus stop. As they rode away I started trying to stop anyone going my direction. My colleague had not returned with the car and the other one had become separated from us in the melee. In desperation I simply stood in the middle of the road and stopped a car. He readily agreed to help me catch up to the bus. When we caught up to the bus it was parked at the entrance to the subway station with no one aboard. Just as I started to race up the stairs to the elevated subway platform, I heard the air brakes release and knew the doors were closing.

My very helpful citizen and I sped away as fast as we could safely go, hoping to reach the next station in time for me to get aboard. As I got out of his car, I heard the train coming in. I ran up three flights of stairs and jumped over the turnstile without paying, much to the displeasure of the toll taker. I boarded the train just as the doors closed. Up to this point I had been too busy to answer my radio. The supervisor was now frantically calling, wanting to know where the subjects were. I could tell him only that I was on the front car of the BMT subway train and hoped that George and Martha were on it also. I carefully worked my way through the cars, ultimately finding George and Martha seated on the rear seat of the last car. I suggested that since this train's destination was Times Square, we should gamble they were going there. I asked that the other 97 men be sent down there.

Why they rode all the way to Times Square I do not know, because when they got off they went north again, past where they could have gotten off. When I left the train at Times Square I was impressed with the large crowd on the platform, most of them being FBI agents. I pointed out Martha and George to as many agents as I could, hoping I now could relax a bit. Once on the street the subjects got into the only empty taxicab in sight. Not one of the agents had a car near enough to be of any help. I simply opened the door to a cab stopped in traffic, got in beside a frightened female passenger, and instructed the driver to follow the subjects now almost out of sight.

FBI agents all carried gold badges. Only Captains and above on the New York City police force had gold badges, so when we showed our badges we got instant cooperation. The cab driver turned out to be an expert driver. Soon he had worked his way up behind the subjects. They proceeded to a bar located on the West Side of Manhattan. Since there were very few customers in the bar we dared not fill it up with FBI agents. Finally, about 2:00 AM, George and Martha came out and got in another cab. By this time we had plenty of cars available. They went to what we called a "brownstone walkup", because it was made of brown stone, and had no elevator. No lights were on in the building. Soon the lights went on in an apartment on the top floor. I could see George pull the shade.

With the couple now apparently settled for the night I thought I would be relieved by one of our late arrivals. No such luck. The word came that Mr. Hoover was following this step-by-step and wanted me to stay there until they came out again, since I knew them better than anyone else.

The neighborhood was primarily Spanish, which made us very obvious, especially when we had to double park and leave the automobile engine running all night just to stay warm. We had to make other arrangements. The only thing to do was to make a parking place and pull our enclosed van into the curb. I instructed one of our men to call a wrecker and have it tow away one of the cars, with further instructions to identify the owner and tell him where his car had been taken. The van was equipped in such a way that I could see out but no one could see in. It had a cold metal floor and no sanitary facilities. Neither did it have blankets or food, but I stayed in there until they came out on Tuesday afternoon. Sometime Monday night I could no longer stay awake. I realized I was dozing while looking directly at the door. Repeated calls came from the Bureau wanting to know if I was certain that they were still inside. I assured them I was certain, unless they had slipped out a back door. Monday night we had to put another agent in the van just to awaken me every time anyone left the building. Once Martha and George came out sometime Tuesday morning, I was free to go home.

Rarely is an agent able to experience an assignment as satisfying as this one was to me. I had single-handedly "saved the day" three times in one day. As tired as I was, I would not have wanted to be anywhere else, nor would I have done it any other way. Several months later Martha and George managed to elude our surveillance teams and make their way back to Russia.

❧   ❧   ❧   ❧

One particular Soviet we will call Petr delighted in living in the "fast lane". We were told the rule was that the Soviet men should confine their sexual pursuits to Soviet women here in a diplomatic status. Petr, for reasons unknown, seemed to prefer other women. He also seemed to delight in making our jobs as difficult as possible. So far as was known, he did little work at the United Nations and was not involved in Intelligence Activity. In short, he was a playboy. It could well have been that his assignment was to compromise as many American women as he could, with the purpose of getting them to work for him, but I doubted it.

It became known through surveillance that he was especially interested in a beautiful Australian woman living in a plush apartment located on the East side of Manhattan. I was looking for an opportunity to compromise him, and this seemed to be it. When I approached the woman she denied any romantic feelings for him but pointed out that he was an aggressive male obviously bent on a sexual relationship. Quite of her own volition, she volunteered to lure him into her bedroom, which she knew would be very easy to do. She offered to allow us to video tape them. The Bureau felt that under the circumstances it would be inappropriate, since he had committed no crime within our jurisdiction. They did leave open other possibilities.

With her help and approval, it was agreed that at a particular time late one evening she would encourage his advances inside his car so that we might photograph him. At the appointed time and place, they parked the car. She had rolled her window down and at what turned out to be the appropriate moment I stepped out of the shadows armed with a large press-size Speed Graphic camera. He saw me an instant before the flash went off. On film was a perfect view of his face, startled look and all. Most of him was wrapped around the young woman. The very day the Soviet mission to the United Nations received some anonymous photographs of Petr in action he was on the next airplane headed for Moscow.

᳚   ᳚   ᳚   ᳚

On April 17, 1967, the New York *Daily News* headline, in two-inch letters read, "**2** RED 'TOURISTS' GROW FBI TAILS - Moscow's No. **2** Spy In Town"

A young man was seen leaving the headquarters of the Soviet Mission to the United Nations late one night. I followed him to a large apartment house on the upper east side of Manhattan. Investigation quickly revealed

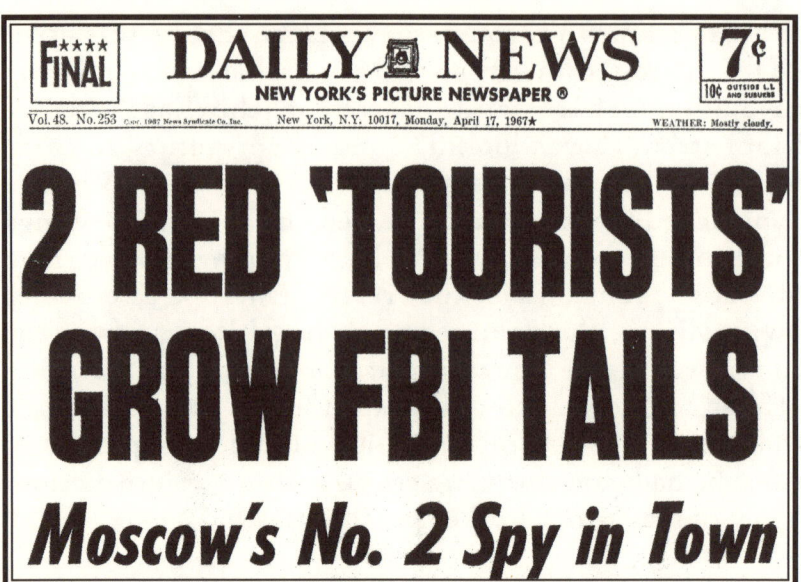

he was a foreign national from one of the Slavic countries. A couple of days later he visited the Soviet Mission a second time. It was deemed advisable at this point to interview him and determine the nature of his business at the mission. Agent Jack Danahay and I went to his apartment. Someone inside acknowledged our knock but refused to open the door. Danahay, a former New York policeman, grasped the door knob, gave it a kick, and we walked in. The occupant and only person there appeared to be of Slavic descent. He declined to answer any questions. We politely "invited" him to our office. Here Jack, who assumed the attitude of "bad, tough guy" and I, the "good, understanding fellow", attempted to solicit his cooperation. We tired after a couple of hours and turned him over to a second team. We sent out for food, determined to wear him down. In the early hours of the morning the Slav interrupted the interview, pointed in my direction and said, "Send him back in here, I will talk to him."

It poured out of him all at once. He was the superintendent of the building where he lived. He claimed to have found some loose papers in the trash conspicuously marked, "TOP SECRET". He was unable to find a cover or even the first few pages, but what he found appeared to relate to plans by the United States Government to bomb China. To him it appeared authentic and well worth an attempt to capitalize on his find. At the Soviet Mission he was greeted with open arms. He had held back most of what he had found, showing the Soviets only a couple of pages. They declined to pay him anything on the first visit, but offered to consider his demand for $100,000.00 if he brought in the rest of it. Little did he know he was dealing with the number two man in all the KGB, who was in New York City only temporarily. As in any operation of this sort in the KGB or the FBI, the highest-ranking man on the scene would be called in to make a big important decision like this case presented.

Soon he offered to take me to the apartment house and show me where he had hidden the additional pages. I suggested he tell me where they were and I would go to get them. He assured me I would never find them. Little did I know how correct he really was. Most superintendents sorted the trash, retrieving anything of value. This Slav was unusually industrious. The entire basement of a block-sized building was filled, floor-to-ceiling, with nothing but newspapers with just enough space to walk between the rows. We threaded our way to a stack near the back of the building. He reached high above his head and pulled the wanted documents from between a mountain of papers. He was correct; I never could have found them.

Back at the office, a thorough examination of the papers failed to shed any light as to where they came from except that among them were notes on White House letterhead purporting to be from President Lyndon

Johnson. On their face the papers appeared to be authentic. Calls to the White House, State Department, and the Pentagon did nothing but alarm everyone. I immediately prepared to transmit it all to the Bureau. The supervisor on duty at night had the responsibility of signing out all communications going to the Bureau. When mine reached his desk he called me. He agreed that what we had was truly startling information on its face. He, however, recognized it as part of a promotion for a new spy novel that had left the presses just days before. He had a copy of the book in his desk. The cover explained it all.

Armed with this, we decided to "milk" this for all we could get out of it. The Slav readily agreed to go back to the Soviet Mission and endeavor to sell the Russians the balance of what he had for $100,000.00, only this time he would hold onto the papers and not allow the Soviets to copy them. A couple of the better pages were selected as the ones the Soviets would be allowed to see. If they wanted the rest they had to pay. As before, he was dealing with the number two official in the KGB.

I'm sure thoughts of a commendation from Nikita Kruschev and what this would do for his career went racing through his mind. It didn't take long for him to come up with the money. The Slav and I walked to our office, with the US Government now $100,000.00 richer.

Knowing the KGB would soon learn they had been duped, we chose to take the whole story to the New York *Daily News* newspaper in hope that they would publish it and publicly embarrass the two KGB agents. The *Daily News* was delighted to publish it. General Vasily V. Mozshechkov and General Nikolai Vinogradow quickly boarded a plane and left the United States. Their arrival in Paris was covered by our legal attaché. It was obvious that both were being summarily escorted aboard an Aeroflot plane by KGB agents for a direct flight to Moscow. I sincerely doubt that either had furthered his career very much.

≈ ≈ ≈ ≈

Vadim Anatolevich Isakov, a Russian national, was a procurement officer for the United Nations International Children's Emergency Fund (UNICEF).

He first arrived in the United States in February, 1962, with his wife and two sons. His job at the United Nations was to purchase chemicals and supplies used by UNICEF around the world. He also had another job, that of a Soviet Intelligence Officer. I never knew how well he performed his work at the UN, but he "goofed" rather badly in his intelligence work.

Soon after the case was assigned to me I became aware that he was in contact with a businessman in New Jersey. It was obvious from the start that Isakov's interests went well beyond his work at the UN. Soon he was asking for titanium alloy tanks that could withstand very high pressures, accelerometers, underwater robots, and a microtonic computer, none of which the UN could use. They could, however, be used in building the new nuclear submarines.

With the cooperation of the businessman we dragged Isakov's requests out as long as we could in order to learn as much as possible about why he wanted these items, and the use they intended for them. What was to be the final meeting between Isakov and the businessman was to take place in a large department store in New Jersey. Nina had helped with many other surveillances, and was on hand for this one. Assuming that Isakov had seen me since I had been investigating him for some time, I needed to remain in the background. Isakov led the businessman to the women's lingerie department. Nina's

199

presence was perfect. She was able to move near enough to hear their conversation and signal to me.

All the items Isakov wanted were classified and strictly forbidden for shipment outside the US. We had no intention of giving him anything on his list. Our purpose was simply to learn as much as we could, then expose and embarrass him. On cue from Nina I moved in, introduced myself to Isakov, and had a brief conversation with him. When I turned him loose he made a quick retreat to the Soviet Mission. He and his family were on the airplane back to the Soviet Union the next day.

This case is typical of many in the files of the FBI. I was complimented, however, when it was written up as a teaching aid for use at the FBI Academy in Quantico, Virginia.

ᕦ ᕤ ᕦ ᕤ

Stanley Ryan, a Canadian citizen, was identified by a highly placed informant as an agent of the KGB sufficiently important to have been paid $1,000.00 per month. Ryan was now "retired", but continued to receive pay from the KGB. Investigation revealed he was in the US illegally, but was soon to return to Canada. In discussion with Canadian authorities it was agreed by all that it would be best to interview him while he was still in this country. Arrangements were made for an agent of the Royal Canadian Mounted Police to join me in New York City for the interview.

During the early morning a colleague and I went to Ryan's hotel. Having used a pass key I was standing by his bed before he knew we were in the room. We had learned that he might have suicidal tendencies and wanted to be certain he would not attempt to harm himself. I accompanied his every move, physically took a pair of sewing scissors from him, and stood next to him while he shaved.

At our office I was joined my Sgt. Harry W. Brandes of the RCMP. Brandes was an especially astute investigator. There seemed to be an immediate bond of camaraderie between us. Brandes was introduced to Ryan by name only without reference to his being with the RCMP. We both anticipated a short interview, being armed as we were with very specific incriminating information. Lunch came and went with no perceptible break in Ryan's denial.

Around 2:00 PM I was called out of the room to take a call from Mr. Hoover, who was interested in the progress being made. I tried with as much optimism as I could muster, to assure him that Ryan was about to break.

When I returned to the interview room minutes later, Ryan's demeanor had changed completely. Brandes said that while I was out Ryan had admitted his involvement with the Soviets and had agreed to tell all he knew, but only after he was back in Canada. Knowing that Ryan might change his mind once he was back on home territory, I told him his offer was not sufficient. I insisted he furnish a signed statement identifying his Soviet principal and at least a brief summary of the type of information he had provided them. This did not come easy, but he was finally convinced he would not be allowed to leave the US until he did. Based on information furnished by Ryan, I prepared and he signed a statement incriminating him in espionage activities. Quick arrangements were made for a reservation on the next flight to Montreal.

At the first opportunity I asked Brandes what had happened while I was out of the room to convince Ryan to "tell it all". He smiled and said that he had moved very close to Ryan, identified himself as a "Mountie", and explained to him what a mean man I really was, and that the only way Brandes could protect him was for Ryan to admit his involvement so they could leave the country.

Brandes told me as they boarded the plane that Ryan thought he was going to be allowed to return to his home, when in fact he was headed directly to a cabin in the Canadian North Woods so remote it could only be reached by float plane. The first report I received from Brandes was in excess of 300 pages with more to come. I was still drawing on the "high" from this case when I received a transfer to the Memphis office.

～ ～ ～ ～

From November to November each year, I often spent my free time planning my next hunting trip. At least this was true over coffee with friends in the office. Each November, six to ten of us would rent an old logging camp, the Little Lyford Pond Camp, located 27 miles northeast of Greenville, Maine. We would hunt for deer and black bears.

No detail was too small to be overlooked in preparations for these trips. The weather could be severe, so the appropriate gear had better not be overlooked. Secondly, an intense rivalry built up among us with everyone trying to outshoot the other. I had restocked a Model 70 Winchester .308 caliber rifle, equipped with a scope, and fine-tuned it until I could hit a nickel at 100 yards with 5 successive shots.

Gail Torrey, who ran the camp, did not want us to hunt on Sunday. So Sunday was spent being sure our gun sights had not been damaged during the trip. The first year I was a member of the group, Gail invited me to accompany him to an open field where we could test our rifles. Gail, a typical native of Maine, hunted with an old lever-action .30-.30 rifle. I set up a paper target with a fairly large black bulls-eye in the center and invited him to try his gun first. He fired three shots. Each was in a different corner of the paper. He reasoned this was good enough, since the paper was smaller than a deer. I fired one shot and he announced I had missed the entire paper. I knew better, having seen it through the scope. He simply smiled a gentle smile when he saw I had hit the bull's eye exactly in the center.

I had hunted all day the following Monday and was sitting on a log just off a trail watching it snow, when Gail and other members came by en route to camp. They had not seen me. They were barely out of sight when a handsome buck walked past me. I fired one shot and got him. By the time I had field-dressed the deer it was almost dark. I dragged the deer to the trail and started to camp. I had not gone far when Gail's son drove up in a jeep and asked where my deer was. He said that when his dad heard the shot he looked about to see who had not returned to camp and realizing it was me told his son, "Get the jeep and go help Thomas. He has a deer down." In the 10 years or so I went hunting there I never failed to get a deer, nor did I ever shoot a deer more than one time.

❧ ❧ ❧ ❧

There are many fond memories of Little Lyford Camp. One day it was cold and snowing heavily when I heard loud breaking sounds. As I got closer I glimpsed a black bear moving through the woods. He was ripping up rotten logs in search of food. I could never see enough of him to get a shot, so I continued trying to catch up to him. I had been told never to try to overtake a bear, because they often travel as much as 20 miles in a day. It was still early in the afternoon and the temptation was too great. It was about 3:00 PM when I finally realized I was not going to catch up to him. Snow clouds were heavy, meaning it would be dark early, probably by about 4:00 o'clock. I knew I had been going generally around the base of Indian mountain, but had been watching the bear so intently I really did not know where I was. Each of us carried the best of National Geodetic maps and compasses since we were in a remote area of Maine near Mt. Katadin, 27 miles to the nearest town and 35 miles from Canada. Thanks to some very prominent outcroppings of rock, I soon determined where I was. I was on the side of the mountain opposite camp. I knew I could never get back to camp before dark but felt I might be able to reach an old fishing shack if the darkness held off long enough. I had never been to the shack, but knew it had a stove, a makeshift bed, and some canned food in it.

Fortunately, I located the shack on the first attempt. It was now just about dark. It was inviting though very primitive. It would surely be better than spending the night in the open woods, which I was prepared to do. There was no way to light the inside of the shack. I carried matches so I could start a fire. While gathering wood for a fire, the clouds changed and it became much lighter. I presumed those in camp would be concerned about me, so I decided I would attempt to follow the trail to camp. It would have been easy, except the snow had obliterated the trail in most places. Since the clouds had lifted and visibility was good, I decided to try it. I arrived in camp about 9:00 PM. Much to my chagrin no one seemed too concerned about me. Gail had convinced them that I could look after myself and would undoubtedly come back in the next day. I appreciated his confidence but was truly glad to be back in camp.

⌒ ⌒ ⌒ ⌒

During one of our later trips to Little Lyford Camp, we had two men from Baltimore who were not FBI agents. One was especially loud, egotistical, and generally unpleasant to be around. He fancied himself as an expert woodsman. One morning he announced he was going to walk out the incoming road, then hunt diagonally across a large wooded area and meet his friend and their truck that afternoon where the trail ended at the base of Baker Mountain. Each of us advised him against it, knowing this was very difficult terrain to negotiate. We knew he had several miles of blow-downs and beaver ponds to go around. Some of us were concerned enough that we were at the truck at 3:00 PM when he was supposed to be there. When he had not arrived and realizing that it would be dark soon, I volunteered to go search for him. The further I walked without having crossed his trail the more I felt the need to find him. If he were walking in a straight line he was certain to miss the truck, go into the mountain, and be lost with civilization many miles away in any direction. I always carried a .22 caliber pistol, which I could use to get small game for food or to signal with if needed. As I went along I fired signal shots, but got no answer. I had been plotting my route carefully with a compass, knowing I had to get out. Just as it was almost dark I saw him standing about 100 yards away. He had heard my shots but gave no sign of recognition. It was bitter cold and he wore only his underwear from the waist up. He was wet with perspiration. I knew then he was hopelessly lost. He had thrown away his gun and his outer clothing, classic reactions of those hopelessly lost.

As I approached him he began backing away. He looked like a mad man. I tried to assure him everything would be all right and to follow me out to the truck. He became very argumentative, claiming I did not know the way out. He was a very large man and I knew I could never force him to accompany me. I told him once again I was going to the truck and started walking away from him in that direction. I discreetly tried to keep him in view and noticed that each time I was about to get out of his sight he would run toward me a little way and then stop again.

It was obvious that if I could keep him doing this we would get out eventually.

I think God must have been reading my compass. A couple of hours after dark I could see the headlights of the truck. I had hit it dead center. When the lost man saw the truck lights he ran past me and got into the cab of the truck without saying a word to anyone. Back at camp he would not eat, instead electing to remain in his cabin. The next morning when we went to breakfast he and his companion were gone, having left during the night. I subsequently tried to follow his trail hoping to find his clothes and the very expensive Weatherby rifle he had been carrying. I never found them. I assumed he had deliberately buried them under the snow and that the subsequent light snowfall had covered them over. He never again contacted Gail, nor did he pay for the time he was there. I am thankful to have been privileged to go to Maine those many years. Every trip was a rewarding experience I shall always cherish.

❧ ❧ ❧ ❧

Without any advance notice seventy-five transfers arrived in the New York office. All were Office of Preference transfers, i.e., where the transferee wanted to go. Transfers were based on seniority.

Initially Nina and I were disappointed mine was not among them, but were actually pleased that we did not have to go right then. We were in the midst of projects on the house that we wanted to finish. Just when we thought we were secure three more transfers were received. When I read to Nina, "Your headquarters are changed for official reasons from New York, New York, to Memphis, Tennessee, effective upon your arrival there on or after this date — May 22, 1967," there was nothing but silence. When I arrived home that evening I was met at the door by Nina and three children with tears running down their cheeks. Each had a reason for not wanting to go anywhere.

We knew we had to accept this transfer or miss our chance for a long time to come. I had just finished Administrative School, which meant I would soon be transferred to Headquarters in Washington, DC. If we had to move, we would much prefer to come to Tennessee than find ourselves stuck in Washington probably for the remainder of my career.

With Nina having graduated from Vanderbilt, and with three children to educate, we felt it best to attempt to get assigned to the Resident Agency in Nashville, Tennessee. Since it was "the Athens of the South", Nashville appeared to be the ideal place to go. Just before I was to leave for Tennessee, and thinking I had arranged to be assigned to Nashville, a second letter of transfer was received. It read "Your headquarters are changed for official reasons from New York, New York, to Columbia, Tennessee, effective upon your arrival there on or after this date – June 12, 1967." Nina's first question was "Where's Columbia, Tennessee?" I had to tell her I had never been there but it was somewhere south of Nashville. When I arrived home that night I was met with the same red-eyed family. Between sobs Nina said, "Do you know what the *Encyclopedia Brittanica* has to say about Columbia? It's the mule capitol of the world and that's a far cry from the Athens of the South!" At the time this was almost devastating. Actually, it turned out to be a blessing.

We sold our house in New Jersey less than a week after putting it on the market. We agreed that Nina would stay with the house until the sale was closed and that I would come on to Tennessee to search for a new home. The truth is, Nina rather booted me out. She knew how much I hated to move and felt she would be better off doing it alone. I have no doubt that she was correct.

I arrived in Columbia, Tennessee, with a car loaded down with plants we knew would never survive in the moving van. One was an "elephant plant" that Nina had grown from a single leaf. It now stretched from the front floorboard of the car over the back of the front seat, with the top touching the rear window. Soon the Holiday Inn in Columbia looked like a floral shop.

We were about to enter upon a whole new way of life. In New York I had tried to match wits with my professional counterparts in Soviet Intelligence, hardly any threat to my person. Now I would be challenged by the dregs of society, bank robbers, car thieves, kidnappers, and others of the criminal world. This was rather like starting anew. Fortunately at the time, the words "FBI" usually struck a note of fear in the hearts of most criminals. They most often responded by doing what they were told to do. That no longer appears to be the case. I learned very soon that personal reputation is a tremendous asset. The criminal subjects seemed to make it their business to know who the local FBI man was, where he lived and what kind of car he drove. I set about trying to create the impression that I intended to deal fairly and honestly but very firmly. I had the good fortune to develop a couple of superb informants. Through them I could send any message I wanted, and it would make the rounds of the underworld in a very short time. In very short time the word was out, "Don't mess around with this new FBI man. He means what he says."

Holloway Cromer was also assigned to Columbia when I arrived. Without his help, adjusting to this assignment would have been much harder than adjusting to New York City. I'm sure he wished many times they had sent a man with more experience in criminal work. I had a multitude of questions, which I'm sure all came at an inconvenient time for him. When I arrived, delinquent cases were awaiting me. The supervisor in Memphis did not like delinquent cases, so he was on me from the start. Soon I would be assigned as many as 65 or 70 cases and would be working a ten-county territory alone.

❧   ❧   ❧   ❧

Departure from an airplane at Nashville, at that time, was down a stairway rolled up to the plane's door. I stood anxiously awaiting the family's deplaning, when it seemed my family was not on board. Everyone else had gotten off. Then Nina appeared at the door with three children and a cat in tow. As she came down the stairs there was a "clunk, clunk, clunk" sound. I soon realized she was carrying a heavy steel crowbar. I felt like laughing and crying at the same time. She explained that just as the moving van left the house, she realized they had left the crowbar. Knowing that my Dad had given me that crowbar which he had made from the axle of an old hay rake, she would not leave it behind. At first the airline in Newark refused to let her board with it but relented when she refused to board without it. She rode to Nashville with it under the seats, hence the reason she was last in getting off.

Searching for a new home was paramount. It was a buyer's market. I had eight or ten "possibles" to choose from. I chose to take her to my least favorite ones first. When she walked into 1003 Sunnyside Drive, she said, "This is it." It was my favorite of them all. The house was almost

1003 Sunnyside Drive. "This is it."

new. The owner had been transferred and it had been vacant for several months. There had been little interest

209

in it by other buyers since it was not air-conditioned. Allowing for this, we made an offer we doubted would be accepted, but it was. Soon we were settled in place. We joined the country club primarily so the children would have a place to swim, play, and meet others their age.

∽ ∽ ∽ ∽

The next twelve and one-half years' work, different as it was from New York City, was equally eventful. An average day consisted of ten or eleven hours of work, plus dictation at home until bedtime, and then often back out at night in response to calls from the local police for assistance. My greatest single regret is that I did not have as much time with my family as I would have liked. Early in my career I instituted a self-imposed rule that I would endeavor, if at all possible, to be home for dinner at 6:00 PM. I missed dinner only a few times, although I often had to go back out after dinner.

Being closer to our respective families afforded us an opportunity to take a real vacation for a change. At various times we traveled to New Orleans, Mobile, Florida, and in 1972 took the first of several trips to the western part of these United States. To date, I have been in every state in the US except North Dakota, Minnesota, and Michigan. I hope to go to those states one day.

Elizabeth Ann entered Memphis State University in 1968. While there, she met and married Edward J. Kiely, of Moline, Illinois. Five years later Susan Carol started college at the University of Tennessee, ultimately finishing as a Medical Doctor. In the interim she married John Dawson Frierson Gray, who was from Columbia, Tennessee. In 1979, my son Lawrence Gray entered the University of Tennessee, graduating with a bachelor's degree in Computer Science. In June of 1987, he married Peggy Sue Cassady of Bowling Green, Kentucky. She brought to our family a delightful granddaughter, Jennifer Sue Cassady, born August 30, 1974.

❦ ❦ ❦ ❦

Between my arrival in Columbia in 1967 and retirement in January of 1980, I drove six government automobiles a total of approximately 500,000 miles. Almost all of it was in Middle Tennessee. At one point, I was assigned eleven counties. It would take in excess of two hours for me to get from the eastern edge of Cannon County to the Southern edge of Lawrence County. I know because I was in Woodbury (in Cannon County) one day when the bank in Loretto (Lawrence County) was robbed. Driving with siren and blinking blue lights on, it took over two hours to get there. When I called to tell the Memphis office I had arrived at the bank they wanted to know where I had been. I've often wondered what they would have done if I had slowed my pace and made less effort to handle all the work they assigned me. Soon after I retired the territory was drastically reduced, and two men were assigned to cover it.

Mixed in with the mundane situations were several interesting, challenging cases and events, some of which were genuinely life-threatening. I retired without ever firing my gun at anyone, nor did anyone shoot at me, although we came close a number of times. The nearest I came to getting shot was at the hands of a 75-year-old man. The Sheriff in Columbia, Tennessee, called to advise me that earlier in the day he had arrested a local citizen in a remote section of Maury County, near the Santa Fe community. At the time of the arrest another man, whose identity was not known, was living with the subject they had arrested. The sheriff's prisoner subsequently advised that his guest was an escaped federal prisoner from the penitentiary in Atlanta, Georgia. Inquiry revealed this to be true. He was thought to be probably armed and was considered dangerous. He had already killed three men.

The Sheriff and I decided this fugative, whose name I do not recall, would not be alarmed to see the Sheriff drive up, since he had been there the day before. I would sit behind the driver with two other deputies with us. The subject's house was located on a steep incline, making the porch six or eight feet off the ground. As we approached, the subject walked onto the porch, bare to the waist. Grid-like scars from knife fights covered his chest and stomach.

The sheriff pulled as close to the porch as he could get. I stepped out and immediately started running up the steps. The subject turned and ran through the house. As I reached the porch I could see he was headed for a rifle, which was laying on a table nearby. My first thought was that I did not have time to reach him before he could get to the gun. I did not like the idea of having to kill a 75-year-old man, so in the split-second I had to think about it, I elected to try and get to him. He picked up his gun and started to turn toward me. The end of the barrel was within mere inches of my face before I could reach the gun and disarm him. En route to the jail, he made it very clear he would have killed me in an instant had he been able to do so. He already knew he would spend the rest of his life in prison.

     ✑   ✑   ✑   ✑

Tom Green was a notorious expert bank burglar. His tools were far superior to most, and I could often tell by looking at a burglary that he had done it. Tom tripped the alarm to a bank in Lewisburg one night. Then, as usual, he hid, waiting to see how long it took for the police to respond. If the police drove away he would go inside the bank immediately, and be out within minutes with the money. The police did not locate Tom but did spot his Cadillac. They waited for him to return and arrested him. Since he had not been in the bank, all he could be charged with was possession of burglary tools. When Tom refused to identify himself I was called in to help. He was demanding an attorney and wanted bond set at once – all things he might do to get out of town.

It was obvious that he delighted in being aggressive and hostile. I chose to try to defuse the situation by explaining that he was destined to stay in jail without bond, until his identity could be established. Further, I was about to take his finger prints and once they were taken, they would be sent to FBI Headquarters in Washington, D.C., where they would be checked, when they got around to it. At that time they were running about three weeks behind. All he could do was wait. I began complimenting him on his excellent equipment and although we had never met, I thought I knew who he was. His ego showed through and he began talking. We talked for the better part of three days, during which time he told me of many burglaries he had committed. He even gave me the name of a friend who worked for the Mosler Safe Company, who would tip him off to banks that were vulnerable to his technique. As we neared the end of our time together, he told me of having tripped a bank alarm in a small town and then hid in a weed-covered lot behind the bank. Shortly a police car pulled up and a very large, obese officer got out. Tom fired his .357 magnum pistol over the officer's head, and laughed heartily about watching this very large man try to crawl under a police car. I did not find the incident nearly as funny as he. This led to a discussion as to what he would do if I ever called upon him to surrender. His reply was, "I will kill you." I endeavored to convince him, with all the sincerity I could muster, that if I called upon him to "freeze", he had better freeze or I would kill him before he could get his gun out.

In due course, Tom made bond and left town. Before long the FBI was looking for him again. Agents in Ohio were able to identify Tom's girlfriend and determined that she was in the local hospital awaiting the delivery of their child. She had checked in under her name and asked for a private telephone in her room. A few days later she checked out with her newborn child, entered a taxicab, and went home. A few days thereafter the mother and Tom came out to take their new child for a stroll. Agents virtually surrounded him. One agent behind him told him to "freeze" while another agent closer to him, told him to raise his hands. He had his right hand in his pants pocket and would not remove it. He explained that he had been told to freeze and that he was frozen. When he was allowed to turn around and saw I was not behind him, he removed his hand. It was then he told the arresting agents of our conversation and the fact that he believed me. He said he thought I was there and knew that if I were and he removed his hand, he would be shot.

FBI procedures dictated that we were not to make an arrest single-handedly. That is, unless we happened upon our subject totally unexpectedly. One such case happened to me in Williamson County, Tennessee. A Marine Corps deserter lived in a remote rural area near the Fairview community. The sheriff and I had been there a couple of times and had received little cooperation from the subject's in-laws, although they were very polite. The subject's wife was expecting their first child any day. She claimed she had no idea where her husband was, but I doubted her.

One afternoon I was in the general vicinity and thought I would simply stop by to see if she had delivered, hoping she would be more cooperative and help in locating him. When I walked to the door, I could see a young

214

man in a rocking chair. Assuming it was my subject, I simply walked in. He admitted his identity, remaining in his chair, gently rocking back and forth. I explained he had to go with me, knowing that if he refused I could be in trouble. He was built like "Lil Abner," about 220 pounds and twenty years old. I was nearing retirement age at the time. Very politely and oozing of confidence, he said he wasn't going anywhere. He was there to stay until his baby was born. When he started to get up I unholstered my gun and ordered him to stay where he was. I explained that I had a family at home and that I intended to be there with them that night. I did not intend to engage in any contest with him. I told him I would shoot him if he tried to attack me. I did not like the situation I was in, but at this point I had no choice but to follow through.

Seeing my gun, the subject's wife began crying and jumped in his lap. She just about turned the chair over backwards. It would have turned over had he not put his arms out behind the chair to prevent it. While he was trying to avoid an upset with his very pregnant wife I luckily got handcuffs on both hands. After explaining I would simply turn him over to the Marine Corps Military Police and he would probably be home in a couple of days, everyone calmed down a bit. As we started out of the house the subject's mother-in-law stopped us and begged us not to go out. The subject's father was outside with a shotgun intent on not letting me take his son away. Pleas of the mother-in-law had no effect on the subject's father. Since he was standing between me and my car, I had no choice but to go out and confront him. With the subject in front of me and very close to me, I placed the barrel of my revolver next to the subject's head and walked out. The subject's father tried unsuccessfully to maneuver around for a shot at me. I finally convinced him that even if he shot me my reflex would surely kill his son. Finally, he agreed to surrender the shotgun. I unloaded it, and threw it as far out of reach as I could. I put the subject in my car and drove away. By the time we got to Nashville, the subject and I had become rather good friends. He expressed his fear at what his father might have done, saying that was the first time in his life he had ever seen anyone "back his Dad down". Few of these details found their way into my report.

❧   ❧   ❧   ❧

Norman Woodrow "Woody" Peck, was a handsome young man from Dothan, Alabama. I first arrested him for automobile theft when he was about 20 years old. I got him a second time for the same offense. By the time he was in his early twenties he had started robbing banks. The bank at Belfast, in Marshall County Tennessee, was robbed one afternoon by two men inside the bank, and two more outside in the getaway car. We soon located the car abandoned on Rattlesnake Hill, which was between Belfast and Lewisburg. The area was so infested with rattlesnakes, police officers refused to get out of their cars and advised me not to get out either. Finally, we got a wrecker to pull the getaway car out so it could be examined. We suspected we knew the identity of one of the robbers, who was a local man, an quickly found his address. I obtained permission to search his trailer, which was parked behind a tavern. Inside were Woody Peck and his wife, Sue Ann Peck. Looking at Woody, I commented "it seems every time I turn around I run into you." His terse reply was, "then stop turning around." The next day we began showing Woody's photograph to witnesses along the getaway route and eventually located a man who made a positive identification. This was enough to charge Woody. He remained totally uncooperative, even after being convicted in Federal Court. His mother attended his trial. Afterwards, she sought me out to explain that Woody was really a "good boy," but had gotten involved in the wrong crowd. I felt sorry for her. I could see my mother

216

in her. She pleaded with me that if ever I could be of some help to him she would very much appreciate it.

With Woody's conviction behind us, and three more subjects still free, I took Woody aside and attempted to gain his cooperation. He was adamant in his denial. I told him of my conversation with his mother, and literally preached him a sermon about what he was doing to her and to himself. In very strong terms, he expressed his resentment of the sermon. At that time the Dodge Motor Car Company was running an advertisement on television using actors with large, white Texas-style hats as the "good-guys". I told Woody that if he ever wanted to get on the side of the guys with the white hats, to just let me know. He was taken to the federal prison at Terre Haute, Indiana, to serve his sentence.

About a year later my telephone rang at 2:00 **AM**. The caller was crying. When Woody could get his composure, he told me that his dear mother had become so despondent that she had doused herself with gasoline, set herself on fire, and died in her front yard. He wanted to know if I could possibly take him to her funeral. I knew it was impossible for me to do it, but set about attempting to arrange for US Marshals to do it. I was successful. A few days later the telephone rang again. This time Woody wanted me to come to Terre Haute to see him. He said he was ready to get on the side of the guys with the white hats. With his testimony the jury convicted the three remaining robbers, one being the brother of a judge in Birmingham, Alabama. A few years later, Woody walked into my office in Columbia, extended his hand, and announced that he was a new man. He had been paroled from prison and now had a well-paying, full-time job. Also, he was a born-again Christian. He thanked me for all I had done for him and then left. I can rejoice at having preached him that mini-sermon, even though he did not want to listen to it at the time.

217

One afternoon, in the middle of the summer, three young black men, two of average size and one tall and very slim, and wearing a brilliantly colored ski cap pulled down over his face, robbed the bank at Chapel Hill, Tennessee. Being nearby, I rushed to the bank. Within minutes, I had a description broadcast over the State Police radio. No one had seen how the robbers made their getaway. Within minutes, an alert State Trooper in the adjoining county radioed that he was stopping a car with three young black men in it. This was followed moments later with the message that two were of average size and the other was tall and very slim. In addition, there was a brilliantly colored ski cap laying on the rear seat. A search of the car revealed the money from the bank stuffed underneath the front seat. Not only did we get back all the money stolen from the bank, but we also recovered 75 silver dollars belonging to the owner of the car, which the robbers had stolen just before the robbery.

Being without help from the FBI, I asked a local police officer to fingerprint the subjects for me. The two of average size submitted without complaint. The tall, slim subject refused to allow his to be taken. Now it was my turn to try. I took him in the booking room, just the two of us, and explained I was there to fingerprint him. His reply was, "It will take more than you to get them." I tried to explain court rulings on the matter and that force could be used to obtain them if this became necessary. I was standing on his left side holding his forearm. He made a fist and refused to open his hand. Being in precisely the right spot, I hit him under his rib cage with my right elbow. His knees buckled and the hand opened up. "You are a dead man, white boy," he said, "When I get out I will hunt you down if it's the last thing I ever do."

My reply was brief and to the point, "It probably would be the last thing you ever did."

Instead of going to trial, all three subjects entered a plea of guilty. Federal Court procedures required me to present facts to substantiate a violation of the Bank Robbery Statute. Feeling the tall subject might make mention of having been hit, I chose to conclude my remarks to Judge Frank Gray by telling him that I had hit the subject and why, and that he had threatened to kill me when he got out of prison. Judge Gray asked the subject if what I had said was true. His reply was, "Yes, Judge, every word he says is true, including the fact I will kill him when I gets out, and I will do it, too." Without a moment's hesitation, Judge Gray said, "And that will cost you an additional twelve years on top of whatever else I decide to give you."

❧   ❧   ❧   ❧

A young Marine Corps deserter's mother lived in Lewisburg, Tennessee. She steadfastly maintained she had no idea where her son was, but would not tell me even if she knew. In time I was able to gain the confidence of a neighbor who saw him going in and out of the house regularly. I was in Lewisburg, when she called and advised that the subject had just entered his mother's house. The late Leonard Adams, Chief of Police in Lewisburg, and I went to the house. When the subject's mother opened the door and saw me she tried to close it in my face, but couldn't with my foot holding it open. The Chief and I walked in, knowing we had other officers waiting outside the back door.

I located the subject in a rear bedroom standing between the bed and the wall, a space of about two feet. He made it clear he was not going to surrender without a fight and if I wanted him I would have to come get him. The moment I laid my hand on him, the fight was on. He was at least six feet tall, with flaming red hair, and weighed about 220 pounds. Before Leonard and I could subdue him, we had broken every piece of furniture in the room. We had walked across the broken-down bed several times. Finally, with my handcuffs on him, we started out the door. Leonard and I were both exhausted. Just as the subject got out the door he pulled free of Leonard, and ran across the yard toward the rear of the house. Being too tired to chase him, Leonard and I followed him across lawns, sidewalks, and driveways in the patrol car, eventually pinning the subject against a chain link fence with the front of the patrol car. Getting him in the car was another matter. I was eventually able to get a secure "choke hold" around his neck and literally dragged him inside the car. I held this position all the way to the jail, which wasn't very far, but it was far enough for him to kick the back out of the front seat, the panel off the door, and even the glass out of the door.

At the jail it took four officers to get him inside a cell. We were all exhausted, so we literally threw him inside and locked the door, even though he was still wearing my handcuffs. After resting a few minutes and listening to him kick the cell door I went back to retrieve my handcuffs. He expected I would come in the cell to take them off. Instead, I ordered him to back up to the door so I could reach through the bars and do it. He refused, and I went home for the night with him still wearing them. I called the Marine Corps Police to come get him, alerting them to the problems we had with him.

The subject screamed and kicked the cell door all night, apparently never sitting down once. I was at the police station when the Military Police arrived. Two black officers who could have been mistaken for Joe Louis got out of their truck. I pointed in the direction of the sound, saying that all I wanted out of the deal was my handcuffs. Within a few minutes the two officers reappeared, one on each side of the subject, holding his feet well off the floor, with him still kicking, but careful not to hit the MP's. One officer stopped long enough to deliver my handcuffs and quietly said, "We will have a short talk with this boy when we get down the road a piece." With this, they threw him inside their "paddy wagon" head first, closed the door, and drove away. I was never to see this subject again but did learn his violent behavior had been drug-induced.

❧ ❧ ❧ ❧

Members of at least three bank robbery gangs drifted in and out of my territory from time to time. One of particular interest was the Dawson Gang, headquartered in Florence, Alabama. The leader was Billy Ray Dawson. He was about 22 years old and lived with most other members of the gang in Dawson Hollow. Since their home was located at the far end of a private road about four miles long, with relatives living along the road, it was impossible to get to his house without his knowing it. After many tries, the Birmingham office had successfully introduced an informant into the gang. Billy Ray was suspicious of everyone and rarely told anyone of his plans until he was en route to hit a bank, rendering our informant ineffective in apprehending the gang in the act of committing the robbery.

Eventually we learned they were to rob the bank at McEwen, Tennessee. The plan was for Billy Ray to steal a getaway car from the parking lot of a factory in McEwen and to make the switch from it to their personal car in a nearby cemetery. It was my responsibility to prevent the switch from taking place. I was to do this by disabling their car with a rifle. I was authorized to use my personally owned rifle, which I knew shot with pin point accuracy.

Bulldozers had recently cleared away additional space for burial sites, leaving a very large pile of tree roots, tree trunks, and dirt. This offered excellent concealment, in exactly the right spot. A colleague had stood his shotgun up against a tree while waiting for it all to get started, and the rain fell so hard the barrel of the shotgun filled to the top with water and bubbled over. Billy Ray did steal a car, drove it to the cemetery, and sat in it about thirty minutes. Instead of robbing the bank, he returned the car to the parking lot. We never did know why he did not follow through. We were positive he did not see the two of us. However, the following week he did rob the bank, but we were not there at the time. The informant told us that Billy Ray and another member of the gang had planned to hide out in a heavily wooded area for three or four days, presuming that by then we would be gone. Billy Ray was known to be armed with an automatic rifle. His hiding place was in a heavily wooded ravine and impossible to get to without being seen or heard. We brought in a helicopter and a police dog from Nashville. With a helicopter hovering very close to the top of the trees and kicking up a large amount of dust and leaves, we were able to progress through the woods with a fair degree of safety. Soon the dog alerted his handler that someone was nearby. When turned loose, the dog raced through the cloud of dust and disappeared under two large trees which had fallen across a ravine. This was followed by screams of pain. When we arrived, the dog was still holding on to a large bite of Billy Ray's buttock.

Following his conviction, coupled with the fact that a number of the gang had been killed, the Dawson Gang ceased to operate.

❦ ❦ ❦ ❦

Dwayne Roosevelt Jones, a young black man, had just been released from prison, having served time for the murder of a policeman. Immediately after his release he returned to his home town driving a new Cadillac

Barritz. It was reported he was armed with a 9 mm pistol at all times and that he had accused the police of harassment when they were seen driving behind, even if by chance. In short, he was a very aggressive, disagreeable person. I began asking questions about him when his name appeared in one of my cases. An informant reported that Jones was incensed when he learned of my inquiry. Soon I was getting information that he was planning to kill my entire family. He knew where I lived, how many children I had, and our routine. He told my informant he planned to bomb our home when the children were all home from college. Since threats were a common occurrence, the administrative staff in Memphis treated the threat with indifference. I felt this one was probably for real.

Nina and I had just gotten asleep when a severe thunderstorm struck. A bolt of lightning struck a tree less than fifteen feet from our bedroom. I awoke with a blinding white light in the room. Nina was sitting in the bed screaming. Our first thought was "bomb". It so unnerved us both I felt compelled to bring the bomb threat to a head. The next morning I called FBI headquarters in Washington, DC, told them of the threat and of my concerns, and asked for their recommendations. We discussed a mutual friend who lived in another state who had a similar threat made against him and his wife. I was asked if I knew how he handled it. When I said I did, I was told to handle this matter the same way, if I chose. I felt confident that I could do it.

I immediately went to the local police and asked that an officer accompany me to Dwayne's house where I planned to confront him. Much to my surprise, they would not go with me nor would they even offer back-up support. I got the clear impression they were afraid to confront him without an outstanding charge. I left asking that they come to check on me within one hour if I had not returned.

223

I had just reached Dwayne's house when he drove up. He had not seen me and started up the steps into his house. By the time he reached the top step I was close behind him, gun in hand. I followed him inside his house and instructed him to sit at the dining room table across from me. I placed the butt of my gun on the table with a considerable degree of authority. I cocked the weapon and began by cautioning him not to say one word until I had finished and told him he could talk. I made it clear that if he made any movement which I thought to be threatening, I would kill him. I meant it. I delivered a clear, unmistakable warning as to what would happen to him if he did anything to my family and what would happen to him if any harm came to me, since FBI headquarters already knew of his threats. I went so far as to caution him about even being seen in my residential neighborhood. I let him know that I would hold him responsible for anything that happened to my wife, no matter where it was or how it happened. He sat motionless and made no attempt to utter a sound. He was known to stutter severely when under pressure. When I finished what I had to say I asked him if he had anything he wanted to say. His only words were, "Un...c...o...c...k it," looking at my revolver.

I had barely gotten in my car when the Memphis office called and advised me to "Call home immediately." I knew he had not had time to get to Columbia from where we were, but my first thought was that he had done something to Nina just before he had returned to his home. Nina was fine but said I should call my informant immediately. The informant had gotten a telephone call from Dwayne moments after I had left the house. The informant's first words were, "You scared the s__ out of Dwayne. I wish I could see him. He is so scared I think he may have turned white."

This encounter definitely had a calming influence on Dwayne. He no longer challenged the police. A few months later the same informant called and wanted to know if I was aware of a home invasion and robbery that had taken place in Columbia the previous night. He said that Dwayne and a companion had broken into the home of an elderly couple and had attempted to rob them, knowing the husband had a reputation of carrying large sums of money. Dwayne had failed to take into consideration the fact that the victim's wife, although elderly and crippled, had a great deal of fight left in her. She hit the robbers with her crutch, knocking a flashlight out of Dwayne's hand. In his haste to get out of the house he left it behind. We found the flashlight under the victims' bed. Dwayne's fingerprints were on the batteries. Dwayne went back to prison, this time under the Habitual Criminal act, meaning he would never be eligible for parole.

❦ ❦ ❦ ❦

No one would ever expect a Soviet spy to have a reason for being in Columbia, Tennessee. In this case we had two, a father-and-son combination, both trained KGB agents.

Late one Saturday afternoon a colleague from the Nashville office called and said he was in Columbia, and needed to see me right away. He explained that Peter (whose last name I do not recall) and his son, both employees of a large eastern US electronics firm, had flown to Nashville on an intelligence mission, the nature of which was unknown. It was highly important that their activities be monitored in a secure manner. The trouble was that the FBI surveillance team had lost them just as they entered the north side of Columbia. I immediately joined in the search for them.

All the motels in Columbia and surrounding nearby areas had already been searched, without their being located. The information given to me indicated they had virtually disappeared from sight in a moment or two. Having lived at the Holiday Inn located near where they had last been seen, I knew of an area located behind the motel where parking for the cabanas was hidden from view. A quick check located the subject's car parked in this area. We quickly installed a radio in my personal car and set up coverage for Sunday.

Sunday morning Nina and I dressed as for church, laid our Bible on the dash of our Buick, and awaited their movements. We were barely in place when they came out, got in their car, and began a day long driving tour of Maury, Giles, and Lawrence counties. Late in the afternoon they led us down an unpaved road in Giles County. Knowing it was not prudent to have an FBI car with a long radio antenna follow them down the road it was time for the Buick to involve itself again. We cautiously drove around a curve in the road and there they sat, almost blocking traffic. The driver had gotten out and was standing near an electric power pole. We passed with difficulty and proceeded on down the road less than a mile. There ahead of us was a large church meeting in progress. Cars were parked everywhere, perfect cover for those of us with Bibles on the dash. We were barely parked amidst the cars when the subjects appeared, turned around, and drove back along the gravel road. I thought they had what they came for and suggested that the surveillance team back off and let them run a bit. They drove directly back to Nashville and caught a plane. I stopped at the electric power pole and got the identifying number off it.

About a month later a Sergeant in the US Army who had been the object of KGB recruitment attempt in Germany, was now assigned to a militarily sensitive facility in Alabama. He was given the location of a "drop site" for messages to be exchanged with Soviet intelligence. This pole was the spot.

226

In the interim it was deemed necessary to install closed-circuit television viewing this pole. This presented unique problems since there were no buildings within at least a half a mile. There was nothing but heavy woods. The bureau decided to send its best technician to tackle the problem. Jack, whom I had known in New York, drew the assignment. Jack was a native of the Northeast and was entirely out of his realm in the Tennessee woods. Soon we located a large tree properly shaped to hide the camera. With power run from the church, we were in business. It had been a long, hard day and the entire crew was very hungry. We went into Fayetteville only to find all the restaurants closed except for a small cafe. The menu was handwritten on a large board posted on the wall, and featured "plate lunches" only. Being from a northeastern state, Jack seemed confused about the menu. He asked me to order something for him. I presumed he was a steak-and-potato man but that wasn't on the menu. I well recall ordering him mashed potatoes, pork chops, turnip greens, and field peas. The servings were generous, almost overflowing the large plate. I wondered how Jack would approach this meal. With his head down he took his first bite. He consumed the rest of the meal without ever looking up. When he did, he handed me his plate and asked, "Can you get me another one exactly like it?"

Soon there was sufficient evidence to incriminate Peter and his son. When approached with the choice of arrest or working for the FBI, they chose the latter. Several productive years followed.

∽   ∽   ∽   ∽

Ernie Anglin was by profession an installer of dry walls in new home construction. Most of his time, however, was spent dealing in stolen property, gambling, and generally being a criminal. He and I were well acquainted, since I had tried to talk to him several times about a host of matters. Having had no success with him, I began trying to recruit his live-in girlfriend as an informant, hoping she would provide me with some helpful information.

At that time, Ray Blanton, the Governor of Tennessee, was under investigation for illegally selling pardons from the State Prison. The investigation had become stalled. Then Ernie's girlfriend called to tell me that the following day Ernie was taking $10,000.00 to Nashville to pay for the release of his brother from prison. I was able to follow Ernie to his meeting in Nashville. Soon the US Attorney had sufficient information to arrest Ernie but offered me the option of delaying the arrest if Ernie would cooperate. Confronted with the choice of being arrested or working with the FBI, and having been given only one minute to decide, he chose to work with us.

In the ensuing months I spent a great deal of time with Ernie. On a Friday he called and wanted me to ride with him a while. He drove over a great deal of Maury and an adjoining county. He was obviously troubled. We arrived back in Columbia late in the afternoon. I was about to get out of his car when he suddenly blurted out, "I've decided to clean up my act. I am going to tell you everything I know about myself and what is going on in this town. I can't do it right now but I will be in your office first thing Monday, and you can turn on a recorder and I will tell you everything." Trying to make the most of this moment, I almost dragged him into my office with a request that he give me some idea as to the information he could provide. He said, "I can put two public officials and a prominent businessman in the penitentiary." He followed that with information specific enough so that I knew he could do what he said.

Late Saturday evening Ernie's girlfriend called me, crying. She said that two masked men had just come to the house with a shotgun and had taken Ernie outside. A few minutes later she heard a shotgun blast and Ernie had not returned. I was at her house within three minutes. It was easy to find his body, shot in the back. A local policeman was already there with the crime scene roped off.

Investigation revealed that after leaving me, Ernie made a fatal mistake. He had gone to a local store and told two of his close friends that he had decided to tell the FBI everything he knew. Obviously, someone did not want him to do that. Because of the identity of the people he had mentioned on Friday, as well as the lack of supporting evidence, I cannot go into detail about them. Two of the three are deceased, and the third is going about his usual pursuit. The ones instrumental in causing this death will, in due course, have to answer to God. Several years later, the driver for the two murder subjects confessed. He and one other had been suspected from the beginning. Both murderers were convicted. Some of this is set forth in the book entitled "Tennpar", by Hank Hillin, who handled the investigation of the Governor.

Blanton was eventually ousted as Governor amid charges of selling pardons, and was eventually convicted of conspiracy to sell liquor licenses, and served 23 months in prison. He died in 1996 of kidney disease.

❧   ❧   ❧   ❧

George M. had spent most of his life making "moonshine" whiskey. While serving a sentence in the Federal Prison in Atlanta, he escaped. It was presumed he would go to his father's home, which was in my territory. The Sheriff and I went immediately to the house, which was surrounded by a high chain-link fence. Posted conspicuously around the fence were signs saying, "Beware of bad dog." Parked there was the car George was thought to have used in his escape. I could see a man moving about inside the house but could not tell who it was. When the Sheriff and I started through the gate we came face-to-face with the bad dog. To say the least, he was intimidating, and gave every indication he was going to attack us. A voice behind the door ordered us to leave or the dog would attack. Feeling this was nothing more than a delaying tactic to allow George to escape, I was forced to shoot and kill the dog. The man inside was George's father. He admitted only that George had been there a short time before but now was gone. Actually, he had stopped there during the early morning hours just long enough to change vehicles. George's father was extremely upset over the killing of his dog. He subsequently brought suit against me for killing his dog. When the case came before Judge Frank Gray, Judge Gray gave him an intense, severe lecture and promptly dismissed the case.

George had a son who lived in Indiana. He managed to drift back and forth between his son's and his father's places, somehow eluding us at both locations. It was virtually impossible to get anyone in the neighborhood to talk about him. Those who were not his friends were afraid of him. The one man who could have given me his whereabouts at all times was the owner of a local general store. This store provided the sugar needed to make the whiskey. Outwardly he was a white-haired grandfather-type who in his low, soft voice, professed his heartfelt desire to cooperate with me but insisted he simply did not know anything about where George might be.

Several months later the local Postmistress called to say that George had just been in the Post Office but had gone across the street to a garage. Being nearby, I raced to the garage, only to learn that he had just left. In fact, the dust that could be seen rising from the roadway was being made by his truck. I immediately loaded the deer rifle I had on the back seat and gave chase, hoping to catch him before he got home. I could follow the dust rising from his truck. Just before he would have reached the country store he would be getting back on a paved road. I knew the dust would stop. I could not have been more than a minute behind him, but when I got to the store he was nowhere in sight. I charged into the store, carrying my rifle. The owner, sitting on the counter as though half-asleep, denied having seen George that day but was curious as to why I was carrying such a weapon. I explained that I was getting tired of chasing George up and down the road between here and Indiana; and when I saw him next I would put a stop to it. He doubted he would see George any time soon, but if he did he would deliver my message.

I promptly called our office in Indiana and suggested that George was probably headed back to his son's place. The next morning our Indianapolis office called to advise that during the early morning hours, George drove up. When he got out of his truck to open a gate, he was told he was under arrest. Instead of following instructions he just stood there motionless. After a few moments he turned around, looked the agents over, and asked, "Where is the man with the deer rifle?" Apparently my message had traveled fast. George returned to prison, never again to engage in the making of whiskey. Shortly after his release some years later, he killed his wife and is now serving a life sentence.

❧   ❧   ❧   ❧

A conviction was obtained in every case I investigated that went to trial – except one. The evidence in that case was overwhelming. It was considered an "open and shut" case.

The Hampshire, Tennessee branch of the Middle Tennessee Bank was robbed by a lone gunman brandishing a German-made Luger pistol.

231

A bank employee recognized the robber as "Mutt" Matlock, a man who had worked remodeling the bank some years earlier. Matlock lived with his sister in Mt. Pleasant, Tennessee, some eight or ten miles away.

Upon arriving at the Matlock residence, I saw an automobile matching the description of the getaway car parked in a shed near the house. The hood was very warm to the touch, indicating that it had been driven recently. A pair of sunglasses and a large bandage, similar to one reportedly worn by the robber, were clearly visible through the windows.

Inquiry at the residence revealed that only Matlock's sister was home. She invited Agent Holloway Cromer and me inside, and was quite cooperative. Mutt, she said, had walked downtown and probably had gone out to get some whiskey. He was known to be an alcoholic. He had borrowed money from her earlier in the day for whiskey. She knew that Mutt owned a Luger pistol, and promptly produced it. She expected him to return momentarily, so we waited.

We knew we had sufficient evidence to make an arrest. When Mutt entered the room we told him that he was under arrest for robbing the bank. I searched him for weapons. He was not armed, but in his left-front pants pocket was a large roll of one-dollar bills. It was obvious that this was newly issued money. A quick examination revealed that the bills were in numerical sequence. I knew the bank had received a shipment of money earlier that day.

I questioned Mutt as to where he had gotten this money. He maintained that it was his "life's savings". I pointed out that he was broke earlier in the day and had borrowed money from his sister. He insisted that he had been hiding this money from her. He stood mute rather than admit this was, on its face, a ridiculous claim, since the money was new and in numerical order. He denied having driven his automobile that day. He said he did not own a Luger pistol. Cromer and I were puzzled, however, by the fact that he had only a small portion of the stolen loot with him.

Matlock chose William "Bill" Leach to represent him. Bill was known throughout the state as an excellent attorney. Knowing the evidence we had, we wondered what the defense would be. It was simple: "Not Guilty".

The late judge Frank Gray was presiding over the trial, which was being held in Columbia, Tennessee. Well before I testified, it appeared abundantly clear that Matlock was guilty. Upon cross examination, Bill asked me one question: "When did you decide to zero in on the town drunk?" I well recall my answer: "When he robbed the Middle Tennessee Bank at Hampshire." The defense presented little evidence.

The jury returned very quickly. This usually indicated a conviction. Instead, the jury foreman, a very attractive young woman, announced, "Not Guilty." Gasps could be heard throughout the courtroom.

Judge Gray, known as a no-nonsense judge, turned red in the face and ordered that every juror be asked how they had voted. One by one they said, "Not Guilty." The judge, obviously upset, lectured the jurors sternly and asked each juror for their full name and address. He then said from the bench, "Not one of you will ever be allowed to serve on a jury in my court again." An acquittal is an acquittal, so Matlock was released.

Soon thereafter, I learned that the jury foreman had a romantic inclination towards Bill Leach, and she was able to convince the remaining jurors to vote for acquittal.

Two or three years after the trial I learned that Matlock had put the stolen money in a paper bag, and on his way from the bank to his home had stopped along the road in a remote section and hidden the money in some tall weeds. When he returned to pick it up, it was not there. It was never known who had taken the money.

During the course of the investigation of the bank robbery I learned that many years earlier Mutt had lived with an elderly couple named Moore. While he was living with them, the Moores had been found murdered, shot in the head with a 9 mm gun. A Luger pistol uses 9 mm ammunition.

Inquiries at the Tennessee Bureau of Investigation headquarters revealed that because so many years had elapsed since the murder, they had discarded the bullets removed from the Moores' bodies. We know that Matlock robbed the bank in Hampshire, but we will never know if he murdered the Moores. We do know that he was a suspect at the time.

Matlock died of natural causes several years after the trial.

A MOMENT TO REMEMBER

While Clarence M. Kelly was Director of the FBI, he visited the Memphis Office where he had been the Agent In Charge during his tenure with the FBI. I happened to be in the Memphis Office and enjoyed a one-on-one chat with him.

Not long thereafter, someone at the FBI academy had a "brain storm" and conceived the idea that the FBI should be in the business of telling Police Departments how to run their agencies. A lengthy, special course was laid out to teach FBI agents how to counsel police departments on "organization, administration of offices, personnel matters, and other related matters." Each office was to send one man. Over vehement protestations I was selected to represent the Memphis division.

Sixty-two or sixty-three men gathered at the FBI academy in Quantico, Virginia. Immediately, each one of us found we shared the same opinion – that this was the most ridiculous idea ever conceived. Not one of us had the slightest idea how to run a police department nor did we intend to return to our territories and embarrass ourselves and the Bureau by trying to implement such an idea. A number of us voiced our opinions at the very outset and were told, in no uncertain terms, that it did not matter what we thought of the program. We would take the course and implement it upon our return. Furthermore, the Instructor expected to receive periodic reports from each of us on the success of the program.

The further we got into the course the more ridiculous it became. It seemed as though the entire class was close to mutiny. We were probably two-thirds of the way through the course when three of us were told to prepare a five-minute oral presentation to the class, setting forth how we would implement this course in our individual territories. Each presentation would be video taped and thereafter critiqued before the entire class. I was to make the second presentation.

I labored diligently in an effort to make a genuine, sensible application to a department in my Resident Agency. I ultimately concluded it was impossible, but chose to attempt an application to the Sheriff's Department in Lewis County. This office consisted of the Sheriff and the Sheriff's wife, who served as the jailer and cook. There were no deputies – just the two of them.

We were told the presentation must be at least three minutes long, but no longer than five minutes. I rehearsed mine ahead of time and knew it would take almost exactly five minutes. It was based on actual facts as they existed at the time, interspersed with what I felt was mild, appropriate humor. How else could the FBI possibly apply this proposed program to a one-man department who certainly needed no help with administration or personnel, since he had no personnel?

Members of the class apparently agreed with me, because I was frequently interrupted with laughter. It was very apparent the instructor did not find it nearly so funny. When I finished he chastised me before the entire class for not taking the course seriously. Even after I assured him I had set forth the true facts relating to the Lewis County Sheriff's Office, he continued to criticize me. He advised me my attitude bordered on insubordination and that was grounds for dismissal from the Bureau. He said he would consult with his superior regarding my future in the Bureau and would let me know their decision the following morning.

When the course first began we were seated alphabetically. Consequently, I sat near the rear of the class. Because of my attitude I had been moved up to the front row. The following morning, while I awaited word on my future, the door opened, and in walked Director

Kelly. It was a surprise visit to everyone, including the instructor. Without even breaking stride, Director Kelly walked straight over to me, extended his hand, and said, "How are you, Larry?" This was a moment I shall never forget. After Mr. Kelly left the room the instructor asked how long I had known the Director. I replied, "Quite a while."

We all left for home knowing we had wasted our time and a lot of the government's money. I am still waiting for word from the instructor about my future as an agent. I was never asked to implement the program, nor was I ever asked to submit a report to the instructor.

AFTER THE BUREAU

One cannot approach the end of 26 years in an occupation he loved without mixed feelings and moments of doubt. Having worked an average of 60 hours per week for 26 years, retirement did not seem such a bad idea. With Larry still in college, I would have liked to work until he finished. But then in January, 1980 I reached the mandatory retirement age of 55. Frankly, I wondered a bit if we could maintain our standard of living on our income. Nina had grave doubts and encouraged me to seek other employment. Hoping now that we could spend time together, I kept finding reasons why I did not like a particular job offer. The longer I waited the more confident I became that I did not have to work. Our blessings seemed to come in increasing amounts. Thus began another ten great years.

I had always given as much to our church as I felt we could afford. Then came a sermon on Malachi 3:10 which reads, "Bring the whole tithe into the storehouse, that there may be food in My house. Test me in this, says the Lord Almighty, and see if I will not throw open the floodgates of heaven and pour out so much blessing that you will not have room enough for it." This is the only passage in the Bible where God says, "Test me." I started to tithe, taking God at his word. Almost immediately all doubt was removed. We always seemed to have more than enough money for our needs and enough left over for God's part. Not only that, but the balance steadily increased. It has continued to do so to this day, right through what could have been a major financial disaster soon to befall us. I will endeavor to give God his part so long as I live.

"Sis" Foster, Nina's aunt / foster mother had died in 1968, leaving her husband Jim (Uncle Jim) to live alone. We promised to take him to their second home in Shreveport, LA when I retired. We drove to Shreveport in the early spring, 1980, and in May returned to Missouri with him. We were preparing to leave for Columbia when he told us he did not feel well and wanted us to take him to the hospital on our way out of town. He died a month later. Had I not been retired I could never have been able to spend so much time away from my job. This was an especially difficult time for Nina. Since Uncle Jim's family knew he had never adopted Nina they tried, and almost succeeded, in taking all of Uncle Jim's assets. The will he had left was not valid in Missouri, but it was in Louisiana. We had left home in early March and now it was July and we were just on our way back.

⌖ ⌖ ⌖ ⌖

A trip to the Western part of the United Stated in 1972 served to whet our appetites to go again. In May, 1981 Nina and I were determined to "do it right". We drove to Boulder, Colorado, over the Rocky Mountains, through Idaho and into Seattle, Washington and then across Puget Sound to Port Washington. After a week here we started down the coast along US Highway 1 all the way to San Diego, stopping where we wanted and staying as long as we wanted. It was truly a special trip.

⌖ ⌖ ⌖ ⌖

In the spring of 1983, Dad expressed a desire to go to McLean, Virginia, to visit my brother Lewis. If it were possible, Dad was the first one to get into the car every time it left. Mama, now 85 years old, was much more reluctant. At first she declined to go but relented when I would not take Dad without her. Mama had never been outside the state of Tennessee. Dad had been to Chicago one time when he was young but otherwise spent his entire life working on the farm. Mama agreed to go only after I assured her we could make the trip without an overnight stop. She had an inner fear of

239

sleeping in a motel, even though I assured her I would get us rooms with a connecting door and leave it open.

This trip was one of the most rewarding things I ever did. Dad, having been a farmer all his life, delighted in seeing new areas and comparing them to his farm in Tennessee. Some places we passed had "far too many trees on them," he said. If they were cleaned off there would be some very fertile, tillable land there. He was at a total loss to understand why there were so many trees along the beltway in Washington, DC. Even when I explained the aesthetic and environmental reasons, he could not comprehend it or at least did not agree with the reasons. Mama was much more interested in cultural matters. Her mind never ceased to be inquisitive. She especially wanted to visit the White House and President John F. Kennedy's grave site. Fortunately, I still had enough contacts to arrange a special guided tour of the White House. President Reagan was away, which was a disappointment.

Next we proceeded to the Arlington National Cemetery. At Arlington, visitors could no longer drive about as they could earlier. All transportation was by bus. My mother could not negotiate the high first step to get on board. When I talked to the Park Ranger and explained the trip to him, he graciously gave us permission to drive about wherever we wanted. I could take her to the very edge of Kennedy's grave.

Thinking I had covered all the points of interest to Mama, I asked if they were ready to start home. Very apologetically she said, "Son, there's one more thing I would like very much to do if it's not too much trouble. I would like to see the ocean." Except for Chesapeake Bay, the nearest shoreline was in Delaware. The next day we drove to Delaware. I went to the wharf in a couple of places but it was obvious this was not what Mama had in mind. Finally, I located a spot where we could walk over the sand dune to the water's edge. I doubted she would want to go because it was a very cool day. This was the spot she had hoped for. With Nina supporting her on one side and me on the other, we negotiated a crude path over the sand dune. When we reached the top, the water was in full view. Mama stopped, gazed out over the expanse and sighed, "It's beautiful. Nothing like I had dreamed it would be." She led us closer to the water. She was shaking from the cold or at least I thought she was. "No son, I'm not cold; I'm so excited!" The tide was coming in and as she got closer I cautioned her she was about to get her feet wet. She took one step forward as the water spilled over her feet ankle-deep and said, "I came here to stand in the ocean." More than once Mama said, and I'm proud it's true, that she had never asked me to do something I did not at least try to do. Had I not taken them on this trip I could never have forgiven myself.

∽　∽　∽　∽

In September, 1983 Nina and I drove to Maine to see the fall colors. This was her first trip to that area. We planned to visit my old hunting camp and then travel south as the colors progressed. The road to the camp was now impassable. A totally new one was under construction. Just by chance, I stopped by Folsom's Flying Service, which I had used before. Mr. Folsom, who was now elderly, was the only person there. We reminisced about our earlier flights, and I told him how much I would like for Nina to see Little Lyford Pond Camp but we couldn't drive in. He asked if we would like to fly over and offered to take us up. We agreed on a price for a fifteen-minute flight.

Nina had never flown in a float plane. She did not believe it would hold together long enough to get us off the water, twisting and vibrating as they do on take-off. Once we were in the air her fears vanished. The view was spectacular. Lush evergreens, sprinkled with red and yellow maples, white birch, and lakes dotting the entire landscape made for a breathtaking view. Little Lyford Camp now had a ski lodge, which ruined it for us hunters. Mr. Folsom apparently sensed that Nina was enjoying this flight as much as Mama did the ocean. We landed an hour later, being charged for only fifteen minutes. New Hampshire and Vermont were as beautiful as always. We concluded a great trip in Gatlinburg, Tennessee.

Late December 1983 was the due date for the arrival of our first grandchild. Nina had gone to Memphis to be with Susan as she was about to deliver. I had planned to hunt a few days in the Columbia area. John Dawson Frierson Gray was born December 23, 1983. I had gone to Memphis feeling like I was in perfect health. In the very early days of January 1984, I awoke one morning to find both my knees swollen to almost the size of footballs. I could barely walk. I had to get back to Nashville as soon as possible.

Dr. Charles Hamilton, an orthopedic surgeon in Nashville, had performed surgery on my right knee several years earlier. Nina knew I was hurting when I could not drive. When we arrived at Dr. Hamilton's office I had to be helped out of the car. I knew I was in trouble when Dr. Hamilton, whom I knew well, looked down at the floor and said, "I'm sorry, I cannot help you. You should see Dr. Houston." Posted on Dr. Houston's door was a sign showing he specialized in internal medicine. Once I was inside, my questions were answered. All about lay books and pamphlets relating to arthritis. Dr. Houston was not in the office that day but Dr. John Sergent agreed to see me. The probable diagnosis came quickly: rheumatoid arthritis, the crippling kind. Thus began a regime of treatment that continues to this day. Because I was unable to tolerate any of several oral medications Dr. Sergent, started me on injections of gold.

Almost immediately I began to improve. By March I was walking, using a cane.

Aunt Alta Thomas, my father's sister, lived in Knoxville, Tennessee, at the time. Knowing of my problem and our search for something I could do with limited mobility, she called to suggest I attend a photographic workshop being offered at the Arrowmont School in Gatlinburg. Her friend Conrad Reinhart, a staff member at the University of Tennessee, was the instructor. Another friend of Alta's, Inez Lovelace, offered the use of her cabin in Gatlinburg. This afforded a variety of challenges, the first being how I could negotiate the stairs leading into the cabin. I left there two weeks later knowing more about photography than I had learned in all my prior years and I no longer needed the cane. We were privileged to use this cabin until Inez sold it seven or eight years later. I never went there without feeling immeasurably better when I left. With the exception of Nina and Dr. Sergent, no one has contributed more to my recovery from arthritis and general well being than Inez. Nina and I spent much of our free time the following years in the Smoky Mountains, often going three times a year for extended stays, enjoying the unlimited photographic possibilities. In 1989 Nina and I hiked more than halfway to the top of Mt. LeConte, a blessing I never dreamed I would achieve.

We had made our third trip west and a second trip to Maine by 1990. Interspersed were several shorter trips. Nina shared my interest in photography and became a good photographer in her own right. Most of all, she was always searching for new places to go with new and not yet photographed subjects. She became very knowledgeable about the identity of wildflowers, remembering every one I had photographed. We both enjoyed the pursuit immensely.

❧　❧　❧　❧

Our second grandchild, Thomas Pierce Gray, born December 7, 1986, to Susan and Dawson, was handicapped. He was diagnosed as a "Charges Syndrome child," one of less than 100 on record in the United States at this time. Among other problems, he was deaf and had a life-threatening heart condition. It was thought he probably would not live a year. It soon became apparent he wouldn't live that long without medical intervention. A pediatric surgeon at Vanderbilt University Hospital in Nashville, Tennessee, opened this tiny baby's chest and found a large hole in his heart. There was nothing to do except use a clamp to close the hole, knowing this was not a permanent solution.

Nina said that if prayer could help, Pierce surely would be made well. I think every major denomination in the world, with the possible exception of the Muslims, had offered prayers for him and they may have also. In spite of a number of other major operations, he seemed to gradually improve.

It appeared he would never be able to sit up. He lacked neck muscles sufficient to hold his head upright. Nina seemed to sense his determination to live and was burdened to find a way to improve his life, if that was possible. We purchased a baby walker and when the nurses would bring him to our house (which was often since Pierce lived near us), Nina would sit for hours holding his head upright. Gradually, he gained strength. First he could sit, then push himself about, and eventually stand. As he gained a bit of weight and became more active it was apparent he was starving for oxygen. His legs would turn a dark blue.

Susan consulted everyone she felt might help, including a renowned pediatric surgeon in Boston. He concluded there was nothing more that could be done for him. As Pierce's, condition worsened, it became apparent that he would die if something were not done soon.

The pediatric surgeon who had performed the initial heart surgery felt it prudent at this point to take another look at Pierce's heart. I had accompanied Susan and other family members to Vanderbilt. We were waiting in a room down the hall a short distance from the operating room. From my seat I could see the door to the operating room. As we waited, knowing it was now past the time they should have finished, I saw the surgeon emerge. He was still wearing his surgical gloves. There was blood all over his gown. He was walking rapidly towards us. When he saw me a broad smile came across his face and entering the room, said, "I have just witnessed a miracle."

When the surgeon removed the clamp from the heart he fully expected the portion around the clamp to have atrophied. He expected Pierce would likely die on the operating table. Instead, the hole had now completely healed and the area turned a healthy pink and beat as strongly as any normal heart. We were told to expect him to start to grow and as far as his heart was concerned, he could lead a perfectly normal life.

Pierce is now thirteen years old. He is fifty-three inches tall, having grown two inches in the recent past, and weighs ninety-two pounds. He attends school every day and is learning to read, write, and do mathematics. Among his many mental capabilities he can recite the birth date of every person whose birthday he has ever known. Although he is deaf and does not speak, he is proficient in sign language.

TRULY A MIRACLE.

I thank God for His blessings and Pierce has been one of those blessings. I thank his mother, father, and brother for the love, care, and attention they have given him. I surely believe that Nina, from her place in heaven, can look down and see him write his name.

Disaster befell us in January, 1990. Nina had cancer. Not just cancer, but inflammatory breast cancer, among the most virulent and fastest-moving kinds. Her oncologist, Dr. David Johnson, in his own quiet, unassuming way, told us she probably had a year to live. We talked. We cried. We hugged. Late one day as we sat together praying, we both suddenly stopped. I told her I felt like there was a light fog in the room and I had a sense of utter calm. She had just experienced exactly the same feeling. There is no doubt that we had just been visited by the Holy Spirit. From that moment on we stopped feeling sorry for ourselves and set about making plans to enjoy every moment God gave us together. Fortunately, except for the first few times, she had no great trouble with the intensive chemotherapy she was undergoing. This consumed all of 1990, with her finishing all she could tolerate in January, 1991. This was to be one of the best, if not the best year, in our nearly 44 years of marriage. Nina and I both felt well. In June we left on a trip we had long wanted to take but had always saved it for "next year", a trip to Glacier National Park, located in the northwestern part of Montana. En route we traveled along highway 212 in Montana and Wyoming described as probably the most beautiful stretch of highway in this country. We went through Bear Tooth Mountain into Yellowstone, our third trip there. All in all, this was the greatest trip of our lives. In the fall we went again to the Smoky Mountians.

In January of 1992, the cancer struck again with a vengeance. This time it was attacking her liver. Little could be done without totally destroying her heart with the medication. She died July 27, 1992, in our home with me sitting beside the bed holding her hand. The last words she spoke were, "I love you." It is my fervent prayer that when God calls me unto Himself that I will go with the same dignity as she. She often said she knew where she was going when she died but she just was not in a great hurry to get there. Concerned to the end about others, she said that she had the easy part, that mine would be much more difficult. Her wisdom reached beyond my comprehension. Throughout her illness I had devoted my entire time to her treatment and comfort, trying every way I could to make life as enjoyable as possible. I had put off thinking about her death until it actually happened. There is no way to measure my (our) loss. I could stammer around here endlessly and would never find the words to express how I felt. Except for faith in God, it would have been unbearable.

I subsequently visited Dr. Johnson to say one final "thank you". I had known from the beginning that he had studied for the ministry before becoming a Doctor. I had seen him pause between Nina's examining room and the next patient and pray. As I was about to leave, he said, "There is something I want to tell you that I never did. When I first saw Nina and told you she probably had no more than a year to live, I honestly felt she would survive no longer than six months." Instead of six months, God gave us two and one-half truly great years. Nina described 1991 as the best year of her life. We all must die sometime. What greater gift could He have given us than two additional years! My children, may we always strive to follow God's word, and when we die leave a legacy approaching that of your mother. Be prepared to meet God, for we will all get the call one day.

Dad died August 21, 1993, at 94 years of age. Mama followed him on December 27, 1993, at age 95.

During Nina's illness her sister, Lillimae Hester, who lived in Newport Beach, California, came to visit in early 1992, staying for approximately six weeks. She left saying, "Call if you need me." Little did we know how soon that would be. She returned to stay until Nina passed away. Without her and my daughter Elizabeth, I could never have cared for Nina at home.

Wedding Day, June 22, 1996
"Young At Heart"

Lillimae's husband had passed away several years earlier, so she knew what I was facing. After her return to California we began communicating by telephone. There were a number of visits to California, and from California to Tennessee which culminated in our marriage on June 22, 1996. A loving, caring, considerate, thoughtful, sharing quality surely runs through the Gray family. Lillimae is endowed with all of these in generous amounts. I consider myself blessed that she joined our family, along with her five wonderful children, Bruce, Bill, Les, Victoria, and Ben.

Lillimae had traveled extensively before we married and remains ready to pack on short notice and be off again to places

(l-r, standing) Bill, Myself. Les, and Bruce
(seated) Lillimae, Victoria, and Ben

not yet seen, and in some instances to places she has already visited. We have traveled a great deal in the United States and Canada. In June of 1998, we were privileged to spend a month in France and Germany. Headquartered in a quaint motel in Paris, we traveled with friends to the Normandy Coast, Omaha Beach, the United States Military Cemetery there, and subsequently to the Loire Valley in France. In the interim we took the "bullet" train to Remagen, Germany in search of battle sites in which I had participated during World War II. The details of this trip are in the "Military History" section of this book.

In the fall of 1996, Lillimae turned a piece of her California property into a nice home in Prescott, Arizona. Prescott is a small town of about 40,000. It is situated along the Bradshaw Mountain range. Our home is located in the "tall pines" at an elevation of 5,700 feet. The nights are cool, even in the middle of summer.

Arizona did not become a state in this great nation until 1912. The gun was the law then and for several years thereafter. Its history is colorful and interesting. There is still much for us to see even though we have traveled over a great deal of the state.

Lillimae is a great companion with whom to travel. With a rare, inquisitive mind, she is constantly in search of detailed information beyond my normal interest. Never have I taken time to follow her lead without being thankful when I returned home, I did not have to tell myself, "I wish I had taken time to read the fine print underneath the displays in the host of museums we have visited from California to Europe." Surely, we haven't missed a single one.

I look forward to returning to Germany and continuing my search for information about my activities during World War II.

To date, LIFE HAS TRULY BEEN A GREAT ADVENTURE. MAY GOD CONTINUE TO MAKE IT HAPPEN.

IN CLOSING

The mind and the memory are amazing gifts. The more you require of them, the more they will provide. So it has been with this venture. Most of us never take the time to sit and share what dwells in our memories. On many occasions I have wished for that opportunity with my Mama and Dad and others who are no longer with us. We should each take the time to listen to the life stories of others. In doing so, I believe we enrich our own lives.

As I said in the beginning, it was not my literary talents I set out to prove, but rather just the telling of my own personal stories and about some of the times in which I have lived. It was my goal to set down on paper thoughts and events I hoped would be of some interest to others, but particularly to my children. It was my desire to give them a bit of insight as to who I am as a man, and not just as their father, and thereby to give them a sense of who they are, and the roots from which they came. I hope this instills a confidence in them as to where they are going and to know that a bit of me always goes with them.

I have now lived over three-quarters of a century. What a ride, literally! From mules to crank automobiles to jet airplanes. Just about every "latest and greatest" piece of technology has been developed, or at least become commonplace, in my lifetime -- electricity, indoor plumbing, telephones, TV, VCR's, computers, etc. - the list would be another book by itself. If there is one thing I've learned, it is that no amount of technology will take the place of the human heart, the human mind, or the human touch. We are designed by the Master, and each of us is incredibly unique. I believe we are each here for a purpose and that we all have an opportunity to make a difference. To begin each day anew with thankfulness in our hearts, no matter what our circumstances, is to make room for the blessings life has to offer.

At the encouragement of my son, I began this journal of thoughts and stories several years ago after Nina's death. I found that the more I wrote the more I remembered, so I continued, and this book is the result of my trip down memory lane. I thank you for taking this journey with me. If you take away one thing from reading this, I hope it is to encourage you to remember your own life experiences, and to share them with others. In doing so, you may learn much about yourself.

My experiences are not necessarily any more or less remarkable than those of so many other Americans who came from similar backgrounds. I will not be remembered in history as an "historical figure" who left an indelible mark on civilization. I'm just an average man, very proud to be an American and to live in this great nation of freedom. It is for this freedom we hold so dear that I, and so many others, fought to preserve. Our freedom comes at a very high price. I often think of those who made the ultimate sacrifice. Anyone who thinks this is not the greatest nation on earth need only travel to a distressed nation. I am sure they will be glad to have a return ticket "home."

Each day I strive to maintain a thankful heart and to remember how truly blessed I am...

LEST I FORGET

APPENDIX

EXCERPTS FROM THE REPORT, AFTER ACTION AGAINST THE ENEMY

by

52nd ARM'D. INF. BN.
9th ARMORED DIVISION

Files of the National Archives, Washington, DC reflect copies of the above captioned report, further identified as "S-2,3 Journals", and a shorter report simply captioned, "Headquarters, 52nd Armored Infantry Battalion, APO 259, U.S. Army, for the months of January, 1945, February, 1945 and March, 1945.

The report for January, 1945 reflects the following information of interest to this document.

"Having been released from attachment to 101st Airborne Division in the vicinity of Bastogne, Belgium on December 30-31, 1944 the remaining elements of the 52nd Armored Infantry Battalion, were assembled at Vic Saulces Monclin, France. Due to the heavy loss of personnel and equipment suffered previously (Dec. 1944), it was found necessary to reconstitute the 52nd Armored Infantry Battalion. 1st Lt. Edward Bills commanded Company A.

"Our mission during this period was twofold: (1) to reorganize and reequip the Battalion and (2) to institute and conduct a complete, thorough and workable training program for our reinforcements.

"Our tactical mission during this period was to take our part in the Division mission of defending the area south of the Neuse River — it was found necessary to give the returning men several days of rest and medical attention as nearly all of them had digestive diseases and foot ailments caused by their physical hardships of the previous month.

"On January 7, 1945 Company A was moved to Vic Lucquay in order to have sufficient space to receive expected reinforcements. Lt. Col. W. R. Prince was assigned as commanding Officer on January 10, 1945."

"On January 11, 1945 the Battalion was moved to Boulange and then almost immediately to Vic Metzervisse. Again it was necessary to move Companies A and B, with Company A going to Vic Elzange on January 16, 1945." [My recollection is that I joined Company A, on January 17, 1945.]

"The remainder of January, 1945 was spent with calibration of weapons, specialized training in mortars, 57 MM and LMG's, scouting and patrolling, squad and platoon tactical training, crew drill, supply discipline, organization of Armd Inf. Bn., bayonet instructions, assault fire and bayonet attack, map and compass problems, functioning and the effect of the Rocket Launcher, assault of infantry in foxholes by tanks, etc. It is considered that this company, at the end of the month, was again a well-trained and equipped unit ready for, and capable of, successful action against the enemy. This unit had no contact with the enemy during this period.

"During January, 1945 no one from the 52nd Armed Infantry was killed or wounded. No prisoners of war were taken.

FEBRUARY, 1945

The after-action report for February 1945 reflects the following:

"Our mission during this period continued to be the reorganization, re-equipping and training of the Battalion. No tactical mission was assigned to the Battalion during this period.

"Our training program consisted of squad, platoon and company problems, formation and employment of assault and rocket launcher teams, attack of fortified positions, street fighting and infantry-tank coordination. A proportionate share of time allotted to each training phase was devoted to night training.

"On February 23, 1945 the Battalion marched to the vicinity of Spirmont, Belgium. The march commenced at noon on February 23, 1945 and the battalion closed at 4:30 AM on February 24 at Lince, Belgium.

"On February 28, 1945, the Battalion moved to the vicinity of Kornelimunster, Germany, arriving at 11:05 PM.

[According to the report the Battalion had no contact with the enemy during February, 1945. There were no Americans killed or wounded. No enemy prisoners were taken. Lt. Edward Bills continued to command Company A. Lt. Colonel William H. Prince commanded the 52nd Armored Battalion and Major Gen. John W. Leonard commanded the 9th Armored Division to which we were attached.]

MARCH, 1945

The after-action report for March, 1945 reflects the following:

"The first day of this period was spent in an assembly area in the vicinity of Kornelimunster, Germany awaiting orders. In accordance with March Order No.2, dated March 2, 1945, this Battalion moved from Kornelimunster on March 2, 1945 at 6:35 PM. and closed in on Krezau, Germany at 9:10 PM.

"On March 3, 1945, at 6:00 PM orders were received to move to Zulpich, Germany, set up a defense of the town and be prepared to attack in the AM. At 9:30 PM the Battalion left Krezau. The mission to attack Zulpich was canceled, with orders to move to Geich, Germany.

"On March 4, 1945, at 12:20 AM the Battalion closed in on Geich. At 1:00 AM orders were given to attack.

"On March 4, 1945, The Battalion moved on Rovenvich and at 11:00 AM orders were given to dismount the vehicles and attack. Company A was ordered to an assembly area at RJ W (west) of Rovenvich and prepare to move forward and clear Rovenvich by 3:00 PM.

"On March 4, 1945, at 3:35 PM the attacking companies had crossed the first phase line (Silver) and were proceeding according to plan. Enemy resistance was moderate. At 5:30 PM, due to complete breakdown of communications, heavy going through persistent rain and thick mud, and loss of contact with Battalion Headquarters, the attacking companies found it necessary to readjust their position and reorganize. It was not until 11:00 PM, or after, that communications were reestablished between Battalion and the attacking companies, at which time orders were given to continue the attack at 4:00 AM. Orders for this attack were canceled and the Battalion was ordered to leave Rovenvich at 3:00 PM, and move toward Oberelvenich, Germany.

"On March 4, 1945, at 3:49 PM Company A closed on Oberelvenich, but met no resistance. At 5:30 PM Company B took 35 prisoners and at 5:45 PM, the Battalion took 40 additional prisoners. At 11:00 PM Company A was ordered to continue to attack with the objective being to establish a bridgehead. Company A will coordinate in taking Woscheim.

"On March 5, 1945 at 1:00 AM orders were to hold present position, dig in and be prepared for a counterattack. Company C was expected to take Woscheim that night. Company B had four men killed and counted fifteen enemy dead. At 2:40 PM the Battalion moves toward Euskirchen. "A" Company was to report when defense set up. Road to Euskirchen was impassable. Orders were canceled and a billeting party was sent in search of a rest area."

After-action Report S-2,3 Journal, for March 6, 1945 reflects the following:

"At 8:35 AM orders were received to move to Esch, Germany, at the rate of 15 miles per hour with no halts.

"At 9:00 AM 2 squads of Company A were being returned to Company control. (The report did not say where they had been) Company A MUST reach bridge between 9:45 AM and 10:00 AM

"At 10:05 AM the Battalion Leaves Ober Wichterich.

"At 1:35 PM the Battalion arrives at Esch. Head of column continuing on mission. At 1:45 PM, you are to continue to attack and seize town NO. 6. Your route is left to your decision and you are to advance as quickly as possible. Reconnaissance reports friendly forces in

Rheinbacht and mortar fire from Reimershoven and Florzheim.

"At 2:25 PM Battalion leaves Esch. At 2:41 PM a Belgium Prisoner of War reports four (4) heavy gun batteries in vicinity of 5136, also four Tiger tanks and infantry in the woods.

"At 2:50 PM the Battalion arrives at Ollhein. At 3:10 PM the Battalion leaves Ollhein and at 3:50 PM arrives at Miel.

"At 5:20 Battalion arrives at Flerzheim. At 5:37 three (3) prisoners taken; claim they are from 1308 Artillery Company.

"At 6:30 PM an unnamed town was taken.

"At 8:00 PM Company Commander returns to Command Post with orders for attack on Mehlem, and call all officers together.

"At 8:45 PM orders given to attack Mehlem. Company A was to spearhead the attack. Company A was to secure the high ground South and West of Mehlem. Rate of march was to be 10 miles per hour.

"At 9:14 PM all men will provide themselves with white arm bands to be worn on the right arm. [This was to identify any enemy forces attempting to infiltrate our forces dressed in American uniforms]

"At 10:30 PM, when ready to move advisable to have Company A establish road block at Western edge of town until all elements clear."

After-Action report, S-2,3 Journal for March 7, 1945 reflects the following:

"At 12:50 AM, orders were given to have everyone relax for a couple of hours.

"At 3:50 AM reconnaissance reports road intended to travel not considered feasible for armored vehicles.

"At 6:45 AM orders given for attack on Sinzig. Our objective has been changed. Our mission now is to seize and secure bridge heads over the Aahr River at Westum and Sinzig. Company A will pass through C company and take Westum. The remainder of the Battalion will assemble in Bodendorf.

"At 7:15 AM the Battalion leaves Flerzheim.

"At 9:52 AM orders given to report location of head of your column hourly on the hour.

"At 10:00 AM Mortar and artillery fire falls on column. Company A and C continue on and remainder of column stopped and knocked out an enemy observation post.

"At 1:00 PM Battalion arrives at Bodendorf. Between Gimmigen and Heppingen moderate mortar and artillery fire began falling on part of the column. This lasted for over an hour. Company C, at Sinzig, ran into heavy mortar, small arms and automatic fire from an enemy entrenched in the high ground surrounding the town and in concrete emplacements at the two entrances to the town. Company knocked out the guns on the high ground and routed the riflemen. The bridge over the AHR River leading into Sinzig was captured intact after a brisk fight. After entering town, C company ran into an enemy ammunition train consisting of about twelve trucks and horse drawn wagons. The enemy column was completely destroyed and all enemy personnel were killed. Company A launched an attack on Westum, took the town and established a bridgehead, thus completing the Battalion mission.

"At 2:45 PM a civilian reported the bridge at 652202 [undoubtely the Ludendorff Bridge at Remagen] was to be blown at 4:00 or 5:00 PM.

"At 8:20 PM orders were received to cross the Rhine River.

"At 8:30 PM orders were given to move out for Remagen. C Company was in the lead followed by Company A." The head of the column arrived at Remagen at 8:30 PM."

After Action report, S-2,3 Journal, for March 8, 1945 reflects the following.

"There was much delay in crossing the bridge because of the congestion in Remagen

"At 2:00 AM the Battalion starts across the bridge, with Company C leading the way. At 3:10 AM a Tank Destroyer breaks through the floor of the bridge and is stuck. There after all troops had to cross on foot.

"At 3:50 AM Company A crossed the bridge.

"At 4:15 AM Company A closed into their defensive position.

"At 10:15 AM Company A reports receiving artillery fire.

"At 3:00 PM B (Another company designation was entered first then typed over with company B) reports three prisoners taken on hill in vicinity of bridge. (This corresponds to the date and time the three prisoners surrendered to me).

"At 6:15 PM Company A took four (4) prisoners.

"At 8:55 PM. All companies were ordered to report hourly, on the hour even if there was nothing significant to report."

After-Action report 5-2,3 Journal for March 9, 1945 reports the following:

"At 1:00 AM All companies were alerted to a report by the Air Force of a large column of vehicles coming from the northeast and the South apparently headed in our direction. Some vehicles were believed to be about 25 minutes away.

"At 5:10 AM Company A reported receiving flat trajectory fire from 75 MM or smaller.

"At 10:45 AM Company A was hit with barrage of fire. One man was killed and two were wounded.

"At 11:25 AM orders were received to move to Kasbach and be prepared to counter attack. Check all weapons and ammunition and be ready to move on command. Company A was to lead the march, followed by Company C, Then Company B. Company A was to be on the right side of the road, with Company C on the left. B Company was held in reserve. The Battalion arrived in Kasbach at 1:05 PM having been bombed and strafed en route.

"At 2:00 PM Company A report one casualty by artillery fire. At 6:10 PM Company A reported receiving artillery fire.

"Further, at 6:10 PM the Battalion's mission was changed to defense, requiring the strengthening of positions. By 9:15 PM the changes necessary had been made. At approximately the same time a five (5) man enemy patrol was encountered by Company C outposts. One prisoner was taken. The others escaped. All companies reported heavy enemy artillery barrages falling on and around their positions throughout the night

After-action report, S-2,3 Journal, for March 10, 1945 reflects the following:

"At 1:00 AM, Company A reported receiving machine gun fire.

"At 4:13 AM, Company A took two prisoners from 62 Pioneer Battalion and sent them to PWE.

"At 5:35 AM, Company A reported that patrols had been unable to make contact with unit on their right flank and would like information regarding their location.

"At 7:00 AM, Company A was engaged in small arms fire with enemy.

"At 7:03 AM a prisoner reports enemy officers preventing their men from surrendering.

"At 9:25 AM The Battalion was attached to the 2nd Battalion, 310th Infantry Regiment. Shortly thereafter the Commanding Officer, 2nd Battalion and the Regimental Commander, visited Command Post and ordered the Battalion the mission of taking HILL 448 and surrounding high ground. Companies A and B were to attack abreast, with Company C held in reserve.

"At 10:00 AM orders included the taking of Hill 363 also.

"At 1:30 PM the attacking companies jumped off, encountering heavy artillery fire but little ground resistance. In the drive to the objective 35 prisoners were taken.

"At 5:40 PM, orders were received to take enemy positions before dark if possible.

"At 6:18 PM the companies reported they were 700 yards from their position and receiving heavy artillery fire. The company moved up to their objectives after dark but due to complete darkness, intermittent artillery fire, breakdown of communications and doubt in the minds of the Company Commanders as to their positions, the troops were brought off the objective and march back to LD. The companies were reorganized and prepared to attack at 5:00 AM."

After-action report, S-2,3 Journal, for March 11, 1945 reflects the following:

"At 7:50 AM Lieutenant Bills was relieved of command of Company A. Command was turned over to Lieutenant Biondi. Lt. Bills was placed in command of Company C.

"At 8:00 AM a bridge at 68.1 was prepared for demolition but was not to be blown except on order from higher command.

"At 10:00 AM an I & R (Intelligence and Reconnaissance) objective guarded by the enemy. Request artillery fire on this objective.

"At 11:10 AM Inquiry made as to why artillery fire requested and not been done.

"At 1:25 PM, 80MM mortar fire falling on our position. At 2:15 PM. Lt. Bills was killed.

"At 10:30 PM Company A reports a strong smell of garlic. Suspect of being poison gas. No poison gas found"

After-Action report S-2,3 Journal for March 12, 1945 reflects the following:

"At 6:50 AM Company A in position along same road.

"At 8:30 AM verbal orders to hold Company C in reserve and plan attack for Companies A & B.

"At 9:45 Companies A & B told to check ammunition, weapons and equipment and be ready to move within 15 minutes, if necessary.

"At 10:30 AM a prisoner of war reports that only 2 or 3 enemy enlisted men holding position. Enemy tank has withdrawn approximately 300 yards and is without fuel.

"At 5:00 PM Companies A & B ordered to proceed, dismounted, to Kretzhaus and given permission to pass through 3rd Battalion, 310th Infantry. Kretzhaus was believed strongly held by the enemy and was the key to Kalenborn and the Autobahn.

"At 5:30 PM Companies A & B leave for Kretzhaus.

"At 6:50 PM Column halted and went into an assembly area at check point 5 to await orders to move.

"At 10:30 PM. Orders were given for attack on Kretzhaus. Companies A & B were to proceed crossing LD 0500 Companies abreast. Company A will seize and secure the town and cut road junction to the North of town. Company B will seize high ground and Railroad track North and East of town.

After-Action report 5-2,3 Journal for March 13, 1945 reflects the following:

"At 5:00 AM Companies A & B, with Company C in reserve, start their attack. Although both companies reached their objective they were unable to consolidate due to heavy and persistent artillery, mortar fire, small arms and tank fire. Companies reported sustaining heavy casualties.

"At 6:00 AM Company A reports intense mortar and artillery fire in vicinity of sawmill.

"At 6:30 AM Companies A & B report they are held up by small arms and direct weapons and heavy artillery.

"At 6:40 AM Companies A & B reported they were progressing slowly against heavy resistance.

"At 8:00 AM Company A reported they are on objective and are receiving heavy small arms, artillery and direct fire.

"At 8:30 AM Company B reported they are on objective and pinned down by machine gun and artillery fire.

"At 9:00 AM Company B took four prisoners.

"At 10:00 AM Company C moved to an assembly area in the vicinity of the quarry.

"At 10:30 AM Companies B and C unable to consolidate their objective due to machine gun, tank and artillery fire.

"At 4:00 PM commanding officer gets permission to use Company C in night attack to take Kretzhaus.

"At 4:15 PM Company A takes four (4) prisoners.
[NOTE: This approximates the time I captured the 9 enemy soldiers in the basement of the first house. Since they were merely directed toward the rear of our lines it would be doubtful they all made it with the intense fire falling at that time.]

"At 5:00 PM Company C was ordered to pass through Company A at 4:30 the next morning and take the town.

"At 6:15 PM attempts were made to organize Bazooka Teams in Companies A & B and to prepare for the night". [This agrees with my recollection]

"At 6:25 PM Your Tank Destroyers will displace forward to right of the saw mill in Company A sector and into the woods to the right of Sawmill. This will be done late this afternoon or as soon as possible.

"At 8:00 PM Commanding officer, Company C and Platoon leaders leave for Company A to coordinate their attack.

"At 9:00 PM S-3 leaves for Kretzhaus to observe the attack by Company C".

After-Action report of S-2,3 Journal for March 14, 1945 reflects the following.

"At 4:30 AM Company C starts the attack on Kretzhaus. Tasks force one gets bogged down. Task force 2 is sent out. [Note: By 4:30 AM or a bit earlier I was wounded and taken to the basement of the first house I had entered.]

A report, captioned "Headquarters, 52nd Armored Infantry Battalion, APO 259, U.S. Army", dated April 1, 1945 reflects the following as occurring in March, 1945:

"By 10:00 PM, March 13, 1945, the entire town (Krezthaus) west of the railroad was cleared out; however the Germans still maintained positions along the railroad and on the roads in the woods East of the railroad. Elements of the German 11th Panzer Division had been opposing the Battalion. The attack was resumed the next day with Company "C" to clean out the woods and secure the roads leading to Kalenborn. This mission was accomplished by 5:00 PM.

"Thus, the spot dubbed by GI's of the Battalion as "HELLS CORNER" was finally reduced and troops to the right and left were free to move on Kalenborn and to cut the Autobahn East of Kalenborn. It was not long after that the Armored break through to Limburg was to take place.

"For the next three days the Battalion was in III Corps reserve and held its defensive position in and around Kretzhaus. The Battalion was relieved of this mission on March 18, 1945 and reassembled at Kasbach where it commenced to reorganize."

[Note — The aforementioned report continued]

"The Remagen Bridgehead Area" - This phase of the campaign differed from the first phase in that the enemy made a firm and determined stand at Kretzhaus to deny use of the Autobahn to the invading troops. With Kretzhaus, the local point for the drive Eastward eliminated, troops and armor literally poured over the Autobahn and into Central Germany. Again the artillery was called upon for a great deal of support, which the Battalion received and which was very effective. The capture of Kretzhaus paved the way for the drive on Limburg.

Company "A" 52nd Armored Infantry, from March 1, 1945 to March 22, 1945 had the following commanders:

1st Lt. Edward Bills - March 1st to March 11th
1st Lt. Eugene Biondi - March 11th to March 13th
2nd Lt. Donald G. Thorn - March 13th to March 22nd

Statistical Data - Battalion.

Personnel Losses:

	Officers	Enlisted	Total
Killed in Action	3	41	44
Died of Wounds or Injuries	1	2	3
Wounded or Injured in action	8	199	207
Missing in Action	0	3	3
Captured	0	0	0
Sick / other non-battle losses	0	98	98
TOTAL LOSSES	12	343	355

Prisoners of war taken, Fifteen (15) Officers, two thousand seven hundred forty three (2,743) enlisted men.

Ammunition Expended (among other):

.30	Cal. Carbine	16,800
.30	Cal. M1, 8 per clip	65,856
.30	Cal. M1, 5 per clip	4,500
.30	Cal. Machine gun	81,000
.45	Cal. Ball	5,400
.50	Cal. Machine gun	44,940

Larger caliber, including mortar and howitzer not set forth."

EMILE A. FONTENOT
4512 Hazelwood Rd.
North Little Rock, Arkansas
Notes From Conversation Aug 5, 2000

The trip to Remagen, Germany ultimately led to the identification of a few members of the 52nd Armored Infantry Battalion that fought in Germany subsequent to crossing the Rhine River.

On August 5, 2000, I had the privilege of visiting Emile A. Fontenot at his home in North Little Rock, Arkansas. With his permission, I am recording his recollections as follows:

He departed the United States January 1, 1945 at Boston, Massachusetts aboard the General USS Black, a troop ship. He felt certain I was on the same ship. It docked at LaHarve, France on January 15, 1945. He remembered it was a very cold day with snow piled high on the dock. He boarded a train parked near the dock. The roofs of the rail cars were full of holes, apparently having been strafed by aircraft. He was aboard this train for about 3 days before arriving in Elzange, France, a small town near Metz.

While billeted at Elzange, he recalls hearing that one of our sentries had been garroted by a German who apparently had come through the Maginot Line. He did not know the details of the sentry's death.

After departing Elzange, the Battalion passed through Aachen, Germany, a town almost totally destroyed by aerial bombing. From here, the Battalion fought its way south and across the Rhine River on March 7-8, 1945.

Company "A" of the 52nd had three rifle platoons. Each platoon had three rifle squads, two mortar squads, and one machine gun squad. Fontenot was assigned to the

60mm mortar squad. The names James Waggoner and Wayne Parkey are not familiar to him, although he does recall a Waggoner who fought in the battle of Limburg, Germany, a week or two after the battle at the saw mill, and who received a battlefield commission. On further reflection, Fontenot recalls another member of company "A" named Waggoner who could speak German, and who often served as an interpreter. He does not know this man's name or what happened to him. He believes this latter individual was from Indiana.

Fontenot clearly recalls company "A" taking a wrong road against the advice of others and ending up lost when the road abruptly ended in a field. It was raining very heavily and the night was unusually dark. He recalled that a squad of three men was dispatched in an attempt to determine our whereabouts. He did not recall who the members of this patrol were, but remembered that two of the patrol were killed. The next morning there was a skirmish with the Germans in the area, with our unit getting the better of the battle. He recalled "stacking" the German guns and destroying them with grenades. The commanding officer was disciplined for this mistake and assigned to another company. He did not recall when this occurred, but believes it was after crossing the Rhine River.

When we crossed the Rhine and were going into Erpeler Ley, Germany, his platoon remained near the town at the base of the hill that overlooked the bridge. They set up a defensive position in a level field, which was dotted with piles of manure. The Germans shelled them all night, and often when looking out of his foxhole into the dark, one couldn't tell but what the manure piles were German soldiers.

The following day, when firing subsided a bit, they went to a "chow wagon" for a hot meal, and while standing in line a sniper shot and killed the soldier in front of Fontenot.

After a couple of days in this general area, his platoon walked back to the bridge towers. By now the US forces had pulled antiaircraft guns mounted on trucks, parked bumper to bumper along the roadway. Now rejoined with the rest of the company, we ran into the 2nd Infantry Division. It was around 11:00 AM when we ran into some stiff resistance. A number of German pill boxes were ahead of us and firing on us. The Lieutenant of Company "B" pointed to "you, you, and you," including Fontenot, and ordered them to advance on the pill boxes. Fontenot's response was, "Lieutenant, I haven't learned a whole lot in the military, but I know that is not the way to take a pill box. If you want to lead the way, I will follow you. My platoon leader is on the other end, and I take orders from him. I'm not trying to be disrespectful, but that is not the way to attack a pill box."

During the night of March 12, 1945, we walked just about all night. Just before dawn we approached a town with a large saw mill operation spread out on both sides of the road. A fierce battle, which became known as the "Battle of the Sawmill", was about to begin. Ahead was the town of Kretzhaus. Fontenot was in a foxhole back in the woods[16] a few yards on the right side of the road. He could see down the road leading into town. He pointed to the hand-drawn map I had made and remembered the small shed2 off to the left, and the large pile of crushed stone.

Three US tank destroyers came up the road[7,8,9]. Some of Fontenot's squad got in behind the destroyers and advanced with them. When the destroyers got almost to the rock pile, a German tank[6], pretty much hidden under a large evergreen tree behind the first house on the right side of the street, opened fire on the destroyers, knocking out all three of them. One man got out of the third destroyer[9]. One of his hands was missing. In addition, when the first destroyer was hit, the projectile passed completely through it and killed three of Fontenot's squad. Not long thereafter, the German tank pulled back.

Company "B" was off to his left and a German machine gun up ahead was "cutting them to pieces". Some time later the machine gun went silent. I told Emile that after the tank pulled back I had gone into a ditch[10] on the left side of the road and crawled up to the first house. He recalled the ditch being there. Further, I told him I had killed the machine gunner and then went down into the basement and routed out nine German soldiers, now prisoners, and sent them down the road towards our line. He recalled seeing "a bunch" of prisoners running toward our forces, but did not count them, but "there were too many for him".

Fontenot and his men began moving out to their left toward the little shed on the map. A radioman was in front of him, running bent over nearly horizontally. A large German gun fired (maybe a tank), and shot the man's head completely off. In spite of this mortal wound, the man continued to run at least three steps.

Fontenot came around the rock pile between it and where the machine gun had been and on around the back of the house I first entered. At the rear, he recalls seeing a number of American soldiers (3 or 4) standing near a wounded German soldier[15]. The German reached for the Sergeant's .45 automatic, and someone in the group had to shoot and kill him.

Fontenot continued across the street and in behind the first building[18] on the right side of the street. He thought the German tank had left the area, but found it had moved back only a short distance and was standing there with the hatch open. The people inide the tank were talking loudly. There seemed to be wounded inside. An American soldier dropped a grenade inside and destroyed it. No one was seen getting out.

After I told Emile of having fired at the tank, he concluded that undoubtedly one or more of my shots went inside and had probably wounded the driver. He had seen this happen a couple of times before.

Fontenot knows of only three men in his squad who survived at the end of this battle.

He continued in combat until the end of the war.

MERLE E. THOMAS

788 July Circle
North Fort Meyers, Florida
Notes From Telephone Conversation Aug 17, 2000

On August 17, 2000, I was privileged to talk with Merle E. Thomas by telephone. He provided the following information.

He took military training at Camp Croft. He departed the United States from Boston, Massachusetts on January 1, 1945, and arrived at a US Army barracks on January 17, 1945. He thought he was in an old pre-war military facility near Thienville, (phonetic) France. He recalled that during a training session, a Lieutenant drove a pipe in the ground with just a bit of it sticking out, and then stuffed a "plastic explosive" in it. When it was detonated, a piece of shrapnel from the pipe hit a soldier in the penis causing gross bleeding. I recall this incident since I was within just a few feet of the injured man. Merle and I were housed in the barracks near Metz, France.

Merle was assigned to Company "A", 52nd Armored Infantry Battalion, second rifle platoon. He did not recall my name and felt he would have, since we both bear the same last name. This means I was either assigned to the first or third rifle platoon.

He well recalls our Lieutenant taking us down the wrong road, which ended in a field. He was not aware that a patrol went out, but remembers that it was raining torrentially, and after a while his Sergeant was called to a meeting. When he returned he told his men that they were seven miles behind German lines. He recalls that his Lieutenant was transferred to another assignment and was killed soon thereafter.

He also recalls the "Battle of the Sawmill". He walked all night and while it was still very dark he approached the area near the sawmill. Other platoons were in front of him, and when his unit approached the road that led north to a rock quarry, and they took that route. From the quarry they started east and as they topped a ridge they came under heavy fire from German tanks and machine guns. They suffered several casualties at this point, but were eventually able to advance straight ahead.

They received three replacements. All three were promptly killed. Merle and his group never passed through the sawmill.

He also fought at the battle of Limburg, Germany, where they again suffered heavy casualties. Of the seven original members of his squad, only three survived. During this battle, he felt a stinging sensation as something hit his shoe. Without looking back he called to the man crawling behind him to look at his feet and see if he was wounded. He called a second time after getting no answer. It was then he realized that a German bullet had passed through the helmet and the head of his colleague, and the bullet had landed in the lining of Thomas's boot.

He continued to fight until the end of the war without being wounded.

A NOTE TO THE AUTHOR

My father has given me a great deal of credit for helping him prepare these stories for publication. In truth, the credit is his. Without his amazing clarity and ability to recall detail, this would not have been possible. Turning his recollections into a completed book has been a bit daunting, but it has most certainly been a labor of love. It has been a privilege and an honor to assist in the recording of these experiences.

As I have reviewed the body of his experiences, I am reminded how truly fortunate we are as a society. Much of what we take for granted was paid for by the hard work, dedication, and sacrifice of those who have gone before us.

I have heard these stories from time-to-time while growing up, but taken in the context of his life's experiences, I have a new appreciation for my father as an individual, and not just as "Dad." I am proud of him, and thankful for his guidance, wisdom, and love.

Lawrence Gray Thomas
July, 2001